SECOND AID

TO SUPPORT YOUR
SOUL SEARCH

Judy Fraser

Published by Landraagon
Design & Cover Illustration Pavllou Landraagon
www.landraagon.com

ISBN-13: 978-91-979875-2-3
ISBN-10: 9197987522

THIS BOOK IS DEDICATED TO THE GARDENERS OF THE EARTH

Acknowledgements

With special thanks to:
The "Management Upstairs" for supplying all copy and illustrations and so strongly encouraging the author to make the material available.

Richard White from Word Edit: Professional Literary Services, the editor of *Second Aid*.

Pavllou Landraagon, Publishing Agent and Cover Designer.

Alex Amengual Newletter, Distributor and Website Maintainer.

David Newberry Diagrams, for providing illustrations.

Gordon Volke and Richard Hall the editors of *Second Aid*'s companion book, *The Soul Searcher*.

* We use the term 'God' The Management Upstairs' as a description for the powers beyond our current understanding that so clearly impact us. We wish to point this out to be able to be inclusive of, and to embrace all cultural descriptions depicting the invisible worlds that influence us.

Contents

Part 1: Learning to Live Effectively
Chapter 01: Security During Changing Times - *02*
Chapter 02: Moving On When Change Is Required - *12*
Chapter 03: What Is Next? - *20*
Chapter 04: Guidelines During Transition - *26*
Chapter 05: Personal Programming - *35*
Chapter 06: Environmental Programming - *44*

Part 2: Living in Rhythm
Chapter 07: Fear - *50*
Chapter 08: Communication - *58*
Chapter 09: Compassion - *64*
Chapter 10: Earth Changes - *71*

Part 3: Motivation and Movement
Chapter 11: Spiritual Health and Hygiene - *76*
Chapter 12: Healthy Stress - *84*

Part 4: Loving Learning
Chapter 13: Stress Management - *95*
Chapter 14: Freedom - *100*
Chapter 15: Positive Thought - *104*

Part 5: Learning to Unite More Effectively
Chapter 16: Planting New Seeds - *109*
Chapter 17: Harvesting - *115*
Chapter 18: Fertilising - *121*

Part 6: Living The Dream
Chapter 19: Group Dynamics - *128*
Chapter 20: Colour - *130*

Part 7: Learning To Grow More Effectively
Chapter 21: Releasing History - *142*
Chapter 22: Laying a New Foundation- *147*

Part 8: Learn It Or Live It
Chapter 23: Reformation - *152*
Chapter 24: Beyond Revolution - *159*
Chapter 25: Placement - *164*

Part 9: Claiming Abundance
Chapter 26: Power Issues - *173*
Chapter 27: Equality - *176*
Chapter 28: Parents, Partners and Children - *178*
Chapter 29: Burnout - *181*
Chapter 30: Prosperity - *186*

Part 10: Living Spirituality
Chapter 31: Self-Awareness - *196*
Chapter 32: Spirituality - *208*

Introduction

Many people consider spirituality a separate entity, an external, when really it is integral to our being. Spirituality is, at its most basic, the language present within us and the Earth, providing a sacred union for those motivated enough to reach for it. Yet only a minority do reach for it, because egos cloud those who cannot recognise that current beliefs and understandings are incorrect, working against us rather than for us.

There are times in life when we feel left in the dark. For a lot of people, it feels as though life just is not what they expected or hoped it would be; instead of grabbing the bull by the horns and living exactly how we want to, we can find ourselves stuck in a mundane job that we do not enjoy, being overworked and underpaid for a seemingly unappreciative boss. Some are content with this, holding the attitude that the key to getting through life is keeping your head down, staying quiet and just making the most of it. Others, though, want more from life.

It is not always work that drags us down, though. Family life is almost always stressful, regardless of one's status. For parents, it is a constant struggle to make ends meet while maintaining the upkeep of the house, laundry, encouraging the children to succeed and finding time to keep the marital flame burning. For the children, it is a daunting task to try to find their place in the world, discover who they are and decide what they want to do. There are the pressures of school grades, social hierarchies and adolescent hormone changes. There can also be the times of stress that affect everyone, such as a family death or an unwelcome diagnosis of a loved one.

Even for those rare families that have most things in order – good financial standing, ambitious and focused children, and plenty of time for each other – life can throw a curveball when it is least expected, and all the money in the world will never substitute good health. Sometimes, life is out of our control, or it is we as people that are out of control, and that is something that we can all agree on, even if we disagree on *why* it is out of our control – some say it is God, others fate, and others simply put it down to bad fortune. Whatever our personal reasoning for why, there is no denying that we are never in control of our whole existence. Therefore, it should be of prime importance to do all we can to be in charge of the parts that we can control without manipulation of anything.

Taking responsibility is harder in practice that it is in theory; it is easy to *say* "I'm taking charge of my life" and quite another to actually *do* it. That is, in a nutshell, the entire purpose of this book. The following text will provide guidelines for you, a unique individual with unique requirements, to decide the next step for fulfilling your potential. This is not an immediate or overnight process; your body has its own memory and it will take time for your mind to incorporate these guidelines and release the old attitudes. As such, the single most important factor in facilitating this process is your own intuition, and that makes the journey deeply personal; your intuition is unlike that of anyone else, and thus it will be a fruitless exercise to try to ride on someone else's success, or try to use their intuition in your journey. Remember that this is an ongoing process to aid the rest of your life, so while immediate changes will be well received and promptly appreciated, do not rest on your laurels by stopping before the finishing line.

Within the text you will come across some diagrams. These are to encourage freeing your intuition by triggering an energetic response to support the text. You may not understand them at first, and you do not need to; observe them and let your intuition do the rest. As time goes on and you progress through the book, you will acknowledge that the text and diagrams have formed an association, facilitating your journey.

While it is desired to reap the rewards of this book as fast as possible, the golden rule is the age-old one of quality over quantity, and in this case the quality is how well you absorb, incorporate and abide by the information, rather than reading as much of the book in one sitting as possible. Allow your mind to be free and open, and it may be helpful to keep a journal – either written or spoken, or both – to keep track of your thoughts and feelings throughout.

At the hectic pace of today's lifestyle, it can be difficult to find time for reading. Most people will want to read when they are at their most relaxed and comfortable, when the little ones are tucked up in bed and the dishes put away; but we seldom remember that things are never complete, that there is always something else that requires our attention. Therefore, it is important to not treat this as any other book, but a written guru or a lifestyle bible, an accompaniment to help us through life. What this means is that the book must be read at any available opportunity, which can sometimes mean when you are relaxed of an evening, but will usually mean grabbing it whenever possible and incorporating it into your schedule. You will need to adapt regardless of circumstance, and employing such a lesson will be a great asset as you change your intuition.

To encourage a feeling of serenity, it may be beneficial to go for a quiet walk or take a relaxing bath before reading; doing a similar activity after reading will allow your mind to open and your intuition to harness the teachings of the text.

These are only suggestions. You will soon unlock your own path and then life will change for you; gone will be the attitude that life is something to drift through, and in its place will be an acute awareness of the beauty of the world, even if you are experiencing great trauma within the moment, so that when you turn the final page of this book you will have learnt how to let go and surrender to the spiritual instruction before you. The curveballs thrown at you will no longer be total surprises as instead you will be able to understand the Earth's clues and realise that the world is bigger than people. With that realisation comes the ability to cooperate with the unfolding mystery that presents itself in front of you, so that you are no longer a dancing puppet in an impossible-to-understand universe but a key player in unlocking your own destiny on the grand stage of life.

Do not fall into the age-old trap of putting off until tomorrow; there is no longer the choice, only the here and now; become more of who you really are by utilising mind, body, heart and soul. Stop seeing yourself as a victim of life or pretending to be a master of it; simply recognise that we are participants who choose to cooperate and collaborate until we progress far beyond where we have ever been before.

Further text and information can be found online at
www.judyfraser.com

PART 1:
LEARNING TO LIVE EFFECTIVELY

Chapter 1: Security During Changing Times

Change

Who am I?
Where do I go from here?

Without losing identity, project a constructive future
at what you consider to be a destructive past.
Focus concentration and give hope, renew flow
within the rhythm and harmony of nature.

The Sea

Possible
Dam - Stagnation - Falls - Rapids - Pond -
Side track - Removal from central flow

Impossible
Reversal of direction

Consider the image above and how it applies to your existence. On your journey of soul searching, and life itself, many things are possible. You may hit barriers, encounter distractions or get pulled off course, but the one thing you can never do is turn around and go back. Keep surging forward and you will find no matter what gets in your way, you will break through that barrier and reach your goal.

The first part of this section deals with change. One of the most important things to us as contingent beings is our sense of identity, our uniqueness and essence that differentiate us from the six billion others on Earth. So important is identity, in fact, that it is perhaps one of the biggest reasons people refrain from embarking on their personal journey of soul searching – fear of losing what makes them 'them'. In other words, people get scared that they will become a different person by the end.

If you are one such person then you can rest assured: the journey does not change you by losing anything; rather, you gain new attributes. Rather than changing, you become the perfect version of yourself, who you are meant to be with all potential realised and fulfilled. Step one, therefore, is to project a constructive future for yourself and what you yourself consider to be a destructive past, without losing identity. Focus your concentration and energy to find hope and renew flow within the rhythm and harmony of nature. By channelling yourself in such a way you are removing the negative attributes of your life and enhancing the positive; identity is not lost because it is precisely your identity that decides what is constructive to your personal future. Your future is your own and no one else's, so only you can create it.

An important fact to remember is that everything in life moves. The Universe itself is moving and so is everything contained within it. Just as some people walk and others sprint, so, too, does everything move at its own pace. In the above image, both the mountains and the water move but, unaware of the other's own progress, they move at their own speed: the mountains so slowly the human eye cannot detect the movement, the water so fast that were we to jump in it would carry us along. The pertinent question is, "Does your current movement resemble that of a mountain or water?"

If we resemble the mountain, things will change around us faster than we ourselves can change. Life will pass us by while we stagnate, and just as a mountainside will erode as the water continually gushes over it, the big changes in our life will be thrust upon us by the progression of others. Other times, though, our life moves so fast we cannot get a fix on it. This can be overcome in the same way that water flows down a mountain and out to sea: it is impossible for water to move without the seabed beneath it. In other words, without the Earth's foundation lending support, water can go nowhere. That same support is lent to us, and we need the Earth's foundation just as much as water does. Like water, once we have begun we cannot stop: if a dam is built the water is blocked until the pressure builds up to such a point that the dam collapses, and while water can stagnate, if it does so for too long it will turn stale and require flooding in order to flow.

Water is the metaphor you need to grasp. Just as the image at the start of this chapter displays, we can find a quiet lake or pond to rest for a while, to ponder the changes – both past and present – and to gather ourselves; we can detach ourselves from the central flow for respite; we may get distracted by others or events that take place; but what we can never do, what is fundamentally impossible, is reverse the flow. We cannot fight the tide, rather we must accept it, find our own place within its bustling waters and ride it to the end of our journey. This is equally true whether we chose to hop into the stream or we were pushed off the riverbank; whether things in life happen because we made them or because they were thrust upon us, we must adapt to the new circumstance to the best of our abilities.

To begin, think about the changes taking place in your life and write down what you like and dislike about the situation. Once they are written down, organise them in order of priority, with the most important as number one. By doing this you are taking your power back and cooperate consciously rather than being a victim of life or trying, in vain, to control something that you currently do not have the ability to. After you have succeeded in organising your list, concentrate solely on the most important item for a period of time that you define. This will allow you to concentrate and focus all your energy onto one area of importance, rather than distributing it across multiple areas. You will notice results much faster and easier in this way as you give your full attention.

After the list is compiled, take the image at the start of this chapter and colour it in however you see fit, but it would be wise to first learn what colours mean. For instance, bear in mind that white is not a colour but the projection of all colours, while black is the absorption of all colours. Photocopy the image so you can colour as many versions as you desire. The lesson here is noticing that although the basic foundation appears to be the same – the image of the mountains and the water – the symbolism in each is unique to itself, perfectly reflecting your emotions at that period in time. The purpose of changing is being liberated enough to be flexible not only with ourselves but also with others, and by colouring the picture multiple times all emotions will be catered for, each picture a new way to grieve for what has preceded it and a way to look at, and work with, the new, all while releasing negative emotion. Fundamentally, this can only be done after we have decided what it is we want from our life and prioritising each one: so while colouring the picture may be fun and nostalgic of childhood, remember to compile the list first in order to progress properly.

Security

Change is one thing, and important to us on a personal level and if we want to accomplish our goals. Of equal importance, though, is security: no one likes to feel unsafe or insecure; indeed, many of us spend our whole lives searching for security or refusing to try something new, no matter how much we desire to, for fear of stepping out of our comfort zone and feeling that wave of panic that encroaches when insecurity grips us.

The trouble is, security and what makes us feel secure is unique to each individual, so there is little that can be said in the way of guaranteed-success advice to make someone feel safe and secure. There is, however, one permanent mainstay of security that is universal through all of us: love. From the day we were born we associated security with the maternal warmth bestowed upon us by our mothers, the paternal protection of our fathers and the general feeling of acceptance and love from all of our family members. From our earliest moments alive we felt safe around those people, and for almost all of us that feeling of security and protection remains for life.

Love is the single most important thing in our life. While we may not be able to define it, we can recognise its impact on us and the calming effect it has on us when we are suffering from anxiety, stress or insecurity. As babies, our guardians would feed us when we were hungry, give us water when we were thirsty, play with us for entertainment or cognitive development, and let us sleep when we needed rest. In order for us to develop properly these base needs were recognised and attended to by our guardians, whether biological or otherwise. Parents know that getting one of those needs wrong, such as keeping a child awake while it should be sleeping, will cause it to become agitated or upset. Thus, we can see that the key to development is obeying the fine balances of nature. As we grow older our independence also grows and we take care of ourselves, and while we can stay awake longer some nights or miss the occasional meal, the same base needs are exactly the same. In short: as adults we are the same as we were as children, albeit bigger, stronger, more mentally aware and so on. We have developed over the years but our biology remains almost identical and we require the same things, including love. Just as we developed from baby to adult, becoming better versions of ourselves, we can also continue to develop throughout adulthood to try to become our ultimate selves.

Physical and inner growth are synonymous with each other and, as our bodies grow, so does our spirit – our emotions and ability to deal with situations expands, allowing us to overcome the challenges that face us all at various points of life. Our security issues require a firm foundation, as the Earth provides to water, to act as a springboard to keep insecurity at bay. Our individual needs must be assessed in order for us to grow within safe boundaries and, just like the previous water analogy, this tidal flow is essential as it clears and cleans our interior in the same way a shower cleans our exterior. Stifling it is akin to water that no longer flows and sits stagnant, growing stale.

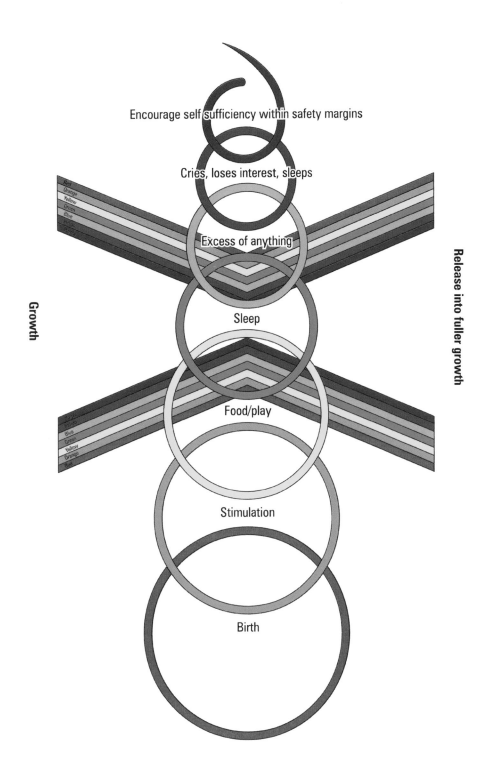

Study the preceding Security Diagram, decide the area of greatest need that you identify within yourself and figure out the steps required to meet this need. By doing so, you will be developing your own security, increasing esteem and confidence, and developing your inner self, paving a firm foundation for harmony and completeness.

One of the most important things to us as human beings is being able to function properly in everyday situations without being overwhelmed or anxious, because such negative emotions can hinder our lives both socially and professionally, and for some people can develop into conditions like agoraphobia or claustrophobia. Indeed, as we sensitise from our growth it can be problematic or uncomfortable to be in busy places like airports, supermarkets or the high street, but we need to be able to function properly in these areas because we must face them almost every day. Most of us are adamant that we do not hate anyone, that we hold no prejudices or we tolerate everybody equally, but really we are repelled – not through conscious judgement – if someone gets too close to us when we do not want them to, and this reaction is heightened if their vibration is incongruous to our own. When we are affected on a spiritual level, we seek to distance ourselves from the person or people in question.

How do we deal with these situations? It requires us to channel ourselves, to teach ourselves how to expel energies we do not want and hold onto those we do; to deduce what is beneficial and what is not, to absorb what is useful and reject what is not. A simple exercise to learn this difficult lesson is visualising oneself in an egg.

Firstly, imagine that you are within the yolk of an egg, so all around you is a golden-white light. The egg white enveloping you is your own personal space: clear, clean, undisrupted. The final layer is the delicate porous shell.

Now that you have pictured yourself residing within the three layers of the egg, inspect for holes or missing parts on the inside. If you come across any, utilise the light as a liquid to cover the holes in the same manner you would use a paint roller to decorate a wall.

Next, you need to look for invasive devices, such as ropes or cords, connecting your egg to another. If you find any, cut the connection and pull it into your egg, and remember to repair the shell afterwards in each spot you need to cut a connection. If possible, push the other end into the egg of the person the device is connected to.

Once the above has been completed, place your egg into the fitting within your egg box. This can be done without any equipment, but if you are feeling fragile then it would be beneficial to first protect the egg with lavender-coloured foam rubber before placing it inside the box. Do not be afraid of isolation within the box; your immediate family will be in there with you, resting in their own mould, while other people and their families will be in boxes separate from your own. Each person in each box has their own unique space, despite sharing the wider space with others. Spend some time observing who is in your box with you, and more importantly make sure you acknowledge that despite sharing space, you also have your own and there is no threat or danger of that changing. Take as much time as necessary to reassure yourself of this.

Finally, return to the centre of your egg, content in the knowledge that you may encounter the presence of other eggs but that they are unable to infiltrate your space unless you desire that to happen, because you have a 'buffer zone' that holds not only you but each other egg safely and securely.

Once the visualisation is complete, you can transfer it to real-life situations to become comfortable in crowded places, knowing that while you are sharing an area with others, you also have your own impenetrable space.

Sustained Effort

Generally, when we are required to do something we give it all we can and then rest, considering the task complete. Quite often, though, we may need to repeat the task until we have completed what we needed to as well as we can.

Consider an onion as an example. As we remove a layer we think that is all there is to it, like an orange only has one skin or a present only has one layer of paper. However, after removing it, we find another skin, which we dutifully remove only to find yet another one. We know there cannot be an infinite number of skin layers, and eventually, after repeating the action numerous times, we reach the centre. What's more, we know that the action is absolutely necessary, for if we just aim straight for the centre then all we will produce is chaos, populated by onion flesh, skin and juice – the clean-up of which will require far more energy and effort than the simple but gentle process of removing each layer of skin individually.

While the onion analogy works perfectly for explaining a task we do, it also works perfectly when looking at human development. As the picture on the following page adequately shows, a child grows physically at a staggering pace between birth and age twenty-one, and, as explained previously, inner growth happens at the same speed. However, what cannot be overlooked or understated is the fact that inner growth requires strong foundations, as all contingent beings do. These foundations are not intrinsic and are not handed to us gift wrapped with a bow upon birth; just as a child is not born with a brain full of knowledge, the foundations must be acquired over time. The foundations must be built, and while we rely on others to help and support us through various stages, we are the bricklayers. The lessons must be learnt, rather than us going straight there, for the exact same reason that an onion must be peeled gently and slowly, not butchered to reach the centre. In this instance, it would be akin to a toddler with a child's medical textbook being sent to the operating theatre to perform surgery, or sending a child at pre-school to university. In order to get to university, a person must progress through the many individual years and stages of education to train the brain to be receptive and accommodate new information, and a surgeon requires even more years of education and training. Human beings are not built with electronic ports that allow us to insert a cable and download information, so we must take the long paths of acquiring information and foundations, starting at the bottom of a large pile in pre-school and progressing to the top, only to start again at the bottom of the next pile in primary school, and so on. This repeated process of progression from bottom to top to bottom again is how we develop the solid foundations that keep us grounded in reality and which manage our various states – emotional, mental and physical – as we, or the situations we find ourselves in, change. In essence, it is simply a way for our inner selves and outer selves to find a compromising balance.

One of the most important ways to ensure a feeling of security is making sure you are comfortable with yourself and your role in life, and a general feeling of relaxation and serenity. The following basic relaxation exercise will help to instil that feeling and it will be worth coming back to this exercise as you progress through your journey.

To begin, imagine that you are safe, protected and healthy and a white cloak that gives you warmth, love and comfort is wrapped around you.

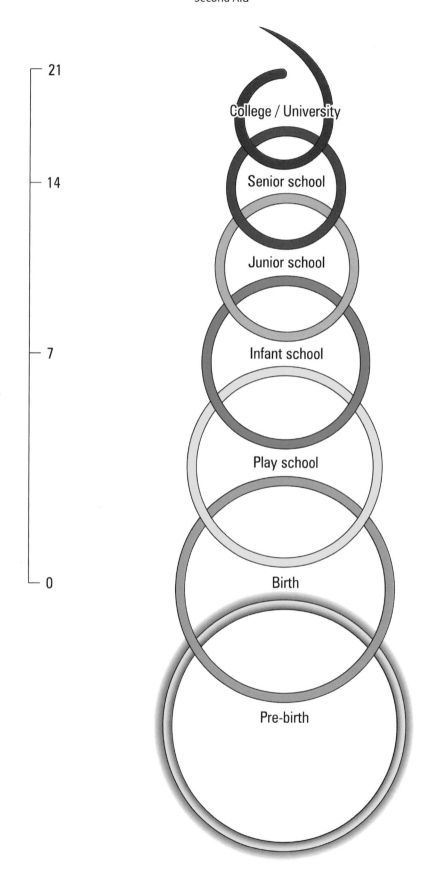

College / University

Senior school

Junior school

Infant school

Play school

Birth

Pre-birth

21

14

7

0

Sit somewhere comfortable, either in a chair with your feet placed flat on the floor and your spine upright with no curve, or on the floor with your legs crossed or in front of you with the knees bent and feet flat on the floor. Remain with a straight back, but do not let yourself become too stiff and rigid.

Repeat the word 'relax' and take three deep breaths in succession, pushing out your abdomen with each inhale, and utilising the muscles to pull it in on each exhale. Starting from your feet, concentrate on each muscle in your body, working your way up the body from calves to head. As you consider each group, tense the respective muscles and then slowly, consciously, relax the muscle and release the tension, making sure you feel the wave of relaxation with each muscular expansion. As you do this, you will realise your body is a pleasant part of the natural surroundings.

If you are feeling negative emotions, such as worry or anger, conjure a very clear image of the situation in your mind, and again repeat 'relax' three times while bringing your breathing under control as above. Imagine the situation changing: making up with a person or another positive change, all in a setting that makes you feel serene, like a forest with luscious greens and a perfect waterfall, or even just your family home – each person is different, so choose what works for you.

The chances are that if you are involved in a situation with someone else where you are angry or upset, you also had a part to play. Repeat the event in your head, carefully reconstructing the behaviour of the other person and yourself, so that you can try to see how the situation may look from someone else's point of view. This objective viewpoint can be extremely useful and enlightening, as our emotions can become heightened and unreasonable when we are in the situation ourselves.

As you do this, pay careful attention to your reactions. It can be difficult to create a positive picture and nice setting while you are focusing on negative emotions, so it will take some practice to get right, but it will become easier with each attempt. Viewing the scene again may be difficult, so remain gentle with both yourself and your thoughts – watch rather than judge. The exercise will lower your frustration or other negative emotions as you do it, so try to be aware of this happening and tell yourself that you have a new perspective and understanding of the situation now.

Once you have completed this and feel calmer with the situation that made you upset or worried, slowly move your head, hands and feet. Slowly open your eyes and look around at your environment, knowing that you are safe, well and in harmony with your surroundings.

If you are not currently in a state of worry, frustration, anger or sadness, the above exercise may be confusing to you. Put simply, as we go through life we pick up and carry a wide variety of impressions – consciously or unconsciously – and there comes a time when we must stop and review them. If we ignore them and carry on as though they are not there then it will be incredibly difficult for us to grow, or for the growth we have experienced to emerge, thus trapping us in a more infantile state that we should be in. That growth was earned, so let it free! Always remember that the whole purpose of *Second Aid* is personal growth and expansion, so there is never a point in your life when it is too late (or too early) to reflect, on the beginnings or the entire past. As such, you can create your entire future.

As stated above, to peel an onion we must remove each layer of skin one at a time, for if we simply karate chop it the end result will be a large mess. A further point on the analogy is that the same is true of life and we experience this at every stage: when we learn the piano, our fingers are limited to the boundaries of a single octave because it would be too much to take them all on at once. When we are young we walk before we can run to give our legs and balance time to develop. When we learn to cook we start with basic meals rather than launching straight into a gourmet feast. We must also start from the ground up to build a solid foundation upon which all else can be situated; when a house is built the builders do not start with the roof, they start at the foundation and work towards the end result. The key lesson in these examples is that if we try too hard to rush, or just go straight for the finish line, we will learn nothing and everything will fail. Any and all changes must be made gently and no faster than time permits.

When we begin something new we are often overcome and consumed by the difficulty of it, but when we work at it piece by piece our ability increases and the task gets easier. In life we must practice our single octave until we become proficient enough to move on to handling two at a time, and eventually the entire piano. In order to work to the utmost of our abilities we have to take responsibility for ourselves so that what we are facing before us takes priority over everything else, for the present is the only place we can make changes. We cannot fill a one-gallon jug with two litres of water, and we cannot take on more than we can handle. However, by taking on what we can handle and mastering it we make room to take on more. This all ties in to what has been said in the previous paragraphs: to take things slowly, at our own pace, and to build a solid foundation. We should be grateful for what we have, because waiting will be easier if we are not pining for something else. Make friends with a skill set that complements your own to help each other progress.

The following diagram showcases the need to break down an area until we are relaxed and comfortable with it, and until we are fully proficient with it. During this stage we will be in the present's shadow, and when we have developed and the time is right, the shadow will be removed to allow us to move to the next octave on life's piano.

How much can you handle?

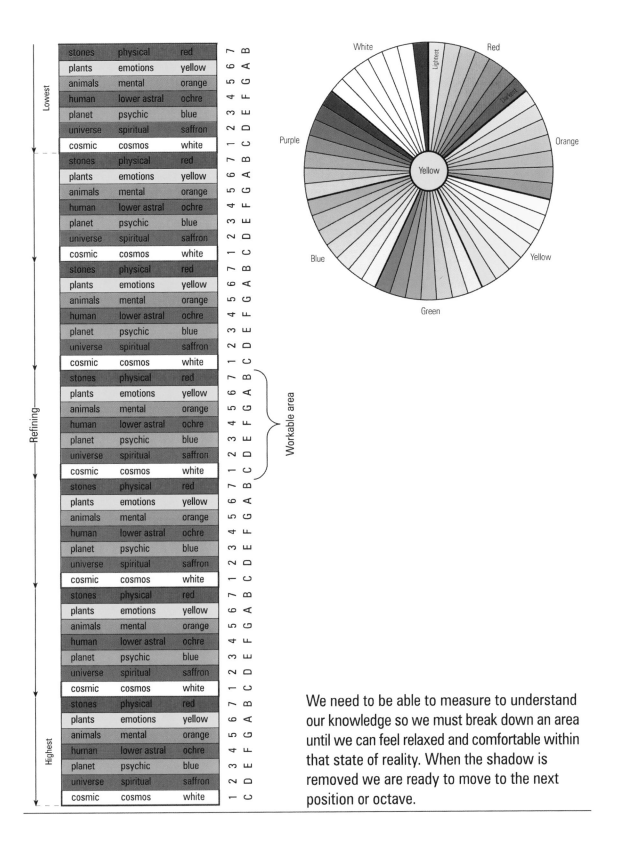

stones	physical	red	7	B
plants	emotions	yellow	6	A
animals	mental	orange	5	G
human	lower astral	ochre	4	F
planet	psychic	blue	3	E
universe	spiritual	saffron	2	D
cosmic	cosmos	white	1	C

Lowest

stones	physical	red	7	B
plants	emotions	yellow	6	A
animals	mental	orange	5	G
human	lower astral	ochre	4	F
planet	psychic	blue	3	E
universe	spiritual	saffron	2	D
cosmic	cosmos	white	1	C

stones	physical	red	7	B
plants	emotions	yellow	6	A
animals	mental	orange	5	G
human	lower astral	ochre	4	F
planet	psychic	blue	3	E
universe	spiritual	saffron	2	D
cosmic	cosmos	white	1	C

Refining

stones	physical	red	7	B
plants	emotions	yellow	6	A
animals	mental	orange	5	G
human	lower astral	ochre	4	F
planet	psychic	blue	3	E
universe	spiritual	saffron	2	D
cosmic	cosmos	white	1	C

Workable area

stones	physical	red	7	B
plants	emotions	yellow	6	A
animals	mental	orange	5	G
human	lower astral	ochre	4	F
planet	psychic	blue	3	E
universe	spiritual	saffron	2	D
cosmic	cosmos	white	1	C

stones	physical	red	7	B
plants	emotions	yellow	6	A
animals	mental	orange	5	G
human	lower astral	ochre	4	F
planet	psychic	blue	3	E
universe	spiritual	saffron	2	D
cosmic	cosmos	white	1	C

Highest

stones	physical	red	7	B
plants	emotions	yellow	6	A
animals	mental	orange	5	G
human	lower astral	ochre	4	F
planet	psychic	blue	3	E
universe	spiritual	saffron	2	D
cosmic	cosmos	white	1	C

We need to be able to measure to understand our knowledge so we must break down an area until we can feel relaxed and comfortable within that state of reality. When the shadow is removed we are ready to move to the next position or octave.

Chapter 2: Moving On When Change Is Required

Indications of the Completion of a Phase

Life consists of many phases and each of us goes through them. However, it can be difficult to know when one phase has ended and another begun, so it is easy for us to be partly or fully in a stage behind the one we should have progressed to. This is not something to blame yourself for, though; it can be difficult enough to acknowledge at the best of times, but busy, stressful lives pulling us every which way but loose can make it incredibly difficult.

So how does one know when the end of a phase is reached? There are subtle signs, such as statements like "I am much less tolerant now than I used to be" or "I used to have a lot more compassion than I do these days." There is usually a message hidden there, but as we only examine the obvious we miss it entirely. Of course, we may sense there are changes ahead of time, as there so often are, but it is imperative that we acknowledge that the old must exit before it is possible for the new to be welcomed in. It is at this point that we can understand one chapter is at its close while a new is at its dawn.

To tell if you have completed a phase of life, look at any changes that have been made in your life lately. In order to do this it may be helpful to keep a journal so you can monitor certain changes. For instance, have you started eating new foods or incorporating more of one type of food into your daily diet? Many would consider this a small change and will not even notice it, but if you think about it you may be aware that you are now eating, for example, more sweet foods. However, even if you do notice it, you may be totally unaware of what it means. Craving sweet foods frequently can be indicative that you are trying to sweeten your life because you feel there is too much negativity in it. Similarly, an increased consumption of spicy foods can be a tell-tale sign that you are bored with current events or impatient for things to change – in other words, you want to 'spice things up' somewhat. On the other hand, bland foods could mean that you want some rest and recovery, a way to slow things down from your busy schedule.

Perhaps your diet is exactly the same but other things in life have changed, like your relationship with friends. There may be new dynamics: you might be finding yourself annoyed with them for no apparent reason, or the idea of spending time with them may make you feel more depressed than happy. When some people experience this they respond by suppressing the emotion, hoping it is just irrational behaviour that will disappear given a little time. There is nothing wrong with such emotions, and certainly they are nothing to be ashamed of or worry about; perhaps the reason they exist is because you and your friend(s) are no longer growing in parallel, but in different paths. This can happen because we change and develop as we age, and it does not mean that you or your friend(s) are bad people or worse than you used to be – simply that you may have now outgrown each other and changes are on the way. As stated above, some will suppress these emotions and hope things will revert to the way they previously were; however what this really means is they are sacrificing the obligation to expand, and thus denying themself the ability to grow internally and become a more developed, well-rounded person.

Have you recently found a new interest or passion which is taking you in a new direction? Maybe you are suddenly interested in learning a musical instrument and pursuing that path? Alternatively (or synonymously) you may have lost interest in an activity you already do for no other reason than it simply does not excite you any longer.

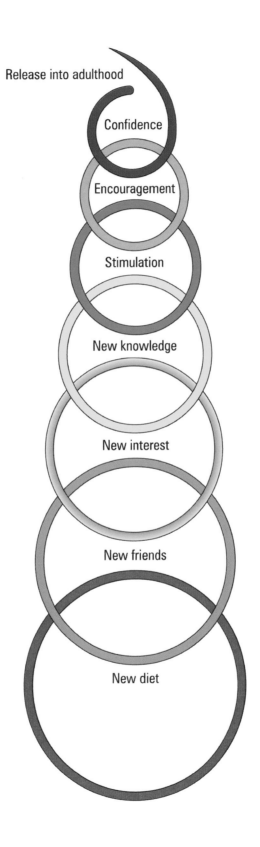

These are just examples of subtle changes in life that can be very important but are easily overlooked. Both these changes and any others you may have noticed in your own life may indicate that you are at the end of a phase, ready to enter a new one.

During these times of change and uncertainty we cannot underestimate the helpfulness of support and encouragement from those who have already passed through a new phase. Consider life like a book: the duration of our life is a single book, and each phase a chapter. We can benefit and learn from those who have already begun the next chapter so they can help us through the transition stage. Remember that in order to find what we are now interested in may also mean finding out what *does not* interest us so we can home in on what is really important. The process may take some time as we will seek new knowledge and it requires, to a certain degree, learning who the 'new' us is. However, the patience will be rewarded as we will meet someone, find something or come across a new place that will signify the start of the next, new chapter. In doing so, we will finish the spring-cleaning of the previous chapter by tying up loose ends and then close it neatly. Universal law dictates that we create a space and then clean that space to allow the new thing to move into it, so do not worry that by moving forward you will be leaving chaos and disarray in your wake.

Decision Making

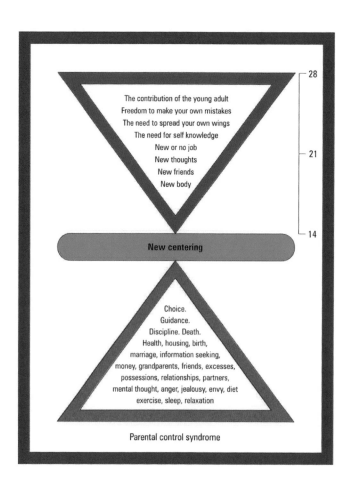

The working framework of years standing starts to crumble

The diagram shows an arena that is roughly double the size of what we are used to working in. In that arena other people have made certain choices for us and disciplines have been thrust upon us: in childhood we are told how to behave and speak; we have little to no choice in where we live, how much money we have and who we should see. These decisions, although affecting our lives directly, are made by those who preside over us and hold us within their care, such as parents and guardians. This is called the Parental Control Syndrome.

As our expansion path begins, we start by taking up more space as we continue in our established routines as well as looking at the next ideal, rather than shrinking and modifying our current routines to incorporate the future movements and plans. In this transitional phase of enlargement we retain what is familiar so we can extract its essence, removing the important bare bones of it and discarding the useless filler, and deduce what the next ideal really means and entails.

Once we have acquired all the information we will be able to decide where to go from here and what is best for us, shrinking back to occupy less space than we did when enlarged with our previous routines in addition to the new ideal. However, the shrink is not immediate and while we approach the decision we are stretched to the limit of our capacity – referring back to the egg analogy, our shell at this point would be straining against every conceivable part of the egg box moulding that encapsulates us, and we are at risk of taking in too much information too quickly. Our saving grace here is that the decision is made slowly, giving us time to receive information from all around and digest it at our own pace; the slow speed of this process lessens the vulnerability we are exposed to from being over-stretched and allows us to prepare for the consequence of our eventual decision. That decision will be the turning point in our future as it is our next step, and it will affect those around us as well as us personally.

Our first attempt at this is between fourteen and twenty-one, with the precise age being different for each individual, and being our first time and with so much to learn, incorporate and attempt to discard, we stretch to the upper limits. It is within this age range that we try to learn for the very first time what we are capable of – physically and mentally – and we find our own knowledge from wherever we think is best, we make our own mistakes and, to begin with at least, we will fight to reside in the upper half of the previous diagram. Simply put, we begin fighting for our freedom and carving our own path.

Now, this is a complicated process that requires much effort, and so, as with most things that require such effort, it may require multiple attempts. Going back to the above image, the process means that you will be bringing the ceiling down and the floor up, closing the gap. This is repeated until the original triangle is once again there, but repositioned from the bottom to the centre. This highlights the change of priorities and our newfound control. It is at this point, and no stage earlier, that we will have achieved the flexibility to take from external sources what we want or need and reject what we do not. This is a crucial stage of our development and just as a university student is able to handle information better than a toddler, this stage signifies a huge step forward for our capacity to embrace and reject, becoming more developed individuals.

At this point, a recurrent theme throughout life must be highlighted. People can be grouped into two categories based on their decisions: whether to grab instant return whenever possible, or strap in for a long-term investment. Typically, the harder a path is, the more rewarding it will be at the end, so the gains will be great but it will take longer to get there. Alternatively, very many people opt for instant gratification because the rewards, while possibly lesser, are immediate. It settles the desire for something straight away and that is considered a pay-off for having less than would be received had the long game been played. Ultimately, the decision rests on each individual, but it is always worth aiming for the harder path, for it shows strength of character and further development, and far more will be gained from it.

Balance

Balance is about finding a point that is compatible with our current state and where we want to be. Consider the following diagram and imagine drawing a line from 'positive thought' to 'pressure', 'joy' to 'inertia' and 'negative thought' to 'freedom'. Lines can be drawn from any point on the left to right, as they are equal opposites of each other. As such, one is where we perhaps might be currently, and the other is the goal. Balance is the mid-point between them, finding a spot where we are happy and able to move forward.

As children we have an abundance of physical energy, always on the go, up to mischief and looking for adventure. From the moment our eyes open in the morning until they close at night, we are in a state of perpetual motion, stopping only for a short break or when our parents call us indoors for food. At that stage in our lives, our entire focus is on our physicality and not our emotional side; no percentage of brain power is devoted to our feelings. By the time we reach adolescence, though, our physical drive, while still there at a high level, has decreased slightly to accommodate our newfound interest in developing our feelings. While as children we had no interest in the opposite sex, as an example, by our teenage years we begin to see them in a new light, and fostering relationships both with friends and now partners takes more effort, which is accomplished by lowering our physical side. After all, some space must be freed to make room for this new development. After a period of time, when we are used to managing both aspects of ourselves, we can make the required adjustments to each level so both are running at the optimum amount, without one hogging too much space and thus having a negative effect on the other.

Lack of dis-ease can equate to
feeling comfortable between opposites

All invisible senses

Spiritual
eg - Positive thoughts

Negative thought

Mental
eg - Freedom

Pressure

Emotions
eg - Joy

Joyless

Physical
eg - Over exertion

Inertia

Balance of
our world

A positive reaction to this change signifies who we are now and where we are in our development. The experience is completed by realigning the physical, emotional and mental outlook and then adjusting what we have learnt from our experience and noting what we still do not know or want to investigate at some point in the future. This returns us to a state of balance while simultaneously acknowledging that we must pursue our development later.

Suffering from inert behaviour may be a sign one feels life currently holds no joy, and the inertia within the negativity will be a further pressure. However, understanding that the entire cycle is being released will allow us to feel more positive and find freedom from the past, creating joy even if we are still over exerting ourselves.

Balancing the over exertion and inertia to close the circuit is the ideal boundary. Prior to this, we will have been working physically with one or the other and our balance would be negative as we flick between over exertion and inertia; and having too much of one means we must find the middle to strike a balance.

Now that the space itself has been figured out, envision a rectangular frame around it to contain it, giving you a clear and vivid image of the space, its size and partitions for each of the contents. Having done this, it is relatively simple to recreate the balance between the opposites again. The next step is to move from the spiritual positive standard holding through intellectual pressure; you may feel emotionally good but physically inert, or emotionally negative, knowing what you want and how to get it but it seems like a joyless activity as you physically seek out the plan of action.

The attitude we hold at this time will inform us of whether or not this experiment is viable as well as telling us if we need any help and, if so, what type. This cautious approach is positive in nature and thus will counter a seemingly negative experience, providing balance between what we know and what we suspect.

Integration

Growth

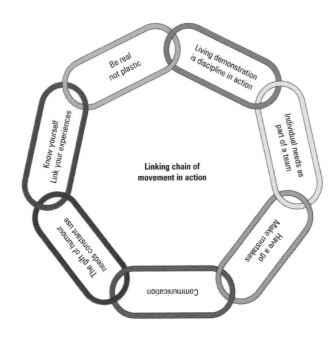

Living demonstration is discipline in action

Be real not plastic

Individual needs as part of a team

Know yourself
Link your experiences

Linking chain of movement in action

Have a go
Make mistakes

The gift of humour needs constant use

Communication

The joy is not always a pleasure

Quite often in life we think have wasted time on something because nothing, or very little, physical was drawn from it. As one example, often people who exit a long term relationship think it was a waste of time because it did not last forever. However, each circumstance is an arena for us to learn from and take experience from. In the case of relationships, far from being wasted, we always move on with a wealth of new knowledge to take to the next relationship, such as how not to let ourselves be treated, how to defuse a situation and how to help the longevity of the relationship.

Things are always cloudier at the time of a given incident, and the majority of people upon becoming single after being in a relationship for any sustained period of time will not view it as a good thing, but will rather be weighed down by negative thoughts with no scope for potential benefits. However, that same person six months down the line will be far more upbeat and positive for the future and feeling armed with knowledge and experience that eluded them previously.

The chances are that within your own life you will be able to recall experiences that at the time would have made the future look bleak but, looking back now, had clear positive impacts on your future. In fact, after these negative experiences, once the dust settles and we see the positive changes, we usually say "It is like it was meant to be." Hindsight encourages greater perspective of the mapping of our individual lives.

Sometimes the only way round is through; we cannot avoid everything, and there are times in life when a particular aspect of learning demands this of us. Sometimes there is the added benefit of learning something from a tough experience, too, and if we push through those demanding times to come out the other side, we may be lucky enough to have a sense of gratitude as well. When working through something such as this book, there will be times when one aspect is harder than others, although what that part is exactly will vary from person to person. However, it is important to keep things in proper context and focus, and one must learn that linking each chapter is akin to a chain: each link must be attended to as its own separate entity before they can be joined together to form a complete chain.

Just like links coming together to form a chain, your past steps are a foundation that create your future. Accordingly, if you want to get a glimpse of your future simply make a list of the things that occurred in your past – events, jobs, relationships, friendships and so forth – and put it together in another way. This is not a crystal ball and it will not show you losses and gains, fortunes and the eventual cause of your death, rather you will have created a revealing picture of the foundation of your next step in life, an unearthing of your forthcoming event.

If there was ever any incentive needed to be true to yourself and not live behind a mask for the satisfaction of others then this is it. If we live our lives perpetually playing a role then it will be impossible for us to pave the next step based on our past, as our past will not be representative of who we truly are. It must be clarified here that roles themselves are fine, but it is of the utmost importance that we remain aware of where the role ends and our real person begins, for if we get lost and consumed under the mask then how can we continue as our true selves?

In order to remain on the right path we are dependent on feedback, especially if we are looking as though we are approaching the point of no return. At such times, we rely on the people closest to us to help us stay true to ourselves. The importance of a team to provide feedback cannot be overstated or underestimated, especially as during periods of growth we must make mistakes to learn from and overextend ourselves to increase our capacity. Also be aware that when people change it is human nature to try to stop, for fear of change or losing who we are. This is fine, but for a limited period of time only while we rest, after which we must get back on the horse to continue; never rest on our laurels and stop completely.

Part of our growth is learning to communicate on all levels, which includes learning to laugh with others. This may seem odd, for we all have our social groups and the ability to laugh with friends and family. However, when we grow spiritually there is the inclination to lose our sense of humour, becoming very dry and serious. In order to continue developing we must either retain or find that humour once more. This is more than watching a light-hearted comedy film with friends, though; it is extremely challenging to increase our level of trust and, until we learn to embrace it, there comes a point when we must really learn to 'lighten up', and this is the essence of finding that sense of humour we all have. It is important not to be so consumed by growth that we become overly serious and overlook the fun in life.

One of the easiest ways of 'lightening up' is recognising that every person is limited in some areas, while our talents shine in different places – some may be great at drawing but bad listeners, others may be natural speakers but awkward in crowds, and so on. While we may envy the skillset of someone else, it is important to remember at all times that we, too, have our own talents that others are envious of. As we all have our skills no person is more important than another, so while it may be enticing, there is no justification in feeling inferior to others, for our talents are what help shape us into the people we are and become. The same is also true of our past experiences: as stated previously, everything we go through is a learning experience and helps us progress, and there is no single section of our life that works as an exception to that rule. This is a crucial piece of information for all of us and it is of prime importance that we understand it and work with forgiveness when it comes to others, as it takes some longer to realise what we have to offer. Part of the reason for this is a lot of times people are looking for what others can offer them personally, but it is an erroneous attitude because it is not the satisfaction of all others that we must strive for or even acknowledge, but rather the development of ourselves and the realisation that we have an impact on many people and the wider picture itself.

Chapter 3: What Is Next

Wants and Needs

Whole Worlds

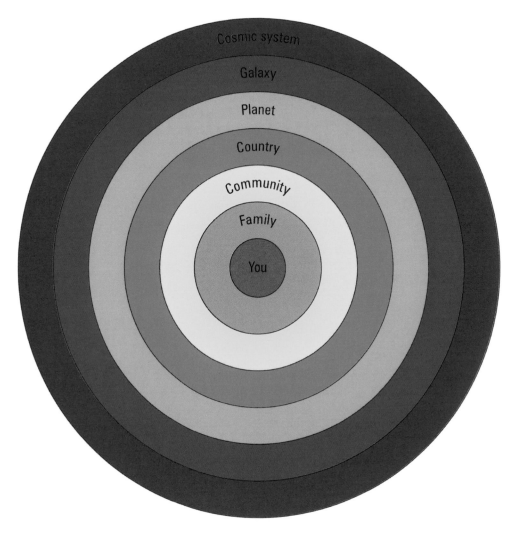

How often in life have you heard, or muttered, the immortal words "It is not what I was expecting", or, "Yes it is nice, but…"? Chances are you have both heard it and said it numerous times, because our wants require adaptation to our needs and, seemingly worse, the needs of others, too. In such times, what are we supposed to do? We want what is best for us, but at the same time one lesson instilled in us from childhood is not to be selfish and consider the needs of others if not above ours then at least on par or a close second. So we are left facing a crossroad: do we continue doing what we always have done, or take a new path?

This is the time for brutal honesty with oneself; decide what will *truly* be of assistance and not choosing something because it is an easy way out. The reason for this necessity of honesty is because those around you may be too kind, which will have negative repercussions in the quest for development, or they may take control of your situation, side-tracking you and making you neglect the entire point – in both scenarios, you come away empty-handed. At times like these, when we are required to make a tough decision, it is all too easy to pawn off our duty elsewhere, but we must always take responsibility for ourselves and particularly the way we behave multi-dimensionally. We are used to taking responsibility for our physical actions, but mentally and emotionally we are more apt to neglect it. However, looking at the above sentence about employing the assistance of those around us, we are responsible for that decision and must embrace it fully, being careful not to make the wrong decision so we can pin eventual failure on it. In order to do this, we must have understanding – until we have understanding we are not responsible, and once we do have it, we are. The reason for this again links to the above about assistance from our nearest and dearest: on this path, we are learning honesty to a more profound level – not just telling the truth in response to a question but in being honest with ourselves also – and once we understand that, we acquire responsibility.

Our emotional state reflects who we are and where we are. If we wake in the morning feeling full of life then we are cheerful, considerate and kind. On the other hand, if in the morning we feel dejected and bemoaning everything in a woeful state, we will be perpetuating a negative self-fulfilling prophecy whereby nobody understands us and we will remain in that state. Worse still, not only will our personal day begin badly but our negative attitude will rub off on those around us, so we will be starting our family's day off badly too, which has a knock-on effect on the people we encounter at work or school. We have the power, therefore, to put the days of many people into disarray before even buttering a slice of toast for breakfast. As such, it is our responsibility to take check of how we feel and, if negative, inform those in our immediate vicinity that we are not feeling our best and would appreciate some space to understand why we feel so low; that way, we are sparing the feelings of loved ones and doing our best to keep their day afloat, as well as winning sympathetic understanding for our honesty and consideration.

The soul searching path is long and a lot to take in, but we must make sure to not let it consume us; if we become so self-involved searching for it that we become unpleasant people, without time for friends or family, we will have lost all purpose as humans and no one is going to be convinced of our spirituality. After all, the journey is about improving ourselves, and one of the most important things any person can do is offer support and kindness to others. The journey will be time consuming, of course, and require much of us, but we must always remember to remain available to those who need us.

This eloquently takes us to the next point: when we want to achieve something we want it to happen immediately or at least extremely fast. Spiritual development is no exception and we will want to progress rapidly, but this is not always practical or possible and we must allow those around us to catch up with us: our development may cause embarrassment to our children, or our parents may need time to comprehend things because what we are going through far exceeds their experience; there are myriad reasons why others need time to catch up, and that is fine. We must recognise it and provide that time. Spiritual development will be your path and that takes time, so you must also acknowledge that your path is leading to the development, in

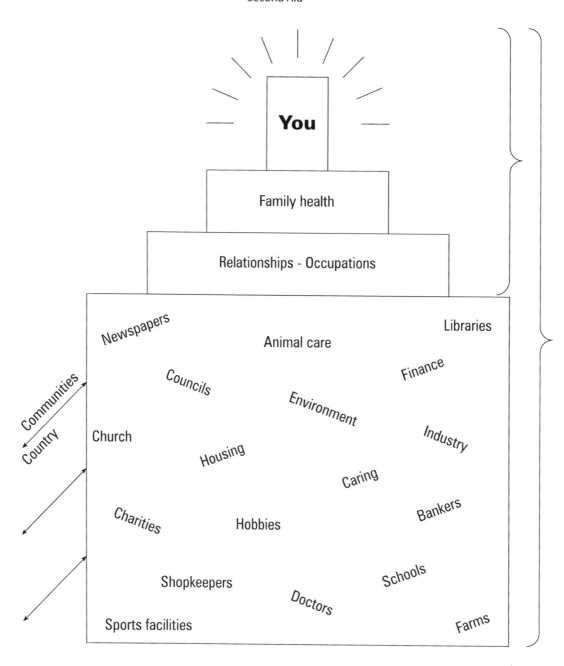

You . . .

Your health . . .

Your town . . .

Your responsibility . . .

Help yourself and your town

other areas, of those in your vicinity. An important lesson is the recognition that time is necessary. The age of Pisces was the age of saving ourselves and the age of Aquarius is the age of working with a group, and while we may consider that a backwards step it is sometimes necessary to do that because one step back can provide the enthusiasm to go further forward at an increased speed, but, as ever, patience is key: let things happen at the pace they are supposed to happen without trying to force anything. We will know when the time is right, and when that time comes we will be adequately prepared to handle the forthcoming pressure.

The following is a self-reflection exercise designed to assist you in identifying your wants and needs:

1) What food would you like to eat at this precise moment?
2) What flower and in what colour would you most like to receive?
3) What quality you most like to possess (e.g. humility, temperance)?
4) What is the most lavish gift you would like to be given?

Each question carries significance and was asked for a specific reason. The food equates to your body's needs; as mentioned already diet has significant bearings on desires. We will crave earthly foods like potatoes and pasta when we are searching for security and fruit and vegetables when we need to purify. An attraction to exotic tastes is indicative of a need to rest and change, and spicy foods signify a craving for stimulation.

The flower in question two shows our emotional state. Of course, roses indicate desire and love, but the white colour represent purity and the deep red signifies passion. Conversely, a daffodil tells of a fresh opportunity, while a tulip, top-heavy by design, means a desire for infilling. A lily shows purity within transition and an iris is a disciplined flower, showing regimentation in life.

The quality we would give ourselves in question three suggests our shortcomings and how we judge ourselves. It shows our inner thoughts on where we need to improve, linking our mental state with our self-worth.

Finally, the gift we would choose to receive in question four symbolises spiritual value and a certain level of trust in the present moment. This question is particularly difficult for people who believe they must suffer or compromise their standards by having anything material to enjoy, lest they not be serving correctly. This notion should be discarded, though; our desires make us human – besides, we will be far less threatening to others if we show interest in everyday things!

Extremes

In order to find our own place we take others' guidance and, recognising that what works for one person will not necessarily work for all, tailor it to our individual specifications and needs. To do this effectively, we need a measuring tool. For instance, to measure, say, three feet on a measuring tape we need to acknowledge the point of zero, and with our emotions we cannot possibly know one until we experience another, for example we cannot know what it feels like to be well unless we have been ill, and vice versa. Similarly, we will not acknowledge feeling good until we have felt bad. Having felt both, we can gauge how bad, or good, we feel in relation to our prior experience. Our experience also allows us to find a centre point, like finding a neutral pH, combining all our knowledge and prior experiences.

Opposites

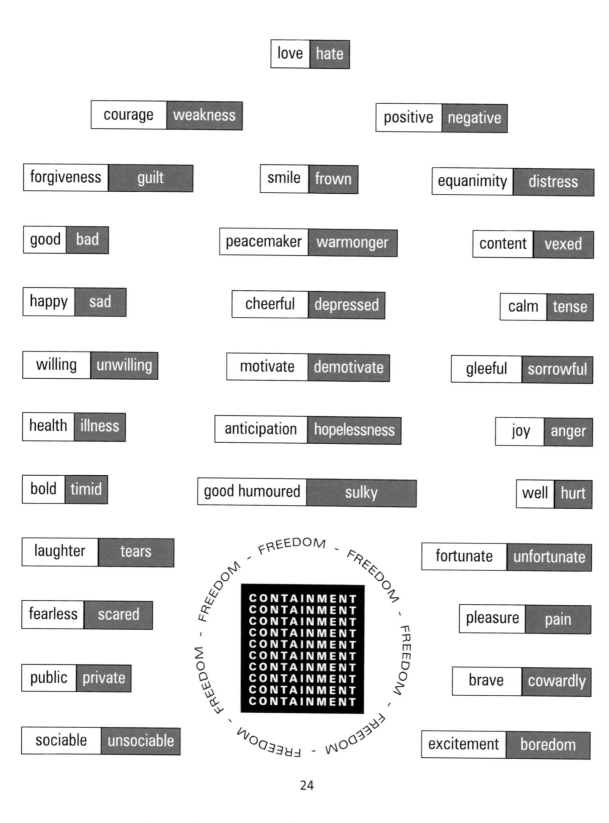

love | hate

courage | weakness

positive | negative

forgiveness | guilt

smile | frown

equanimity | distress

good | bad

peacemaker | warmonger

content | vexed

happy | sad

cheerful | depressed

calm | tense

willing | unwilling

motivate | demotivate

gleeful | sorrowful

health | illness

anticipation | hopelessness

joy | anger

bold | timid

good humoured | sulky

well | hurt

laughter | tears

fortunate | unfortunate

fearless | scared

pleasure | pain

public | private

brave | cowardly

FREEDOM - FREEDOM - FREEDOM - FREEDOM - FREEDOM - FREEDOM - FREEDOM - FREEDOM - FREEDOM - FREEDOM

CONTAINMENT
CONTAINMENT
CONTAINMENT
CONTAINMENT
CONTAINMENT
CONTAINMENT
CONTAINMENT
CONTAINMENT
CONTAINMENT
CONTAINMENT

sociable | unsociable

excitement | boredom

Changes

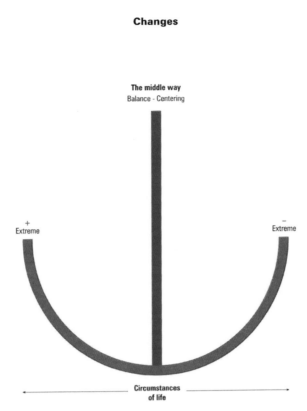

Unfortunately in life we experience negativity, in the form of bad experiences, negative emotions or feeling unwell. Our job, therefore, is to take these negatives and turn them into positives in any way we can. However, if we are in a state of prolonged negativity it can be difficult to remember the positive, and in such a situation we will benefit from a healer to free us from the constraints, acting as a booster in a similar way to a rocket having a booster to overcome the Earth's gravity pulling it down. Once out of the atmosphere, the booster drops from the rocket and it is able to work independently again, and this is the same principle as a healer for our emotions.

The following is a simple physical exercise on gravity fields, with the purpose of increasing your sense of security and protection.

Starting in the squat position, face your palms outward and slowly elevate your body, straightening the back and stretching the arms out to the side until they are fully extended at shoulder height. Once fully extended, raise your arms above your head so the palms meet and then stretch overhead.

Next, turn the palms outward again and bring them back down until extended at shoulder height again.

Then bend your knees and lower your arms until you are back in the squat position and your hands can touch the floor, with your palms facing inwards.

Having completed one repetition, turn your body ninety degrees and do the movement again, turning ninety degrees each time until you have completed it four times facing four directions.

Finally, once you have stood for the last time, remain standing for a few moments to recognise the new rhythm.

Chapter 4: Guidelines During Transition

Laws That Let the Lessons of Life be Learned

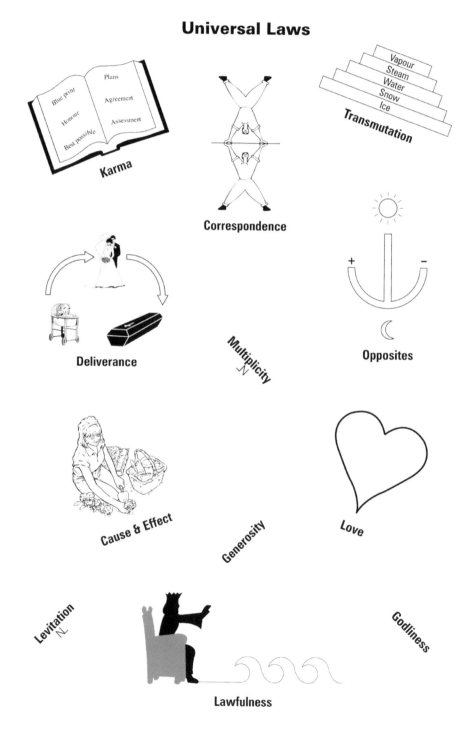

Universal Laws

At some point or another in life we have to question our fundamentals. Most of what we are given we received in early childhood, and some of it we rebelled against as we got older and developed our own sense of identity. However, as we grow and work through personal traumas we must at some point sit up and ask what lessons we could be learning, and what the guidelines are. We must keep learning in an attempt to understand it all, and we must learn under specific rules that allow us to grow while simultaneously harmonising with the abilities and values we already possess. The stress that we encounter both now and in the past serves as motivation for us to seek out a level of comfort that we deem acceptable within our expanding capacity. Sometimes we can feel out of control, especially in the knowledge that we are contingent on forces that are superior to us. However, just as each cell in our body is unique but still part of our body, we, too, can borrow that premise and come to the realisation that we work with the Law of Correspondence.

Essentially, the Law of Correspondence is 'as above, so below'. To give a small example, if only one-tenth of our soul is here on Earth, then nine-tenths are not being used by us at all. Thus, whatever we do on Earth makes it easier for the soul above us, which is then in turn reflected back down to us, making things easier still. However, this rule with positivity is also true with negativity, and so long-term suffering will make things harder than they already are.

Knowing this, we can create our own paths within the overall pattern, meaning we can be our own judges. This also highlights that it is in both the interests of ourselves and of others to be extremely candid, else we could receive energy that we should not be receiving. Karma works within the individual's life, the community and the entire nation with one set of rules. Imagine the Law of Karma to be the blueprint for us, much like the blueprint an architect will use when designing a house, and the Law of Cause and Effect being in this metaphor the building of the House of Karma, right down to being affected by such occurrences as weather, workmen and materials. Depending on the severity of the external factors, and acknowledging that the blueprint may need to be revised more than once, the house may take more or less time to complete than anticipated. It does not matter so much about how long it takes to complete; the important thing is that it will be completed and it requires our involvement to reach that final stage. Therefore, rather than give in to temptation and wait passively for life to happen around us, we must be aware that the Law of Cause and Effect requires total involvement for us to understand cause.

The next law is the Law of Deliverance, which we see in action once we recognise that life has stages of progression from birth to death – as with everything, life has a beginning, middle and end. This is more than just youth, middle age and senior years, however; at the beginning of our life we usually do not keep track of time as we are too busy enjoying ourselves. In the middle we learn more about discipline, and at the end we require help from others as we may forget quite where we are in life's sequence.

We can understand the Law of Opposites by going to the extremes. This allows us to make our own conclusions on what is best for us without too much outside influence; at this point, we recognise the mantra of what is good for one is not necessarily good for all.

It is neither a secret nor a surprise that we develop by using past experiences, extracting the positives for future use and acknowledging where we went wrong, then progressing forward. The Law of Transmutation defines this, and it is where the ceiling of previous lessons now becomes the floor of the future: where we reached the upper limits in the past, we have now progressed enough to go to the ceiling above just like climbing the stairs in a multi-storey building.

The Law of Lawfulness is where we learn movement within the solid nature of a moment and find new form. It is where we learn what we can and cannot change; within this movement we remain static and, unaware of how to leave behind past experiences, we become extremely uncomfortable and constrained.

The Law of Generosity encourages us to not be solitary and confined, but to be linked in harmony with the kingdoms of the animals, vegetation and minerals and to the energies present from other dimensions. This law links with karma, in that we reap what we sow: if we treat others with kindness and compassion we will receive as much back, but if we treat people badly we will receive that, but not necessarily from the same place we sent it.

The Law of Generosity has a knock-on effect, too, in as much as once we have learnt how to link we will recognise that with increased knowledge comes increased responsibility and compassion for the Earth and all its inhabitants, and this is the Law of Love. Love is the glue of the Universe, and the Law of Godliness dictates that love must include everything and embrace all, not be selective in what is included. With this new knowledge and responsibility, our opinions are only good for personal measurement to see how what we think and perceive has changed; instead of being able to judge others we must care for all equally and irrespective of their actions, acknowledging that we do not and cannot understand everything. This is where the Law of Levitation shows that we are to rise above our problems to get past them, rather than pretending they do not exist and consequently being stuck in one place for longer than we should be.

Lessons of Life – A Production Line

Lessons of living:

1) Solidity: the remassing of form
2) Candidity: our own truth, not that of others
3) Datewise: realising that we follow greater patterns and routines
4) Good intentions: the motive of what we try rather than the results
5) To have a good go: get involved, aim high and trust in our abilities
6) To know that we will gain the knowledge we require as it is required, prompted by the will to look for it
7) To do as we think is right and not be too influenced by others
8) Datelink: the linking of experiences making use of the essences
9) Communicating what we know to others
10) The love of all
11) The linking of harmony to other dimensions
12) Care of all the creatures on Earth

Picture the inner-workings of a manufacturing industry. A supply of raw material is delivered to the incoming goods warehouse, perhaps on a forklift, and production workers begin the significant task of turning the individual materials and components into complete products that have mass appeal in order to sell commercially. There are the typical industry issues that need to be navigated, too, such as the specific area of work on that day being dependent on who is available at work and who is required to build a given section depending on their skill set, in addition to people who may not be at work that day. The flow of work also hinges on schedules, industry standards that must be complied with, health and safety laws and officials, and the personnel carrying out checks throughout the process. This happens each and every day for every product we purchase, but it is the unseen process.

While this is happening in the factory or warehouse, the sales department will be deducing the differences between the home and foreign markets, conducting market research to determine the best way to get the product to market and sell significant quantities. This will involve many man/woman-hours of carrying out the research and creating presentations, graphics and packaging. The sales department is trying to work out how to sell many units and the production team is busy putting the product together, while the public relations department and quality control sections will want to achieve basic minimum standards. In order for any of this to take place, though, the welfare department must be prepared to support the production's work ethic, which must include a canteen as well as a sports and social club.

The above procedures are true for the majority of manufacturing industries, but they are also true of the way we process information. As energy or ideas are received they must go through the processes outlined here before they are refined and allowed to be released into another arena of life. We must be patient and realise that things require time to mature; we often reject ideas because we think we do not have the time necessary to let them develop and cultivate, but ideas, like products, have a long process to go through before being in their final state. If we are too impatient we will be continually searching for perfection, and never finding it, rather than being willing and able to utilise what is at hand. This is what we must do instead, just as industry managers do not wait for perfect materials to be built but use what is already available, refine it and then release it.

Energy Exchanges

As we progress through life we are almost always unaware of our potential. In spite of our ignorance, though, it is always there just waiting to be found. We all know we have potential, of course, but we may be eluded on where it is and just how much we have. A good start to finding it is asking, but asking others is not limited to friends and family but also God in prayer.

In order to do this, set aside some quiet time every day, making sure you will have no interruptions, and simply ask for the finest and highest level that we are capable of. Then it is just a matter of waiting to receive. While in the process of waiting you can help facilitate proceedings through daily meditation, as this is just the process of both seeing and listening until we learn what is required. This should be done in conjunction with transmitting, which is the reporting back and asking what is required and how to go about it. It is important to bear in mind that in this type of meditation we try to love each part of our being in its present state. Be careful not to confuse this with complacency and no longer trying to improve, just that in the meditative state we are attempting to create harmony throughout our self. This is an important stage because the energies above us are always there, but what we will connect to depends on our state of mind and being. Look upon the process thus: meditation is a state of receiving, praying is a state of transmitting and contemplation on how to fuse them together completes the process.

Our energetic circuitry must be as clean as possible. The section of ourselves we have with us on Earth is our own responsibility and, just like our friends and partners, we are going to be more attractive when clean and welcoming. The added benefit is that our planet is so polluted it is a difficult task for the Management Upstairs to get in, so by becoming a point of light ourselves we stand more chance of attracting them down. Having acknowledged the above, once we make the decision to improve at soul level and cleanse, we go deep into ourselves, and to do this we must be willing to start a new chapter. We must forgive ourselves for past mistakes and grievances, acknowledging that we were younger and not as aware of things as we are today. During this process there may be a struggle between our physical body and our inner selves, or soul, in which the inner will be ready to progress to the next chapter but the body protests, instead wanting to recuperate from the last experience. When we feel this we must work hard to bring the intent into the physical body; we must earth old experiences through our body and grab the light from above. We will almost certainly notice changes in how we feel during these times, with either very high levels of energy or none, causing us to feel very high or very low respectively. Consequently, we may notice ourselves being constantly hungry or completely off food, wanting to sleep all the time or just wanting to remain conscious as much as possible.

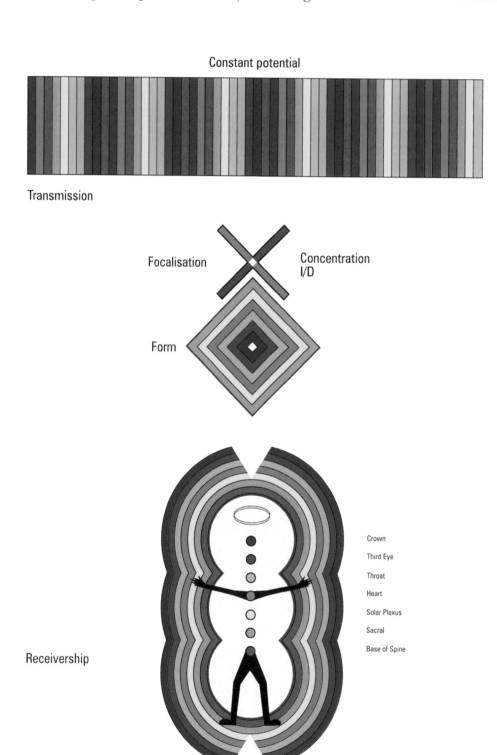

Our balance at this point will be out of whack and we must utilise the nourishment of the Earth Mother to restore our energy balance, stabilising us so we may continue forward.

Of critical importance at this stage in the journey is that this is a quiet time, where we want to withdraw from social gatherings and want to be alone.

When we reach stage two we will attract in situations to dramatise the current situation and want feedback on how we fared. This process will conjure up memories, and we will either act as we are used to, not letting the past go, or we will keep our newfound inner standards and release the old experiences, emerging like a moth from a cocoon: a new, beautiful self, emerging from a former body to progress through life's next step.

In the third stage we will attempt to accept the presented circumstances, trust the new representation and surrender to the will of God.

Inter-relationships

Often in life we feel the need to prove ourselves to others, but such an attitude blinds us to the point that we only see what we want to see, with anything that goes against what we want to see blocked out. There are times we are able to continue our relationships without this getting in the way, but at other times we need to break it down in order to rebuild from scratch. This building from scratch becomes a whole new experience in itself, as it forces us to realise that we, as human beings, are inter-connected to all forms of life, from each other to insects to the rocks and minerals we walk on. Not only are we connected to other things, so, too, are they: the plants, for example, are their own life but inter-relate with the soil and ground they grow in, with the balance of life affected by both. At its most basic, this lesson is the food chain: humans, mammals, insects, reptiles, plants, minerals, everything has its own independent life that both affects and is dependent on others for its own survival and the balance of life as an entire system, as shown in the diagram below. We need to realise from this that we are a small but intricate part of a wider system, and we need to respect and relate to all forms of life.

Naturally, as we can expect by being inter-related with other forms of life, humans are not the only ones on Earth capable of healing. However, a quick look at the above image will explain how the suggestion came about: the kingdoms of nature are on the lower half of the diagram and we respond at an instinctive level to these, while we respond to internal promptings of the Greater, shown at the top half of the diagram.

The mineral kingdom is shown in red in the diagram, which represents the longest and lowest sound; the oldest known form of healing was to carry an ill person to a standing stone with a hole that passed right through, to put the body through the hole and to then carry it home again. While it may not be considered very medicinal now, the reasoning was simple: minerals are the base note of the Earth; if we lose our rhythm we become sick and a way to restore the natural rhythm is to 'remind' the body of that base note, in a similar way to tuning a musical instrument by adjusting the tension on the strings so it resonates at a different pitch.

It is our nature to try to please everyone and simultaneously be everywhere, but it is crucial that we recognise this is not possible. Our goal is to find our own path, and although it may well be similar to that of others it will not be the same: each path is unique by some determining factor(s). Just as there is not one road to any given location, there is not one sole path for people to follow – the question is choosing which one. Do we build upon past experiences? Base the future on what is required of us currently? Predict what the future holds and go that way? There are multiple choices for us, and the important thing is not to get weighed down by the enormity of the situation, as that will just lead to us being ill, perhaps fatally so. This is particularly true for people of a certain age, where such restraints as mortgages, loans, careers and relationships make it feel as

Horizontal polarity

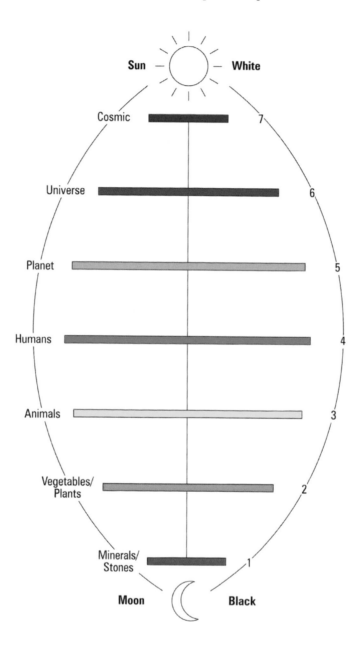

though it is impossible to change anything and this can cause such pressure that a heart attack is brought on as the only way of release. However, a simple change of attitude can permit proceeding in a new way, one that satisfies and stimulates while allowing one to fulfil the responsibilities. There is a hurdle here, though, and it is a big one: it requires the courage to accept that we are led by a higher standard than before; that whereas previously we made our own small decisions, we have now surrendered to a power larger than we can comprehend that will take our life in a direction that will provide us with increased levels of happiness.

Exposure

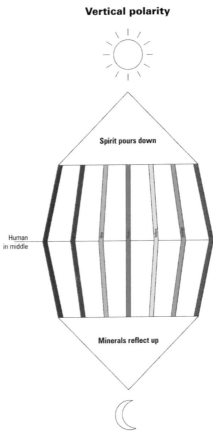

The above diagram shows how mixing separate forces creates a strong foundation for us to grow safely. Darkness allows life to be nurtured, providing room and space to grow uninterrupted, while the light provides warmth and strength. Just like grass exposed to constant heat, though, too much sun will cause the new life to burn and possibly die, while too little will result in malnourishment and possibly death; therefore, exposure to both must be controlled and balanced until we are developed enough for it to be safe to make direct contact. In terms of our daily lives and understanding, this means that there will be times when it is necessary to divide and separate so we can logically deal with the problems of each colour in front of us. Just like the darkness and light, we can update the colours we do and do not need as we work on finding the balance that we require, in a similar way to a baby learning to walk having to learn how much pressure to put on each leg in order to remain upright and not fall down. Learning to gauge our reactions means we are starting to contribute to the whole, which in turn means we are becoming part of a solution rather than adding to the problems.

The above diagram shows the white light that beams down on us, from which we take what we need to grow. The moon is the other influence on us and our planet, absorbing our excesses and reflecting back to us how well we are coping. A poignant example of this can be found in teenagers, more specifically how they dress: early in life children will be dressed by their parents, then develop their own style based on the influence of parents, friends and the environment they find themselves in. Somewhere during the teenage years, something changes and they invariably choose to dress in black – reflected in a typically unhappy attitude as they try to find themselves and their direction in life; once they have found some answers or made some decisions that are satisfactory, a white shirt will be added to their wardrobe, and life is simply black and white. Finally, when they have finished taking what they need from the incoming energy and removed the old undesired energy, they will begin to wear other colours once again. While this pattern repeats itself throughout our lives, it is most prominent and noticeable in teenagers.

Chapter 5: Personal Programming

Personal Programming

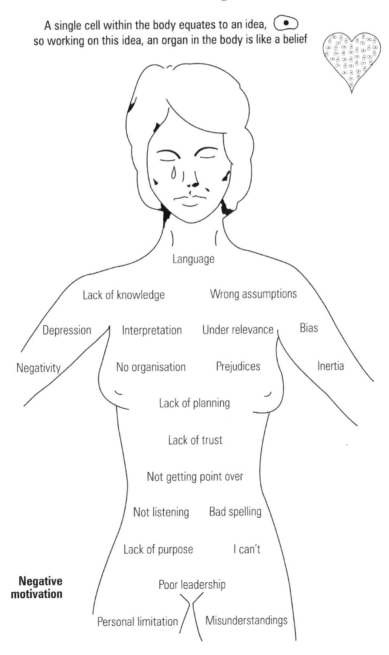

Communication negatives

A single cell within the body equates to an idea, so working on this idea, an organ in the body is like a belief

Language

Lack of knowledge   Wrong assumptions

Depression   Interpretation   Under relevance   Bias

Negativity   No organisation   Prejudices   Inertia

Lack of planning

Lack of trust

Not getting point over

Not listening   Bad spelling

Lack of purpose   I can't

Negative motivation   Poor leadership

Personal limitation   Misunderstandings

Although we may feel as though truth is absolute, in reality it is relative: changing as we grow, experience new things and learn new lessons. The truth we had in childhood adapts as we develop into adults so that our truth now is different to what it once was. Thus, it is imperative we update our personal programming to avoid the danger of the self-destruction we face from denying ourselves our new truth. It takes much courage to change and often our cells hold memories that are now irrelevant or void, such as the negativity and lack of confidence stemming from a child at school once telling us we were not good enough at something. Despite growing immeasurably since that time, we can hold onto those feelings of rejection. It is important, though, to rid ourselves of this: if the cell harbouring that emotion resonates with the cell next to it we can have a sick organ, and if they relate to adjacent cells the problem can spread until we have a sick body, despite the fact the information that created the sickness is no longer even true.

Each one of our numerous cells holds memory of the whole, but not each one will agree with its neighbour as that has come from a different area. If we are negatively programmed, which we all are to some degree because we are wont to believe the bad things said about us, the negative can be magnified easily. Hence we need to take care of both our bodies and what animates them, through exercise, meditation, meeting new people and seeing new places if we are active enough to follow such practices; in the event that we are unable to do these things, seeking the help of therapists can help. Indeed, therapists can be so beneficial that the most effective course may be a combination of both the active methods of movement and the passive method of therapy.

Changing is not easy; as the old saying goes: old habits die hard. It is entirely possible but it takes much work and changing a deep-rooted belief takes a lot of time and effort. But the longest journey starts with a single step and we must start from our current position, with the knowledge that our situation is not perfect and neither are we or those who surround us. We require different viewpoints, and by gathering with others into a group, each bringing our own skill and talents, the differences can be tended to and we can create something that is much more than we could ever present alone. Our confidence needs to be boosted to such an extent that we can eventually retain that particular vibration as our standard one, so we no longer fall back onto the negativity we are so keen to hold onto from the past.

Our growth is at its most rapid when we are surrounded by encouragement and support. We then move into the challenge and this is where we discover how well we can do on our own in spite of the negativity we have retained from the past. It is only once these two stages have been undertaken that we are safe in everyday situations, and if we desire to learn the esoteric secrets of the universe then we can simply study our own body: the mineral kingdom is linked to our skeleton; our bones resonate with the Earth's stones; if the plant kingdom links to the glandular system, which is the memory where inherited fear is stored, then we will need to periodically release it, not least because we know that the highest incidence of glandular fever occurs in youths taking important exams and young adults committing to marriage, both of which are people taking responsibility for themselves with no room to blame others. Finally, it is believed our nervous system is linked to animal instinct, which can be found in our inability to relax. This has huge implications for the physical body as the overload shows itself in our circulatory system, with the heart's four chambers losing rhythm leading to an irregular heartbeat.

Thus, we can see how we are linked to the Earth that we inhabit, and with this knowledge our spiritual journey will be made a little easier.

Refining

New situations often present themselves to us and they can come in many forms: new relationships, friendships, opportunities, job interviews, or even just a night out. These situations are exciting and stimulating, but the more we are exposed to any given situation the more we find we dislike about it, and here we are faced with a choice: do we compromise our ideals in the light of experience by continuing with the situation, or not?

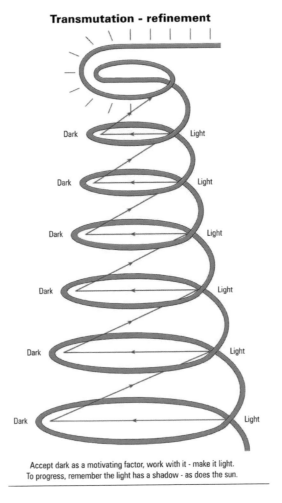

Transmutation - refinement

Accept dark as a motivating factor, work with it - make it light.
To progress, remember the light has a shadow - as does the sun.

Accept dark as a motivating factor and work with it to make it light. In order to progress, remember that light, like the sun, has a shadow of dark.

As we move forward we find that what we originally thought was dark has now merged into light, so much so that we cannot separate the two and they appear to be just one and the same entity. This repeats itself until we eventually wonder what we know. At this point, we encounter the shadow of past experience that we have already gone through, and this conjures up doubt of whether we actually learned anything, because old emotions and feelings have once again become apparent. However, feeling them for the second time, we are to release those emotions rather than experience them again, because it is the *shadow* and not true dark itself. Nonetheless, we will require help here for an extra energy boost that is required to clear and clean the space and be ready for a renewal.

It is a common human fear to be scared of the dark, but we must remember that dark is light at a different level of density, and while making changes ourselves, such as getting married, moving house or getting a new job, will have no effect, changes imposed upon us through events such as death, rape or another moment of loss or sadness, the change is too sudden for us to take in at once and so our energy circuitry will be disturbed.

This delicate circuitry can become unbalanced at childbirth itself, as we spend nine months in the dark serenity of the womb only to suddenly be pushed into the bright lights of a hospital room to be greeted by numerous faces, many of whom will be holding surgical items. The light and noise are not subtle but as stark as they can possibly get, so it is of no surprise that our balance gets disrupted. Worse still, if our mother was frightened during labour or birth, or the delivery was difficult, then we may need the services of a soul therapist to fix our circuitry before we can develop as fluidly as we should.

Regardless of the trouble of birth we do recover from it and settle down. After learning security at home we experience the confusion and stress again by being sent to school, with unfamiliar surroundings and people and, worst of all, we are away from our parents for hours at a time. Once again, though, we learn the rules of school, become familiar with the teachers and make friends in our class and so we relax and settle again. This is a life-long pattern as we repeat it when we leave one school and enrol in another, then university and finally each time we get a new job. A similar learning curve is experienced when we do things for the first time, such as buying our first house or losing our virginity or receiving our first paycheque. At any and all of these moments we once again enter darkness and must progress to the light once we adapt to them.

Progression

Progression

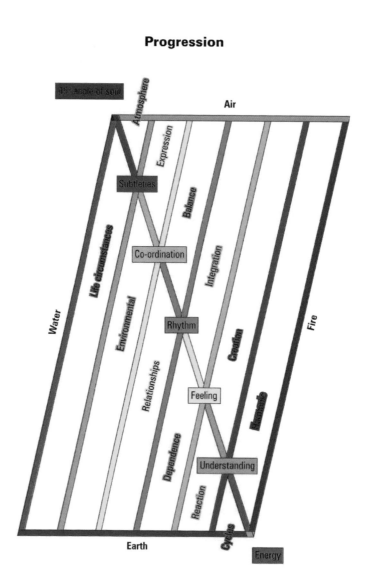

In our individual lives the circumstances we encounter build an atmosphere in which we can express ourselves to others by trying to find a balance between dependence and independence, so we can integrate and react harmoniously with others. Once this stage is reached we are able to go back over our past and determine if our energy creates a feeling at a rhythm that those around us find comforting, or at least do not object to. This will then inform us whether or not we need to adjust further for an accommodating environment. It is at this point of the journey that we start to appreciate the subtle changes afoot that determine our circumstances. Such circumstances are anything from a new job to a new partner or any other opportunity we can think of; quite simply, it is just a matter of moving us along to the next stage, which allows us in turn to break the shackles from our past that we do not need for our future.

Our sense of security depends on us having a framework we can operate in, which also depends on us having processed our fear or not. If we have not done this then we will have fear pockets trapped within our bodies, relating to past experiences rather than current or future ones. The Earth nurtures and supports but sometimes we will experience a situation where we feel like everyone is out to get the better of us. In these cases it is extremely difficult for us to express our needs, which will cause grief for us and others around us. We require air to purify this space, allowing us to slowly inhale the new situation and exhale the reactions we are used to but are now counterproductive or at the very least unnecessary. Fire is the combustible energy of love, which provides us with the time required to create a new, cleaner space where we can harmonise the new with the lessons learnt from the past. Once we have built the new framework to operate in we harness raw energy, and it is at this point that we can begin to understand it, which will lead to a feeling of comfort if we manage to get the rhythm right, but discomfort if we do not.

At this point we coordinate the subtleties of the ideal, which is having an energy that is good for us and those in our vicinity, and combine them with what is possible in our current scenarios. We can then 'let go and let God', knowing that the higher power will take the reins from here. It is difficult to get this right at the first attempt in our polluted environment, but if we manage it then we will receive something to serve. If, however, we get it wrong, then we must try again, learning from the past attempt and content in the knowledge that the chances of success increase each time. As ever, as the new framework is built we will once again move into an area of darkness, resting and regenerating until it is time to move forward again but with strong roots that keep us balanced and secure as we progress.

Visible and Invisible Health

Good health is determined by the absence of disease (broken down into two words as dis-ease, a picture emerges of what ill health really is: a lack of ease within the body). The real question for us is "How do we free ourselves of disease and accept where we find ourselves?" The first step is to learn not to compare ourselves with others, for we are all different and talented in different areas; what we can do is find qualities we admire in others and imitate them until they settle into our expression naturally. This is the second step: taking the finest qualities and connecting to them in a detached manner, being inspired rather than copying. We can then decide what is in our personality that we no longer like and work at removing it, which may mean distancing ourselves from people with behaviours that we do not want to have, just until we are strong enough to avoid slipping into past patterns or picking up unwanted behaviours.

Evolution requires us to utilise all the help that is available, from the Earth itself and the abstract disciplines. Evolution entails us getting to know both ourselves and others better, and we must begin by identifying our skills and recognising how we can serve others to the best of our ability. The world itself runs on sexual energy, and when we harness it this is what gives us the impetus to move. However, when used disruptively it causes sexual disease, so we must be careful to maintain our health standards, of which the greatest lessons are derived from a bygone era, preached to us by the elder members of our family and even in the famous exercise programme created by Charles Atlas: start the day by taking six deep breaths by an open window, get plenty of fresh air and sunshine, cleanse at least once a day, drink pure water and eat fresh fruit and vegetables. These simple things will help keep us healthy, motivated and happy, while a close-knit group of friends with similar interests to our own will provide further joy and contentment, but it is also important to make sure we do not disrespect others just because we are happy.

Cosmic forces & Earthly forces

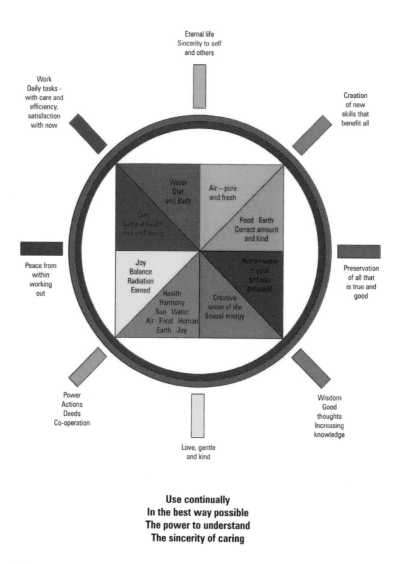

Eternal life
Sincerity to self
and others

Work
Daily tasks -
with care and
efficiency,
satisfaction
with now

Creation
of new
skills that
benefit all

Peace from
within
working
out

Preservation
of all that
is true and
good

Power
Actions
Deeds
Co-operation

Wisdom
Good
thoughts
Increasing
knowledge

Love, gentle
and kind

Water
Diet
and Bath

Air – pure
and fresh

Sun
General health
and well being

Food Earth
Correct amount
and kind

Joy
Balance
Radiation
Earned

Human know
thyself
and use
potential

Health
Harmony
Sun Water
Air Food Human
Earth Joy

Creative
union of life
Sexual energy

**Use continually
In the best way possible
The power to understand
The sincerity of caring**

Change is practised by learning new skills at any given opportunity, and if we focus on the positive and starve the negative of any energy and focus then we will rapidly become wise, for it is the positive that really facilitates growth.

The saying 'actions speak louder than words' is extremely accurate, for it is what we do and how we act that defines how others perceive us, not the words we utter or how many inspirational quotes we can reel off at any given time. We must claim and state our own self-worth and evolve as necessary. By living in the present moment both the past and future are rendered irrelevant because we can only proceed one step at a time, with help from the Light Source and Mother Nature. No matter how far we want to travel, we must walk before we run and even when we sprint we only move forward by taking one step at a time.

External Indicators – Eyes to Feet

Discomfort in our situations, or disease within our body, reflect as warnings that there are imbalances within us. If we recognise this in time then we can investigate what is wrong and fix it; for instance, we can tend to a mild ache before it develops into unbearable pain. What can compound the issue, though, is that the left side and right side of the body can cross over, so one side reflects an issue in the other side. This can cause us to experience pain in the left side when the root of the problem is actually in the right side, for example. We must, therefore, pay attention to everything and recognise when an issue is real and when it is mirroring a problem elsewhere. One way we can do this is by filtering everything that we see and hear, filtering it to the point that we absorb what feels right and rejecting the rest; we must also learn to not live so seriously but instead have fun, laugh frequently and make an effort to socialise and make new friends whenever the opportunity presents itself.

Having followed all the clues we must try to make sense of them and determine how relevant they are to us, and we can facilitate this by discussing it with a friend or loved one, as a detached viewpoint can be extremely helpful. The following list provides some possible meanings for pain or reactions, but keep in mind that they are only suggestions and possibilities, not absolutes, and they can be used in conjunction with Louise Hay's *Heal Your Body*.

Body Area	Right Side	Left Side
Eyes	Tells us to give a second look at another method of achieving the said objective	Will make a less detailed but more all-embracing scrutiny
Ears	Male, dominant, aggressive and outgoing	Passive, non-dominant, more introvert
Nose	Smell more closely; test the atmosphere	Let the standard alone without interference
Neck	An inability to assimilate all that is going on within the body	An inability to sort out the thinking mind which seems overloaded
Shoulders	Anger at prevailing conditions	Carrying a load that feels uncomfortable
Shoulder blades	An impression received is not to our liking	A need to pursue yet a reluctance to proceed
Shoulder to elbow	A need to be shown how to proceed	An asking to be nurtured and guided by experience of our past
Breasts	A little space is needed to allow the way ahead to become clearer before proceeding	Time to assert your own standards on your environment
Stomach	Too much is happening and the body is not able to process the experience	A need to drop one's load of experience to date but not knowing how to proceed

Elbow to wrist	A need to think and assess for yourself	A need to learn and accept the experience of others to give you more material to work with
Hands	More theory can be assimilated for usage	Let go of the logical mind and get more practice with the basics
Hips	Allow yourself the freedom to be carried by others	A time to carry others
Buttocks	Sit on the situation until all the facts are clear	You need to look, for until you express your curiosity you are unable to make headway
Thighs	Deeply felt worries, which take up time. Worries of damnation by the family	Use of emotional energy, which has worn down self-esteem. Worries of the damnation of God
Knees	Not enough deference to the wishes of others	Too much bowing and scraping without thinking why you are doing things this way
Knee to ankle	A feeling of a need to live and experience rather than be told by others	A need to be guided by others and then to personally review
Ankle	An impatience which needs checking	A reluctance to move onwards
Feet	Leave alone for now	Walk onwards

External Indicators – Hands and Feet

Continuing from the above, the vibration of our body is often present in the use of our hands and feet, both as the need to be nurtured and also a showing of how we feel. For instance, when walking we can choose to tread lightly or stamp our feet; when shaking hands we can offer a limp shake indicating low self-esteem, a firm shake indicating our confidence, or clasp so tight that we are indicating superiority. Our hands and feet are important in displaying our emotions and they also inform us of change.

Hands

	Right Side	**Left Side**
Thumb	If courage is shown it will be magnified a thousand-fold	An indication of the foundation of loyalties within the familiar
First finger	Indicates a new way of observing should be pursued	Way pointer for the next logical step
Longest finger	The change to mind control as opposed to brain repetition	Pointer of instinctive action stored up in historical memory
Fourth finger	Shows new devotion lies beyond existing experience	A wedding of polarities is made possible by uniting the male and female energies, so creating the possibility of a third force being introduced
Little finger	Now is the time to bring in the invisible world	A way of getting your own way is arising

Feet

	Right Side	**Left Side**
Big toe	A sympathy to the element of air or ethers	An indication of the ability to pass over into the more subtle zones with ease
First toe	A sympathy to the element of fire	Link to the composite of all past experiences to extract the essence
Second toe	A sympathy to the element of water	Link to the animal kingdom
Third toe	A sympathy to the element of earth	Link to the plant kingdom
Little toe	An indication of grounding to the needs of a spiritual being on the Earth	Link to the mineral kingdom

Chapter 6: Environmental Programming

Extension

The seventh level is the next stage

**Five fingers and five toes taken to the
sixth level becomes the hand or foot.
The seventh level is the next stage - eg Body**

Mineral	Brown	Magnetic	Feel/touch
	Red		
Plant	Orange	Emotional	Smell
Animal	Yellow	Mental	Taste
Human	Green	Psychic	Hearing
Planet	Blue	Spiritual	Seeing
	Indigo		
Galaxy	Purple	Cosmic	Collective
Cosmic	White	Another dimensional influence NEW RULES	

The body's physical systems, like the circulatory and respiratory systems, are animated by an energy force that we are only just beginning to understand and comprehend, although in eastern cultures this has been known as 'chi' for centuries and is used for healing in acupuncture. Our bodies depend on greater forces to function properly, and we must ensure we are well equipped to be able to handle the effects, for although it is an awe-inspiring experience it can also shake us to our core; the inner being that instructs is invisible and it is often the most powerful motivator in our lives. Connecting the invisible with the visible is an individual experience that differs from person to person and is later done in conjunction with others as part of a collective growth. This is what Jung referred to as the "collective unconscious".

Although we all have five senses, some of them are overdeveloped and some are underdeveloped, as evidenced by people lacking one altogether, such as blindness, noticing an increase in their ability to use another. In such instances we might find ourselves relying on one sense primarily but we need to be careful not to do this; instead we must distribute the weight as evenly as possible across the senses, which will also allow the weaker senses to develop, in much the same way as using only one muscle will cause others to weaken but using all will encourage them all to develop at the same rate. This allows us to create a solid foundation from which we can develop.

There is a simple self-reflection exercise that can be performed to determine what senses are weaker and to develop their strength.

Firstly, can you touch others and allow yourself to be touched? If you cannot, for whatever reason, receiving regular massages or something more active like exercise, gardening or household work can be effective.

Secondly, is your sense of smell well developed? If you think, or know, that you do not smell correctly or as strongly as you should, aromatherapy or cooking can help you engage your sense of smell and develop it. By doing something that forces you to engage with scents and aromas the sense will have to work harder and thus grow stronger.

Thirdly, when you eat, do you taste the food you are eating or swallow it as fast as possible? For this sense – taste – the root of the problem could be linked to internal developments, for instance your needs may not have been met as much as you would have desired when growing up. An effective way of changing this is by talking frankly, either with a close loved one or a counsellor, as this will help to release repressed information that still has a hold over you.

Fourthly, do sounds please you? Although hearing is one of our prime senses that in our more primitive time would help us to detect and escape danger, noise pollution in today's world makes it easy for us to be distracted and lose our ability to filter out important sounds from the mundane. Meditation is a powerful tool that will help you heal past damage, and soothing, calm music will also help fine tune your sense of hearing.

Finally, do the sights that surround you please you? Like hearing, seeing is a primary sense that has now been clogged up by man-made sights or sounds that we do not like but consider normal, such as items in the media. At the most basic level, our homes should be decorated and furnished in a manner that makes us feel good and calm, and this is a good first step at identifying beauty and wonder in life. Once we have made the changes within our personal property, we can focus on seeing them in the wider world.

Look again at the image at the start of this chapter, The Seventh Level is the Next Stage. Now imagine creating one for yourself, paying careful attention to the colours, shapes and priorities unique to you. When the image in your mind is clear and constant put it down on paper, either as a drawing or in words, whichever you find easier.

Time Plan – Positive Code of Practice

The following is a list of positive affirmations you can try to live by, collected by various disciplines and put together by people who have survived a once seemingly insurmountable problem.

1) Just for today I can
2) I will pretend I feel happy just for now
3) I will adjust to your needs for now
4) I will not expect you to adjust to what I think my needs are
5) I will stretch my mind and try to concentrate
6) I will make the effort to think something new
7) I will do a good turn and not get found out
8) I will take a little exercise
9) I will not show that my feelings are hurt even if they are
10) I will not let on I feel miserable just for now
11) I will try to be agreeable just for today
12) I will make myself look as nice as I can
13) I will be clean and wash my hair so I feel as nice as I can
14) I will wear my nice clothes and not save them for a special event
15) I will talk quietly and in an unaffected way
16) I will act courteously
17) I will not criticise
18) I will not find fault today
19) I will not try to improve anyone else today
20) I will not organise or regulate anyone else today
21) I will make a plan today so I will not have to hurry or be indecisive
22) I will not be afraid for today – tomorrow has not yet come
23) I will not feel guilty for today – yesterday is past
24) I will enjoy what I can now – flower, tree, colour, sun, youth, seas
25) I will be thankful for the beauty I can see and what I have been able to enjoy
26) I will see what I can give rather than what I can take
27) I will have a quiet time today, be silent and reach for harmony

Our external behaviours must be monitored until we can absorb the changes that are taking place within us, which may be visible or invisible. To help us with this we may need to follow instructions or other guidelines before we can maintain a new standard independently, in the same way a child needs stabilisers while learning to ride a bicycle. On our spiritual journey of evolution we need stabilisers to help remind us what it is we want to be like, and this is especially true if we have 'slipped'. Slips are normal and are part of being human, and we must remember that it will not ruin anything: one doughnut will not undo the hard work of a diet, unless we get so discouraged by a moment of weakness that we cease to continue making the effort.

Some may notice that some of the items on the above list contradict each other or the information contained within this book. The reason for this is simply that we must build security measures en route otherwise we can easily lose our way. Rules and guidelines can greatly assist us, for if we try to do something completely alone without any guidance we can quickly and easily start using others or let them use us for us to feel safe, rather than helping anyone to grow as people. People who are particularly close to us will let us get away with more than strangers or new acquaintances, but it is only when we are ready to free ourselves that we can find out just how far certain people will let us go before their support runs out.

The Effect of Colour

As briefly mentioned already when discussing the colours teenagers wear, colours affect us deeply. Neither white nor black are actual colours: the former is the result of reflecting all colours while the latter is the result of absorbing them all, but both deal with all colours of the spectrum. Colour itself is a universal language that is recognised across all verbal languages, and it affects us all every day. For example, we all recognise the colours of a first aid kit or toxic waste, and worse still is that waste can collect in the environment, not from oil spills or landfills but through our own emotions. Consider those in hospitals, for example; it is common for patients to develop new illnesses while in hospital or for them or visitors to worry, and these emotions and feelings are stored in the materials of the hospital. It is for this reason that it is so important we spiritually cleanse the spaces we inhabit.

Colour is an instruction found naturally in our surroundings and ourselves, containing wisdom that has always been available but waiting to be unlocked by us as individuals. This wisdom can be unlocked more creatively if nature's subtle elements are studied. For example, magnetic attraction can lure us to eat certain foods and studies have shown that foods we normally find appealing become unappealing if they are dyed a different colour. Just as we use colours for such things as first aid kits and toxic waste, nature also uses colours for different functions, which we have adopted in day to day situations. Take yellow reflectors used by cyclists for instance: they are yellow because that is a colour of high visibility that we can see easily from a distance and our fastest responses are gut reactions. Nature uses this itself, with snakes being a prime example. Illumination is an extremely important part of our lives, not just to enable us to see better but affecting us more deeply, as evidenced by the existence of Seasonal Affective Disorder (SAD), brought on in the times of year when there is less sunlight. The role of light on our health and well-being has been extensively studied by the lighting industry, hence our having bright fluorescent lights that permeate every crevice of our space. However, these can have negative consequences because they contain very little blue or red light, which can cause physical imbalance in people, which is why there are some reports of people experiencing headaches and vomiting as a result of them.

Colours are used deliberately in certain situations; for instance factories will use orange to indicate hazardous areas, red for anything related to fire and yellow for anything that requires immediate attention like a risk of falling over something.

Offices use light colours on the walls to aid stimulation, and the reason the desks are usually neither light nor dark is because with light walls and a darker floor, the eyes always adjust back to the mid-tone, which in an office is the desk, where the employer wants your focus to be. Such a shade also lessens the rate of blinking and fatigue, which increases productivity.

In schools, especially primary schools, primary colours are liberally applied around the building. Children respond very well to colours and the bold, bright primary colours stimulate the minds of the students.

Hospitals also have a deliberate use of colour. For instance, the green gowns worn by the hospital staff, as well as used for bedding and patient gowns, complement the red of blood, which minimises distress by patients at the sight of blood. The shade of green also removes the after image that we are prone to when looking at one thing for a prolonged period of time, which surgeons do when looking at a wound in surgery. The green or blue tiles on the theatre walls are used because they reduce glare from the bright lights used to provide high visibility for operating, whereas white tiles would produce a lot of glare, distracting the gaze or hindering the vision of the surgeons. Hospitals should employ the use of bright colours in wards to stimulate the senses of the patients, which can reduce restlessness, boredom and keep patients' minds sharper.

Colours are used all around us for a myriad of reasons, most notably to ensure high visibility but, in schools and work places, to help with concentration, stimulation and mental sharpness. Colour is also used effectively in factories and on the roads to minimise accidents and hazards.

Colour Chart

Personal Preferences of Colours	Energies expressed	Balance Colours
Violet	Intuition and sensitivity	**Reds** Physical/emotional satisfaction
Indigo (Night sky blue)	Self-management and conditioned disciplines	**Wine or rust** Relaxation or self-accomplishment
Blue	Intellectual focuses	**Orange** Manifestation of actions
Green	Humanitarian service	**Gold** Personal self-satisfaction
Yellow	Self-searching and communication	**Green** Self-healing and balancing
Orange	Action, form and structure	**Light blue** Creativity
Red	Physical/emotional focus	**Violet** Inner awareness

PART 2:

LIVING IN RHYTHM

Chapter 7: Fear

Fear

Surrender of defences

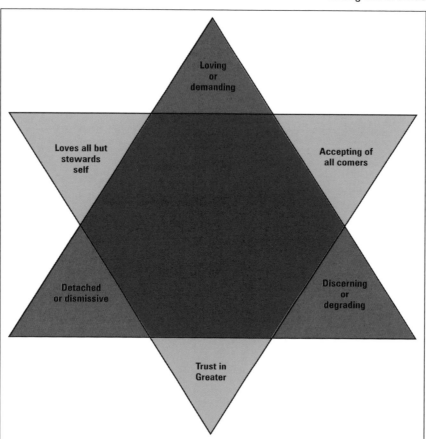

The Judge
Administers all;
demands attention

The Blamer
Insures self-love through
acting out dramas

Loving
or
demanding

Loves all but
stewards
self

Accepting of
all comers

Detached
or dismissive

Discerning
or
degrading

Trust in
Greater

The Controller
Masters and dictates;
organises all

The Manipulator
Treats all comers
as servants

Fear is an intrinsic emotion felt by all creatures, humans included. Although we consider it a negative emotion more often than not, getting in the way of something we need to do, like medical check-ups, or want to do, like giving blood or bungee jumping, it is something we both need and are taught to ignore. For example, without fear we would be reckless in life, taking chances that could put our lives at risk needlessly, yet as children we are frequently told that there is nothing to be scared of and instructed to dive headlong into each new opportunity with joy and abandon, with disregard for any fear we may encounter. The denouncement of fear is more pronounced for males than females because the gender stereotypes are all too often that men should not be scared of anything, always ready for confrontation and to defend the women who are in his company. Indeed, all too often when someone admits they are scared of something they are quickly ridiculed, despite it being a perfectly normal emotion that we all feel at some point or another – whether we admit it or not. Thus, at an early age we learn to suppress fear instead of acknowledge it. This can be damaging, though, as fear can be extremely helpful in telling us when we are pushing ourselves too far.

It is normal, for instance, to feel nervous when undertaking something new, and we notice that fear subsides when we become familiar with a situation or task. Driving, for example, is a task that makes almost everyone nervous when they first get behind the wheel, but after practice and some time spent on the road we quickly adapt and get used to it, and we no longer fear it. However, when we are young almost everything is new and it is normal for us to be anxious frequently, for there is a lot to take in. But our parents will try to suppress our fear by telling us to ignore it, rather than allow us to accept it is normal and will pass of its own accord. As we are so dependent on our parents, when they tell us this we absorb negative vibrations and can develop a fear of fear itself, which, although our parents are trying to help us, is counter-productive because it does not help the child accept fear or overcome it, but instead fear it as its own entity.

Instead of being fearful of fear, we must acknowledge that we, or our children, are experiencing it – whether justified or not. If we had our childhood fears supressed then we will need to learn again our creative expression and communication so that we may adequately express when we are fearful or nervous. It is important to work on this, because fear is another tool in our growing arsenal to facilitate our journey and growth, not the paralysing burden we are often told it is.

As we begin to learn more about any given subject our fear subsides and is replaced with confidence and knowledge. This in turn reduces the chances of something unexpected taking place and catching us off guard; instead, we are prepared to deal with whatever consequences may crop up. However, when we make a conscious effort to go down the path of self-discovery, our fears seem more real and larger than they were previously, to the point that we may become so gripped with them we believe that we cannot resolve them fully. It is an apparent catch-twenty-two: we were taught to suppress or ignore our fears so we think this is the right thing to do, because if we acknowledge it we worry we may be feeding it. This puts us in a difficult position, unsure how or where to begin.

In order to proceed we need to understand that it is the same energy used to feed our fears that we can use to banish them and correct the imbalance. The first step is to stop denying our fears and instead admit them openly, at least to ourselves if not to others. Employing the guidance of a counsellor can be rewarding also, because after admitting the fears there will be a huge amount of resources that can be examined and processed during the counsel, and you will soon notice the fears disappearing as they are used more proactively at aiding the evolution.

We all judge and blame others as we attempt to steer our lives in the way we think they should be going. It is very easy for us to demand attention so we know people are aware of us and, hopefully, loving us; but we also easily resent others, especially if we are close enough to them that we blame them for stalling our progression. At such points, we may try to manipulate everyone to suit our own needs, or we may feel dejected that others are putting us beneath their own needs.

We are in control of our own choices and we must decide whether to love all equally for the sake of love itself, not because we want something in return, or to demand to receive love as our right. The difficulty here is managing to treat every person independently and being able to give love to those we are not attracted to, meaning we can share our love even with people we have no great affinity for. This is what it means to show equality for all.

This is a difficult process and one in which we are almost certain to be confused and doubtful of our own abilities; we will wonder if we have the mental strength and reserves to forge ahead and find our answers. It is important to dig deep and find that resolve, for it is certainly there, and when the conclusion has been reached the road there will feel more than worth it.

Instincts: smelling, touching, tasting

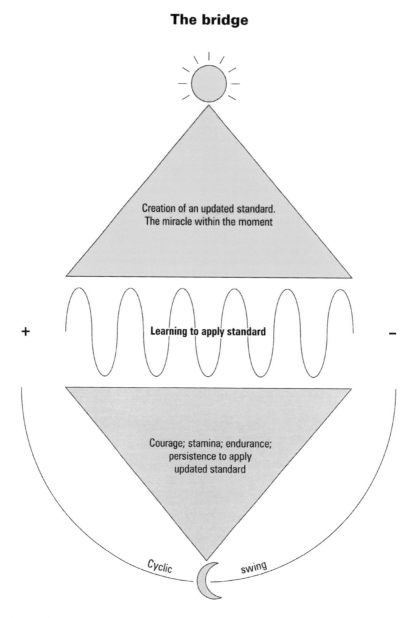

The bridge

Creation of an updated standard.
The miracle within the moment

+

Learning to apply standard

−

Courage; stamina; endurance;
persistence to apply
updated standard

Cyclic swing

Although we are not dependent on our senses of smell and taste, by utilising them we can interpret a lot about our environment and its vibrations. Firstly, we can assess what attracts and repels us – are we comfortable in this particular place? Can we make improvements? We often feel a sense of comfort and discomfort, what we usually refer to as a 'gut feeling', and by homing in on our senses we can determine if this gut feeling is worth dismissing or following.

Food presents a good example that we can all relate to because we all must eat. If someone prepares our favourite meal we will enjoy it, but if that person is sick or in a negative state then we may find the food does not taste as good as usual or that it disagrees with us, not by causing us illness but making us feel negative emotions or stress. As the meal is our favourite, we can comfortably deduce that our state of unease was not caused by the food but the person who made it.

All of our senses have the dual purpose of receiving and transmitting, and we should try to home in on the messages relayed. For example, there are some days when we crave affection and enjoy being touched by others or want to touch them, but other days we shy away from physical contact in any form – either giving or receiving. Observing this permits us the opportunity to look at our mental, physical and emotional reactions and then establish the cause of them. This is one reason why it is so important to not lose touch with our senses, because doing so will drastically impair our perception. Indeed, our mind cannot be healthy unless the body is, and that means the senses, too. In order to keep them sharp, we need to remember that prevention is better than cure; in other words, it is better to look after them than try to fix a problem later on. Protect your vision by reading in well-lit areas and not straining; your ears by not listening to music at deafening volumes and try to focus on soft, soothing music whenever you can; your taste by savouring food instead of devouring it as fast as possible; your sense of touch by taking care of your skin, touch and caress different materials to keep the sense stimulated; and your sense of smell by aromatherapy or other fragrances that keep your nose focused.

In recognising what we no longer want or desire we have set in motion a journey of updating standards, acknowledging that things have changed and we have to cooperate in order to find out what our new standards of wanting are, because in the meantime we only know what it is we do *not* want, not what we actually *do* want. This is not an easy task, but there is no reverse gear: we must endure and forge ahead until eventually we learn our new standard, at which point we can act on it and tell others how we have changed, no longer asking for their opinion and guidance to move us along.

The journey of progression is one that cannot be stopped, but we can change our attitude towards it to make it easier. We have the choice to hold a grudge against others or even ourselves for not being trouble-free enough as quickly as we would like. Our attitude can be one of arrogance or superiority in an attempt to hide our pain from others, especially those we fear may disregard our needs. However, this can all change the moment we become willing to embrace the journey. By being willing to take responsibility we can learn to relax, go with the experience and enjoy our time spent with others.

Letting go can be difficult, so it can be beneficial to break it down with the following three questions: firstly, what is it you are holding onto? Secondly, are you willing to surrender and co-operate with the process? Thirdly, will you collaborate with those around you with increased awareness?

If you can answer these questions positively you will find the process easier and more comfortable.

Hearing Beyond Sound

One way humans differ from other animals is the fact that we do not rely wholly on our five senses for survival. Rather, we have a sixth sense which serves as a message centre for the other five and it processes incoming information that they have relayed. It is then up to us to decide what to do with these messages through our thoughts, emotions and actions.

Indeed, we have evolved to manage our senses on another level: not only do we depend on them for survival and avoiding pain, but we also use them to our own advantage by acknowledging only that which we want to. Take, for example, our ability to block out someone talking to us if we do not like what they have to say. This is not perfect, though, and we frequently hear sounds that we wish we had not, but once we have heard them and recognised them we can often mentally lower their volume so they do not affect us.

Our hearing extends past the normal scope of the auditory sounds our ears pick up, and this is known as 'clairaudience', meaning we are the audience to many types of sounds, including vibrations. With this ability it is important that we are selective, blocking out that which we do not need. Just like a sponge can only absorb so much water, we have a saturation point with our hearing and when it gets to saturation point we need to stop what we are doing and do something quiet, like reading, meditating, going for a walk or having a nap – anything that is quiet and without distraction. Of course, the ideal situation is to be able to be selective from the outset, as this way it will take far more time to reach saturation point and we will not be using so much energy. So listen to only what is interesting or necessary, and always listen to your own internal voice.

Earth represents tangible evidence, water links the continual scene, air the invisible realities of life and fire the essence generator. Our five senses communicate with these and convey back to our inner feelings, which we trust. We then test or detach ourselves to discern how our feelings are the love of the finest quality, and we are then able to select the thought transmissions and transmit what we clairvoyantly know to be the best, trusting that our own abilities will be enhanced by others, so that all efforts will become united.

Framework of potential union

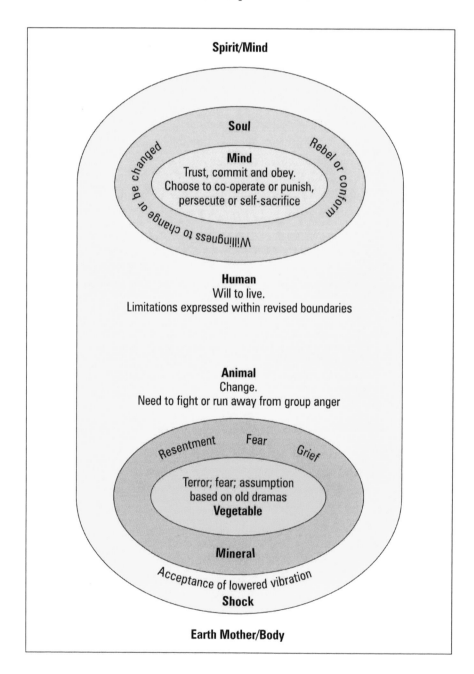

Follow through

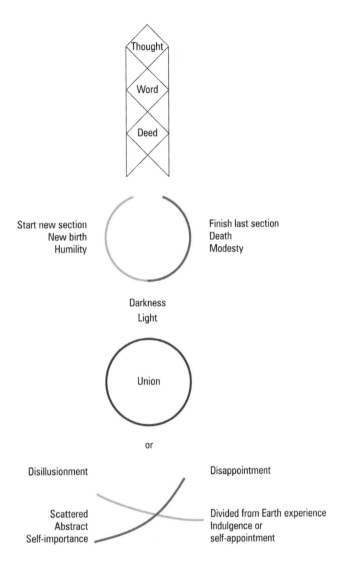

Relaxation

As you go through this journey the invisible will become visible, you will hear the unheard and understand the unknown – all of which define the word 'psychic'. You will be able to smell the atmosphere and determine if you are safe or unsafe within it, and you will redefine the boundaries of self and others, finding your own worth as you value the worth of others, too. Genetic and environmental influences will be acknowledged and released as you create a new space for yourself, which may or may not involve people from the past, as people will not necessarily change at the same pace or in the same direction as you. You will surrender your impotence and in doing so will reclaim power from beyond your sensory awareness, and if you stay still, patiently, you will be shown how to proceed; in the meantime, do what is required of you in your everyday life.

In this stage, it is highly recommended to practice the relaxation technique provided in the first chapter.

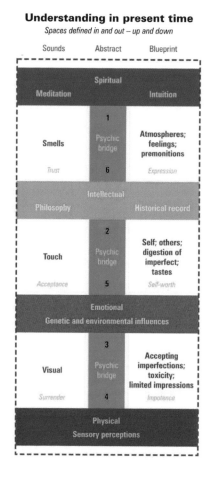

Understanding in present time
Spaces defined in and out – up and down

Seeing

Our sense of vision extends beyond what our eyes can see as we also try to see past where we currently are. The problem with this is that life moves so fast we can feel dislocated, doubting our role; on the other hand, we also know the feeling of elation when we get a clear glimpse of the future and recognise who we are, where we are going and what part we play. In order to see that glimpse, though, we need to find the stillness that resides deep inside, and to find that we must be able to adapt, perceive with unclouded vision that shows the past as complementary to the present and the present as an opportunity to build the future how we desire.

We must be careful in these times to see not only the needs of ourselves, but those of others and the groups we live and work with, because to 'see' means encompassing all of this. A certain bonding takes place when we can perceive things in others, especially if they themselves cannot see it. It requires a lot of courage and hard work to maintain that foresight, but one lesson that reaps huge rewards is making a point of working with groups so we can learn how to work better with others and handle criticism without losing confidence. This can be boosted further by getting in touch with nature, perhaps by gardening. Expanding our vision beyond what our eyes can see will provide us with a harmonious and rewarding way of life.

Repeat the following: I am willing to forgive all – others and myself. I choose to let go of resentment and trust that life will lead me through the fear and support my forward movement as I evolve.

With this affirmation, the shackles of the past will be unbound so that you can step out of history's shadow and into your own light.

Mutual agreement

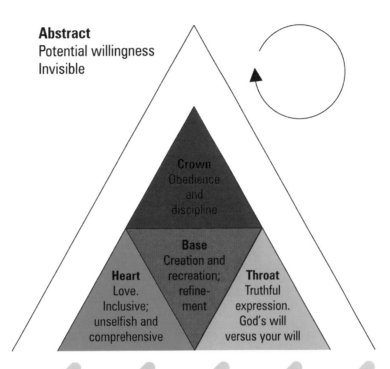

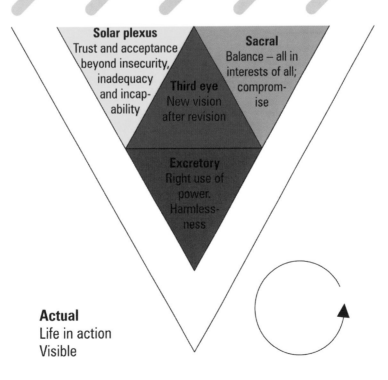

Chapter 8: Communication

What is Communication?

Being able to communicate our thoughts and observations concisely, comprehensively and simply means others are more likely to understand us than if we spoke in a convoluted manner with our words having no sense of direction. Communication extends beyond the spoken word, though, and we can send a clear and direct message through body language, touch, or by ignoring someone completely.

Sometimes we will find ourselves in a position of authority or knowing something that others do not, and in such situations we must utilise all of our senses and not just the one(s) that we find easiest. Indeed, rather than using what comes easiest to us we should choose the one that is easiest for the recipient(s) to understand, whether that is a lengthy discussion or just a knowing smile. The important part here is to know who we are talking to and realising what they respond best to, then dipping into our arsenal of communicative tools to relay the message.

In a guarded and stewarded organisation with a fair authority, any feasible ideas are works in progress, adapted to suit the needs of everyone so that decision making honours everyone involved. In order to set objectives to reach a common aim a rhythm must be found that enables all involved to harmonise their efforts, which will aid progress to the goal. It will be on the leader to be able to see the impending pitfalls and steer around them, thus minimising the likelihood that anyone will suffer, and if the leader is in tune with their sixth sense and able to work with their inner guidance then the project will be useable within the environment.

A small but beneficial self-reflection exercise to complete at this stage is as follows:

Draw a layout of an imagined place and write down the compass points on it. Add to it any features you desire, such as a pub, church, school, bus stop and so on. Once the picture is as you would like it, imagine you are walking within it and ask yourself the following questions:

1) What does a specific feature, such as the school, represent to you? Answer with one theme only.
2) What is this feature saying to you?
3) Is that feature currently active or inactive?
4) When was this site last in communication and what was the message?
5) Where are you recording this experience on your physical body?
6) Why is it necessary for you to be there now?
7) How do you proceed with this information?
8) What is the next step?

Signals, Signs and Symbols

As our senses develop they work harmoniously to sort through the various incoming information and we often refer to this as 'intuition'. A bond often develops between groups of people who are in each other's company a lot, in which each member has this intuition and it eventually acts as a means of shorthand communication between them, where they may finish each other's sentences or know what one is thinking or about to say without anything being verbalised or indicated.

Spiritual belief in oneness

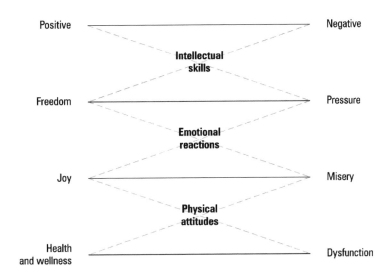

Although useful, it is foolhardy to not validate the accuracy of the transmitted information with those we are communicating with, and it must be observed to never use this ability to intrude on the privacy of another person. We must also train ourselves to observe so that we may understand the knowledge we have at our disposal, because then we can observe the signals alerting us to upcoming movement and change. Such signs are readily apparent but are easily overlooked: crying when nothing has happened to make us upset, but this is done as the body's 'spring clean', removing grief to create room for the impending change; increased hunger and eating incessantly despite no change in our physical movement; experiencing pain when we cannot think of anything that has hurt us, but this is because we are breaking restrictions to make way for the change; or we may excrete in a way that makes us believe we are ill. Some of these signs can be a symptom of illness, so we must make the distinction and see a doctor if we are unwell, but if we have a clean bill of health then we can consider these signs of change in our lives, and although we cannot speed the process up it is beneficial to be aware of what is happening. This is not the easiest task if we do not remember having chosen change, and if we have indeed forgotten then we may start being resistant to it, for no one likes having changes forced upon them. As such, it is worthwhile learning to understand our body, so that we can home in on any changes and determine their cause.

Due to the fact that we are content and happy when things are going well, signs and symbols are manifested on an individual or a group to show a problem and change is required. However, the change may be at a pace that is so intolerable to some the symbols are misunderstood, creating negative representations, causing issues for everyone. The main problem here is that the group can become dysfunctional, so it is critically important to keep change at a pace that everyone is comfortable with, rather than one or two people moving ahead at a speed that causes problems for others.

We must be patient for others, or indeed ourselves, to develop, because we can only assess once everyone is able to speak *and* listen, not just one or the other. Our sense of smell helps us to separate fact and fiction, but if the prospect of growth scares us we often try to mask the surrounding atmosphere, such as when teenagers wear too much perfume or aftershave to hide their apprehensions about themselves or the situation they find themselves in.

We express through body language what we hear from others, and so we will display either a feeling of safety or insecurity. Due to this, it is imperative that we take responsibility for our body and how it behaves, because it informs us of how others feel about us and informs others of how we feel about them. Knowing this can cause difficulties, though, because instead of just being able to speak how we wish we must instead think about every aspect of communication: what we say, why we say it, how we say it, and possibly taking responsibility for others if they are not yet at that stage.

Although learning can be difficult, we quickly start processing information in an effective manner once we have the ability to deal with distortions, static pressures and interference, all of which are encountered in the receiving process and will check both our tolerance and resistance. Our abilities will also be checked and rechecked as our internal growth is challenged until we know we can cope with any contingencies we encounter. It is at this point that we will learn about subtleties, such as tone of expression and body language, noise levels and various other subtle aspects present in our environment. Following this we start to examine the symbology of the audio-visual impact.

As information is received we initially recognise it through our sense of touch or feeling. Someone who does not like being touched is usually either in a vulnerable state of being, whereas someone who actively *wants* to be touched frequently is usually in need of comfort and there is a low standard for who is acceptable. By taking in the smells of the atmosphere we can decide whether to be defensive and stand our ground or to resist the battle and try another day. It is only after this that we really start to talk, because it is at this time that we have to decide whether to agree or disagree with what is said. If we decide to disagree then we must have our counter-arguments primed and ready from the outset, and we must also decide just how far we are disagreeing: is it just the opinion of someone, or the actual person, too? This is not an easy stage and the stronger our state of being, the more confident we are, the better we will be able to handle the situation. Conversely, if we agree rather than disagree our senses will be in a state of harmony.

Our sense of sight is used for assessing people: are they well informed and do they present lightly, with all senses synchronised and harmonised? If the answer to these questions is 'no' then we will be slightly defensive, checking each piece of information with each individual sense before concluding on what the next step should be, which slows down the harmonising process when compared to someone who can answer the above questions with 'yes'.

Our Environment

The prevailing environmental conditions constantly need updating to be in keeping with our advancing abilities to cope with different situations. The difficulty lies in the fact that some conditions make proceeding difficult and we need to learn how to cope with this.

We will always need to prove ourselves in different environments and we must bear in mind that this is not done by trying to take control and be assertive but to appear inept to those who want to control, always hungry for more power. This will permit us the time required to be sure we obey our integrity and find the path that is right for everyone, while also reassuring us that we are still on that path despite the tremendous pressure we face from others.

A defined space
in which to operate

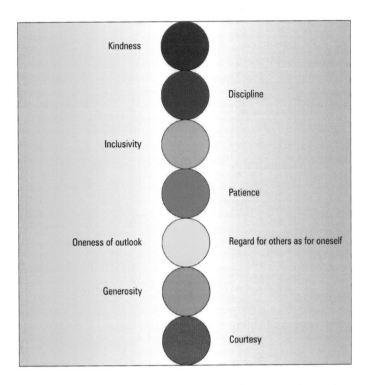

While we deduce what we should keep residing in the past and what is haunting us from that time, we can appear to be inadequate. While others may taunt us for this strategy, keen to find an easier path for immediate, but short term, effect, they overlook that in the long term everyone will be trapped in an endless repeat of circumstances. There are people who try to make things happen quicker than they should because they believe it fits their purpose. These people are selfishly thinking only of themselves rather than the entire group, and it is not unusual for such a personality to abandon the collective if it fits their ideas. While they may walk away, the group cannot abandon them until it has made a decision on the next step.

We find that after this stage the people we are surrounded by are the go-getters, the people who strive to do what needs to be done and can be relied on no matter what the circumstance. At this point, old insecurities will surface so that we may let them go, and as a result we will enjoy updated relationships where everybody feels equal. With everyone on the same side there will be no need to attack others or defend our own position, and disagreements can be aired safely without fear of confrontation. With the common goal known amongst all involved, discussions and disagreements of policy and implementation can take place in a friendly manner for there will be no disagreement on the total objective.

Many may question why it is worth all this hassle; after all, it can be hard enough updating a standard at the best of times, without having to live it out in the environment on top of that. The way to answer the question is by asking more: do you like the way you instinctively react when a negative situation arises? Or are you naturally suspicious, looking for hidden agendas or a cynical attitude? If the answer to either of those is 'yes' then a collective arena is necessary so you may react in different ways in different situations until you are confident you are trustworthy.

You will also learn at this stage that how you behave at home and how you behave outside in different situations is acceptable, because everyone can accept you for who you are without the need to try to pretend to be someone different.

The Core

The holistic being

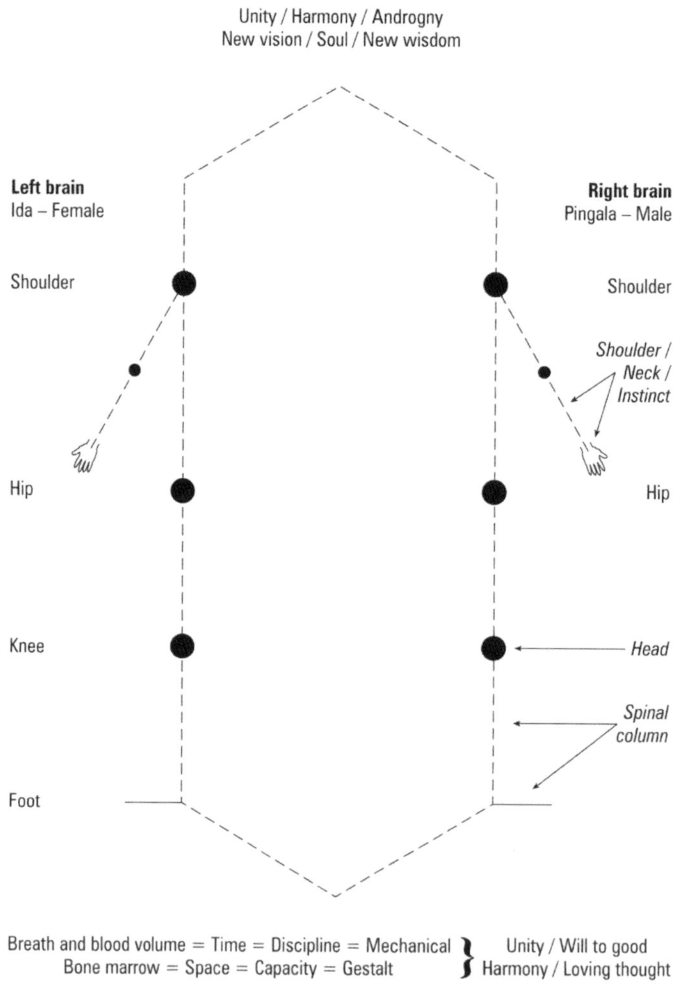

Unity / Harmony / Androgny
New vision / Soul / New wisdom

Left brain
Ida – Female

Shoulder

Right brain
Pingala – Male

Shoulder

Shoulder /
Neck /
Instinct

Hip

Hip

Knee

Head

Spinal
column

Foot

Breath and blood volume = Time = Discipline = Mechanical } Unity / Will to good
Bone marrow = Space = Capacity = Gestalt } Harmony / Loving thought

At this point in the evolutionary journey it is necessary to redefine personal expectations and determine what is possible at this stage in time. This may entail reviewing ideals as we review our own potential, which will enable us to re-negotiate honestly with people who take interest in what we can offer.

The illusions we hold must be dispersed as we collaborate with viable possibilities, but before that we need to honour the disillusionment we have experienced, because it has supported us and allowed us to proceed to reach our current position. Despite the journey, we are now encouraged by new opportunities with such ease we wonder just what we were ever worried about. Nonetheless, it is essential to be grateful for the state of grace under which the core can be cleansed and ready to go further, even if we do not feel particularly gracious.

The heart must help, not hinder, the work of the invisible realms; the mind must possess the ability to remove the pain felt by others that we have contributed to but is no longer our responsibility. Although we may have despised systems that were beyond our control to embrace, they permitted us to develop our integrity and ability to learn what we can trust, so however much we may have hated them in the past, we must acknowledge that through them we know what to accept, allowing us to now be ourselves freely.

By fusing the inner experiences with the outer environments we remove old clutter from inside ourselves, and our hearts blossom into wells of goodwill that we can direct to all without prejudice, which in turn allows us to find the rhythm that will take us to the next chapter. We have now acquired the courage to do what we deem the right thing; if someone expresses the opinion that we are not good enough, we smile and continue for we know we did our best and we are neither better nor worse than anyone else. Rather than become defensive, if we are told we did not perform as well as expected, we listen patiently and digest the information. We are similarly patient when others embark on a quest to find a more effective way and we are willing to welcome them back when required, acknowledging they may now have a different role as a result of their new knowledge. If that new role is not satisfactory to them, we walk away when our intuition tells us the correct path, which is the one with least resistance.

Mantra:

May the power of the One Life pour
through the group of all true servers;
May the love of the One Soul characterise
the love of all who seek to aid the Great Ones;
May we fulfil our part in the One work through
self-forgetfulness, harmlessness and right speech.

Courtesy of the Lucis Trust.

Chapter 9: Compassion

To Enable an Inclusive Approach

Caring means that we apply our standards to those around us too easily under the assumption that they adhere to the same ethics and way of living that we do – and of course, that may not be the case at all. While we can empathise, sympathise and care with and for others, we cannot control them or assume that we know all details about all people. We are all different, and one person's hobbies and interests will not always be coherent with those of others. A lesson we must learn is to love everyone without comprising ourselves with interactions, which is what this chapter will be exploring.

The 'co' in 'compassion' refers to 'company' or 'companion', or in other words, a group home. This may refer to our body, home to our organs; a group within a family; a group of friends; or anything that brings people together. We do not need to do anything within the group except be there and encourage the other members, sticking with them through the good times and the bad. An appropriate saying for this is as follows: "Hold on tightly while it is clearly yours to steward; let go lightly and willingly when the situation changes once more".

During this journey to make soul guidance a priority it is quite usual for people to turn to celibacy, and this is down to each individual's judgement. Be aware, though, that once the cellular structure's memory is cleared there is no reason to remain celibate; the companionship and emotional bond earned through sexual relations can be enjoyed and you can be content in the knowledge that we are being guided in an appropriate manner.

When we try to renew our enthusiasm – not just for sex but for various things – our attitude of compassion towards ourselves can either sap or reignite fundamental issues. For example, are we to apply the same standards of love to ourselves as we display to others? The answer is a resounding 'yes', because we *are* one of the others, and so we simply must be treated in the same way. In order to do this, we must shed ourselves of guilt and accept that the past is done, we did our best and it was good enough, even if we did not think so at the time. We are no longer the same people, and our needs, skills and requirements have changed with us.

At this point it is worthwhile to answer the following self-reflection questions:

1) What is reforming around you – work, family, yourself, your relationships?
2) What or who do you need to let go of?
3) Are you willing and cooperative or obstructive and demanding?
4) Are you flexible and willing to be shown what is required by life?
5) Are you resentful and stubborn or do you listen to the inner instructions?
6) Will you obey or not?
7) Will you suffer or enjoy the moving scene?

The Longest Journey

It may not always seem like it, but the longest journey any person will ever undertake is from our head to our hearts. Our notions of what enjoyment means is so strong that we insist on it from a heart level, which bears the potential of us becoming selfish, or a head level, where we are willing to take it at the expense of others. As such, both must be cleansed.

Brain | Heart

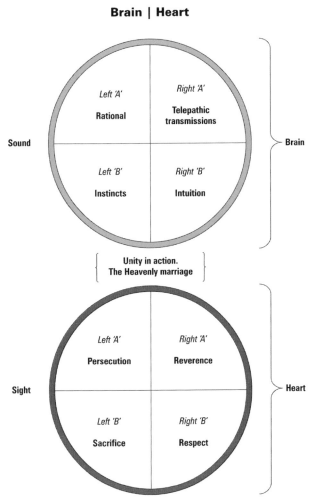

We often find that we feel pleasure even though we were not actively looking for it, or had not set in motion a plan to create it; rather we found it in whatever we happened to be doing. The reason for this is that we surrender to what is happening when we know it is happening, and although we do not necessarily know what it means we do realise that if we are experiencing something we should enjoy it. To this end, we meditate on things we are required to, acknowledging that at the current moment we do not need to understand; indeed, with no alternative we simply have to accept that our soul is working in our best interest, even though we all experience things that we deem negative, wondering why, if we are guided, we were steered into those situations. As explained at the outset of this book, though, there is no such thing as a negative situation, for we learn from these experiences and that is how we grow.

The purpose of meditation is to connect to inner love – the love that guides us and will never sacrifice our integrity for popularity or anything else. However, because meditation insists on intimacy and vulnerability we can find the experience somewhat raw at times as we confront scenarios from the past that hurt us in one way or another. If we listen to our inner voice we will learn why we were exposed to the situation in the first place; perhaps it was to guide us in a new direction but for us to understand why, or perhaps it was to restore karmic balance. Whatever the story, there is always a reason.

The grief that we encounter is kept in the pelvis, head and neck; it is the viewpoint of personality where we have understood the inhumane attitudes and actions of some others but were powerless to adjust them. We could have released the suffering if we had recourse to our soul, and we could have accepted guidance to free us if we had trusted our soul, but if we try to take pleasure only in a physical sense then our pride will be prohibiting us from receiving help.

Reviewing and Rebalancing

Brain balance

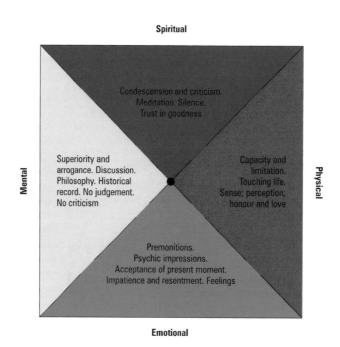

Part of our journey entails balancing the active side – the side that wants to control – with the passive side – the side that is content with the moment and does not feel the need to do anything. If we expect a peaceful coexistence then we may receive it; if the soul is convinced that the ego has understood the role and responsibility of the soul guidance in bringing us this far and that it has done what is right for us despite our shortcomings, the soul will once again get to work at progressing us further.

The only way to prove to the soul that the ego wants its partnership is through our actions in life – like any person, the soul will not believe words attesting to a changed attitude when all it has seen is an uncooperative personality that will do nothing collaborative without resistance. Some personalities think they have the right to knowledge they have not earned, so instead of putting the hard work in they will instead try to take it from others, either through conniving methods or simply trying to take it by force. In the process we may hurt others or we may be abrasive because of a memory we are harbouring. Sometimes we do not even realise that we are being so abrasive and antisocial, thinking we are being rational and kind, until someone or something shows us how despicable our behaviour has been.

Before moving on, practice the following exercise:

Draw energy to the top of your head and imagine expanding all the central junctions of energy that follow the central column of the body. Lift the energy out of the head and let it flow down like a fountain of water. As the energy returns into the body via the feet and anus dedicate it to the highest good for all, then draw it up the body so it exits the head and flows down again. This process will open a creative pathway through the body.

Through the forehead send a wave of bliss to your partner – if you do not have a partner an imagined one will suffice.

Repeat a wave of bliss at throat level.

Repeat a wave of bliss at heart level.

Repeat a wave of bliss at solar plexus level.

Repeat a wave of bliss at spleen level.

Repeat a wave of bliss at the base of the spine.

Imagine the waves coming in on a tide of bliss and then returning to the ocean, repeating endlessly. Feel a sense of gratitude at this point.

The six waves of bliss and six tides represent a transformed shadow that obscured the light – or, if you prefer, the twelve angels at the gate in Heavenly marriage. If both you and your partner complement the masculine and feminine sides within you then you will be loved both at day and night, male and female, Heaven and Earth. You are both parent and child, lover and beloved.

The Heart Space

The heart arena

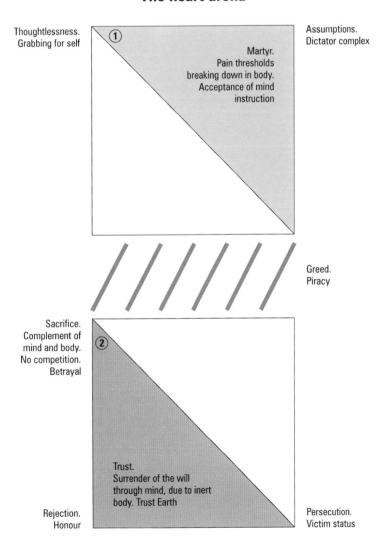

67

In order to prevent a painful experience from the past happening again we may develop a strong shell and become an overbearing personality to others, or wear a hypothetical mask to hide our true feelings and to enact an air of superiority over others. It is easy to disrespect others and make them feel inferior or abused, and we must be careful to avoid this. An example of this is using other people to conjure up familiarity by association, for example when we hear the words "I worked with...", this allows us to feel elevated from our own status to that of someone more respected or well known. However, if we worked without soul we would allow them to maintain their anonymity rather than sacrifice our integrity to ride their coat-tails.

Consider the following questions on space:

1) Who has invaded your space lately?
2) What, if any, was the damage caused e.g. bruising, cuts or other harm?
3) Did you confront the invaders if it was possible, or other authorities if it was not possible?
4) What was your attitude to the invaders?
5) How did others respond e.g. with advice, lack of interest or something else?

We Can Get What We Expect

Negative expectation within service

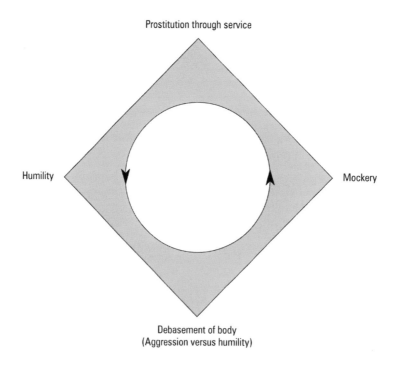

Prostitution through service

Humility

Mockery

Debasement of body
(Aggression versus humility)

For us to be compassionate requires that we acknowledge those around us; to administer tough love to help people do the right thing and not the thing they necessarily want to hear; and to be immune to pressures from others. Our decision to cooperate with the soul and Greater Power and our sensitivity to the energy surrounding us does not equate to immunity where only the good enters our personal space. On the contrary:

trust is the only insurance, gracious acceptance the only assurance and the only guarantee is our willingness for the soul to guide us in the right direction.

If we harbour a lot of resentment then we lack the necessary humility that allows us to recognise that the soul knows more than we do. Although we want to and will be treated like a partner, we must acknowledge that we have less experience and wisdom than the soul, which has access to higher levels of spirituality. However, by being cooperative we will earn access to it, but until then we must be modest and not jealous.

Here are some questions on self-knowledge and reflection:

1) Would you be described as humble, by yourself or others?
2) Would you be described as modest, by yourself or others?
3) Do you think of yourself as a team player?
4) Do you have a loose and cordial association with your team?
5) Do you like to control, dictate or manipulate circumstances?
6) Do you question whether you have the right to input?
7) Would you consider yourself pedantic and selfish or flexible and inclusive?

Practise the following visualisation exercise:
Imagine your spinal column as an inner flute that can be played; envision it embedded into the butterfly shape of the pelvis, and the mouthpiece of the flute has been blocked so the butterfly 'wings' need to move in order for the flute to be played. Open and contract the urethra and as you do so ask the question of how you can integrate the inner male (the one that acts) and the inner female (the one that explores), freeing all that is not required from the body memory. Ask to free from the body old relationships and patterns, parental influences and anything else no longer required. Hand over control from mind to body and welcome new experiences through inner streaming – imagine light streaming from Heaven to Earth that you are joyfully riding. With this exercise you will bond male and female, Heaven and Earth and past and future.

Are We Willing to be Tried and Tested?

Although we know we only learn by doing, it can be difficult knowing what to do and how to go about it; this is compounded further by the inevitable difficulties we encounter as we progress to mastering something, which can make us wonder if we are on the right track after all. On a spiritual plane we want to both experience bliss and be a confidant to the angels, but the question is whether we will be acceptable to them. Before we get to this point, though, we will face potential challenges such as so much intellectual ambition that we become too competitive and cut-throat to our peers, or we are too selfish and greedy, or bullying and pushing others around or letting them manipulate us. To be elevated to the spiritual level we must overcome these.

The emotional challenge from family and friends is to release those who have moved away from the group while embracing those who are entering. On an intellectual level we must be alert for those who will take advantage of others for their own gain or those who crave attention by orchestrating unnecessary drama. The physical challenge is set for us in the confines of everyday demands, whereby we see how far we can go before we reach our limits, set by our health or the health of anyone in our care, be it a friend, family member or pet. These initiations are not to be taken as personal attacks; rather they are tests to prove to the spiritual beings that we are committed to them and to ourselves, as well as enabling us to develop more compassion. As we progress through the tests we can take stock of the weaknesses that we need to work on and strengthen, but we cannot judge as we do not know what is required of us – that will all become clear as we move forward. Until then, we must practise our compassion. If we are able to do so then we are more likely to be accepted into the spiritual plane.

Smooth flowing movement

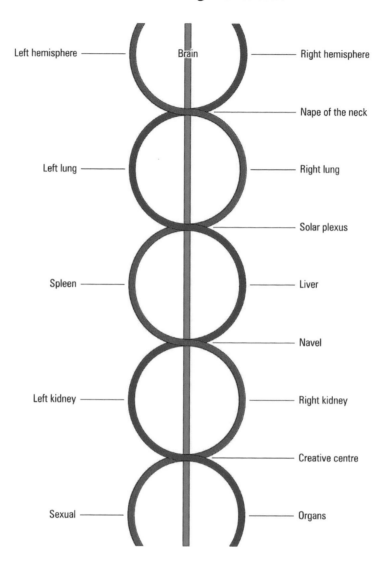

Left hemisphere —— Brain —— Right hemisphere

—— Nape of the neck

Left lung —— Right lung

—— Solar plexus

Spleen —— Liver

—— Navel

Left kidney —— Right kidney

—— Creative centre

Sexual —— Organs

Chapter 10: Earth Changes

I Am the Centre of My World

Balance of abstract to actual

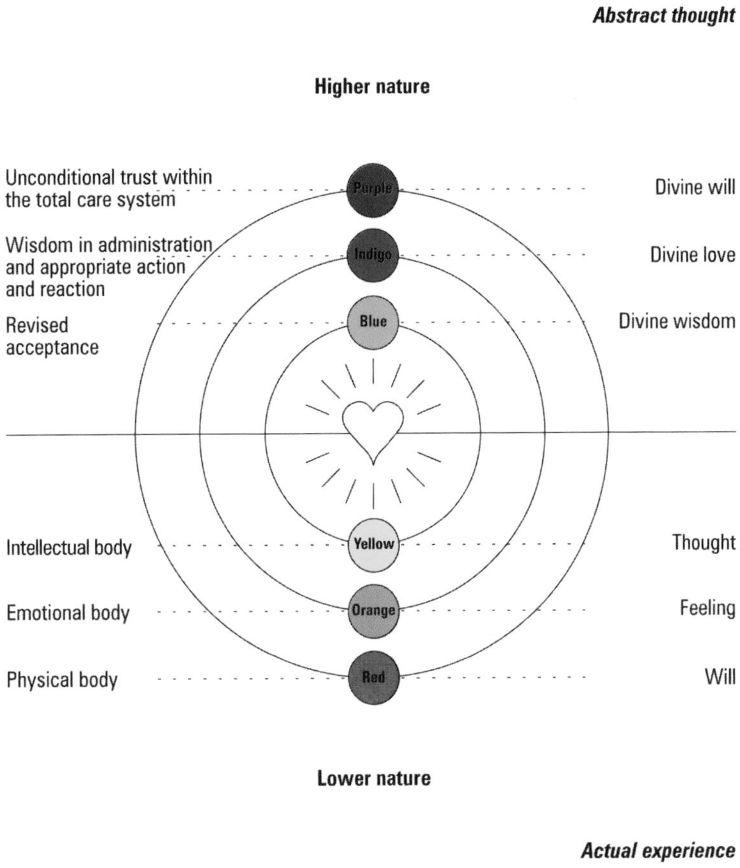

Abstract thought

Higher nature

Unconditional trust within the total care system	Purple	Divine will
Wisdom in administration and appropriate action and reaction	Indigo	Divine love
Revised acceptance	Blue	Divine wisdom
Intellectual body	Yellow	Thought
Emotional body	Orange	Feeling
Physical body	Red	Will

Lower nature

Actual experience

For each change that we experience in life we must create a principle to live by, which needs to be constructive and supportive to us. In order to do this effectively we must know how to conduct ourselves and our business; the people we meet can give us feedback so we can modify and improve upon our foundations. At first we will be met with opposition, the purpose of which is for us to grow, refining and redefining ourselves as well as giving us practice in expressing ourselves honestly, to ourselves and to others. During this transformation stage we will need to convince others of our good intentions and to help them as much as we help ourselves.

By convincing others of this we will be encouraging them to take their own action, which will break down any barriers that exist between us. This will in turn lead to harmony and unity, increasing understanding and decreasing suspicion. However, this is not an easy process because, as with any major change, there are going to be difficulties along the way. One potential problem is our own attitude of self-importance which may stop us seeing that there is a requirement to negotiate with others if their standards are radically different to those we hold. This pushes us into a state of self-assertion and we may resent this as we see no need for criticism and so may feel as if we are trapped, forced against our will to do something we do not think we need to do. Part of our resentment may come from feeling as though we are revisiting somewhere we have already been, where we initially developed things like sympathy, humility and patience. Recognising what we learnt here the first time allows us to reflect and feel gratitude for making such progress despite such difficulties as we faced at the time, as well as allowing us to assess the people in our vicinity to decide if we wish to continue being in the same group as them or not.

The decision-making process at this stage is to help us know what the next step is so it may happen gently, not with a large bump to get our attention.
The following is a small exercise on goodwill:

1) Imagine everyone in your group is concerned with the good of everyone rather than only their own goals and objectives.
2) Envision goodwill for all; imagine a ray of light emanating from the centre of yourself, with you in the middle of a circle.
3) Ask that each person can see what to do and how to do it, as well as they will be courteous while doing it.
4) Ask that everyone involved organise the updated format peacefully and with goodwill.
5) Make a note of your thoughts and feelings for each of the four stages.

Do I Want to be a Part of the Problem or a Part of the Solution?

When we are faced with a situation that we cannot control we usually want to get the best out of it that we can, but we may not necessarily try to obtain the best for our close allies, so we may have to think on our feet. If we have practised repeatedly and are influenced by people who have proven themselves in the past then this will work to our advantage, but we also know that things rarely work out that way and we often have to just do what we can with little preparation.

The questions we are faced with then are: what is the fusion between the abstract spirit world and the physical world? How do we transform our past actions and reactions? For the latter question, we may have done the wrong thing even in bad conditions, indeed we may have done better in a bad environment simply by enjoying what was available and reducing the challenges we had to face. Suitable frustration will turn this to our willingness to be flexible during events, having no desire to control, instead content to go along with the situation as and when it changes while keeping the end goal in mind. First, though, that aim has to be created, and while any individual can do so, the objectives need to be agreed by all and each person must work at them daily. However, if we are the type of personality that wishes to be a leader not a follower then we must ensure we keep that competitive streak at bay otherwise no progress will be made. We must work cooperatively and not intrusively. By being invasive, challenging or angry we will invoke hostility from our team mates also, so it is important to remain passive – but alert – and make sure we are working with everyone's best interests in mind.
Consider the following self-reflection questions:

1) What is the major source of frustration for you recently? How does it affect you now?
2) What makes you angry? Do you feel the same about it now or do you respond that way because it is what you are used to?

3) Have you revised and revisited your fears? If so, how have they changed, if at all?
4) Have you been trying to avoid your fears?
5) In what areas do you feel lonely?

Others' Behaviour

There will be times when we are greeted by a situation where others are behaving in a manner that we disagree with and we may feel forced to challenge them. This is a situation that we are almost all certainly familiar with, and it highlights that we observe others and use their behaviour as a benchmark while applying our own standards. Although almost universal, this is the wrong thing to do; in order to alter an outward experience we need to look inside ourselves, for very often people are the behaviour they demonstrate.

Naturally, different emotions exhibit different behaviours. Grief can only be dealt with over time and this emotion is felt whenever someone we care about leaves us – either physically moving to another place or exiting the physical world altogether – and we find ourselves feeling hollow and wondering how to move forward. What we find though is that if someone else needs us, whether personally or just that we need to attend work, we can brighten up and discard, at least temporarily, the negative emotions and, in the right situation, even laugh and have fun. This shows the grief has not engulfed our body and with each passing day we will feel more positive energy, until the time comes when we find ourselves at peace.

All too often we encounter selfish people who are looking for personal gain and with little to no qualms about obtaining it. These type of people come in different cloaks: some may be sitting comfortably and getting through by barking orders at those willing to play servant; others will pretend to be a team player but are often absent; others still will say flattering things in a bid to manipulate a situation to suit themselves. We must be aware that selfish people are not always those in front of us, rather we can be just as selfish. So selfish can we be that we become so used to giving instructions we can think of no other way to live and are just too comfortable with how things are, or perhaps so *un*comfortable that we worry changing something will make matters even worse. In order to escape this catch-twenty-two we need to state our desire to change, and although we will be aware the next step will be different and quite likely difficult, we must have faith in our ability and know that we will make it through.

A desire for immediate satisfaction and personal greed often leads to a cruel personality. All of us will have undoubtedly mishandled situations in our past and this can lead us to harbour negative expectations, where we believe the next encounter will be as difficult or negative as the last one. This is a false assertion, though, because the whole world evolves and with it all its inhabitants evolve, even if we are unaware of it. There becomes a union between what we have been through and how we dealt with it, from which a third force is created. As difficult as we may fear things will be, we need to learn to 'Let Go and Let God'; we have no idea what each situation or scenario will entail so we cannot try to control it before it happens.

"Come to the edge", he said.
They said: "We are afraid".
"Come to the edge", he said.
They came.
He pushed them . . . and they flew.
Guillaume Apollinaire

Now focus on these questions:

1) What suspicions do you hold regarding the problems of working in a group?
2) Are you disappointed that those suspicions are true, if you know them to be?
3) Are you disillusioned that the suspicions are, as of now, unfounded?
4) Have you judged anyone to be wanting on the basis of gossip?
5) Have you slandered people other than those whom you have problems with, or do you face the person directly to discuss matters?
6) Are you sad at having to wait for relief from past inhumanities and for a next step to synchronise?

A Brave New World

To have unity between our past and our future we must apply the same standard of acceptance to ourselves as we have for others. For instance, if we love and care for others, or have at any point in the past, then we know we are accepted and acceptable too, so we must live to that standard. In this manner, as we progress through life it is inconsequential if we agree or disagree with the system, for we have no choice in it and must simply trust events – there is, after all, no way for us to change them.

Clinging to the past leads to a feeling of guilt for not suffering for a length of time that we think is required, and this is especially true in those instances where loved ones seem to be going through an event that is more troubling than it is for us, but we do not help them by suffering alongside them. However, the true way in which we can help is by being living proof that difficulties can be overcome, and overcoming them to the point that we can be free from them entirely. By showing that this is possible we can encourage and inspire others to release their own shackles. However, we must be aware that the path we took for release is not universal and each person must find and follow their own path; accordingly, our presence may be restrictive to them so we must learn to read the situation and know when to lend a hand and when to take a step back.

Consider the following self-reflection questions on change and how you cope with it:

1) What parts of your life are changing their boundaries as a result of changing circumstances?
2) As you contract into your management of time within the designated space, what has changed and needs to be released?
3) As you expand, what gaps are apparent? For instance, altered family situation, feeling dislocated and the desire to move elsewhere, a feeling of hopelessness regarding the future etc.
4) What are you grateful for and currently content with?

PART 3:
MOTIVATION AND MOVEMENT

Chapter 11: Spiritual Health and Hygiene

Progress

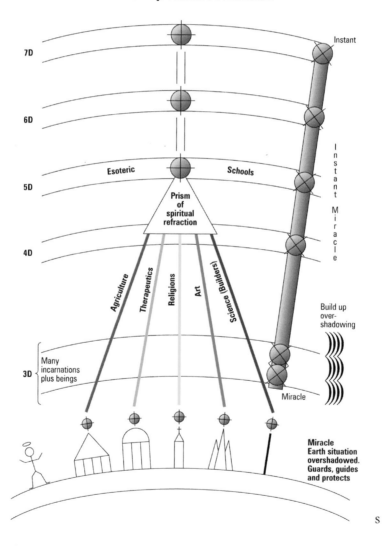

Prism of spiritual refraction

Mastering ourselves can be achieved by developing our skillset while also cherishing those with skills that complement ours. Our abilities are supported by life in every spectrum, i.e. on a spiritual level and also mankind's history, even though we are not aware of this on a conscious level. Nonetheless, the balancing act we must perfect is being neither arrogant nor cocky nor diminishing ourselves by underestimating our contribution.

If we feel we are going it alone then we are in danger of becoming uptight, but knowing that we belong to a group allows us to relax. Although we comprise just one cell of the greater organism we must still perform at our best; the dichotomy is that we are inadequate and somewhat useless in the grand scope of all life, but as a part of the Greater we are incredibly powerful.

Being sensitive to various things at any given time, with or without consistency, serves as protection for we must step aside and let the work take place. The reason for this is that we have no clue what is going on – and if we did we would try to gain control or manipulate others to try to work out the outcome, all of which will just mean we are in the way.

Our truth is relative and based on our understanding, meaning we are relative presentations of the Light force we possess. It is fine when things disintegrate around us because the Light is carried within individuals and things that have been achieved, which gives us freedom – the sacred space is provided to us regardless of our location, physical or emotional, if we have proven ourselves to be worthy. This keeps us free while allowing us to take the essence of our learning to the next chapter in our lives.

Now consider the following questions:

1) Do you feel you are regularly judged unfairly?
2) Do you judge others in matters that do not concern you?
3) Do you feel blamed for things you have no control over?
4) Do you blame others rather than take responsibility?
5) Do you instinctively criticise and condemn others?

History

Evolution is never destructive but rather is the process of repeating cycles that facilitate cleansing and transformation. Nature can be tough but it is never harsh unless such an action is required for the group's wellbeing. In order to enjoy new things we must release what we no longer need to survive, including out-dated dogma, prejudices, criticisms and resentments. We must also release our need to fix things for others and trying to change things to suit ourselves. Such acts are divisive, harming the innocent and those who have already freed themselves.

Part of the process is working out what we are attracted to – modern or antique? Local hospitality or trips to exotic places? Routines or spontaneity? What attracts us indicates which energies we resonate with. Cosmic light works on our central nervous system as well as the endocrine system, and it will, over time, build up enough pressure to create a pain threshold in order to block the flow so we can confront it and forgive and release the flow or not. This updated rhythm brings cycles that give the opportunity to achieve personal, community and planetary evolution.

Consider the following questions on over-care:

1) Do you try to 'fix' things and manipulate circumstances for your own end?
2) Do you feel manipulated by others?
3) Do you try to 'rescue' others or feel they try to 'rescue' you?
4) Do you try to protect those who surround you unduly or feel stifled by the care of others?
5) Are you usually content or are you constantly trying to make changes in those around you?

Point of potential change

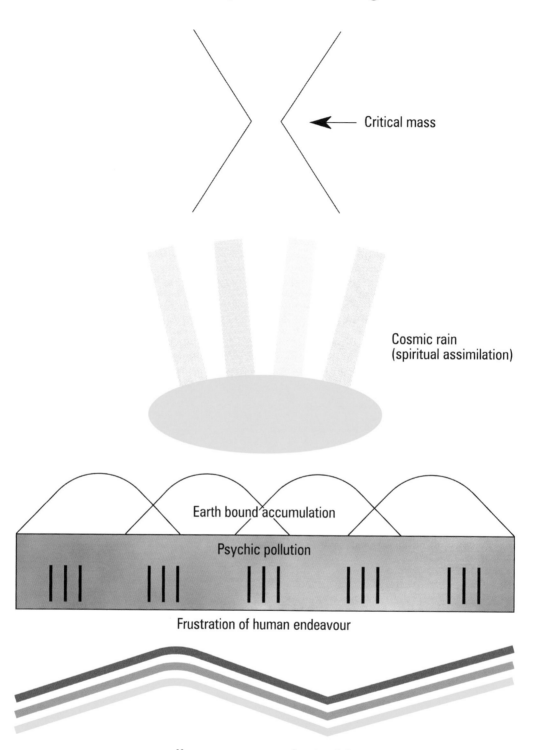

Critical mass

Cosmic rain
(spiritual assimilation)

Earth bound accumulation

Psychic pollution

Frustration of human endeavour

Human resource and potential

Conversion of experiences

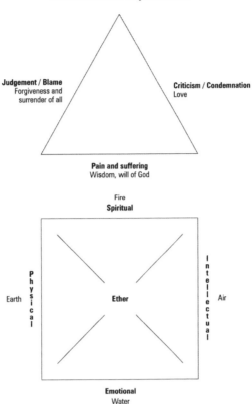

Judgement / Blame
Forgiveness and
surrender of all

Criticism / Condemnation
Love

Pain and suffering
Wisdom, will of God

Fire
Spiritual

Physical

Earth

Ether

Intellectual

Air

Emotional
Water

Who Can I Blame?

Although we all blame, judge and condemn others at some point or another, once we have finished doing so we must take responsibility for ourselves and see if our actions against others have come back on us. If they have then we will end up spending time seeking change, which we can control once we have perfected it through practice. Alternatively we may seek someone else to fix it, and in such times we are none too choosy about who we select. A worthy person will support us and encourage us to reconnect to our own inner resources, which they may do by reminding us of our own strengths and what we have overcome in the past. This is useful for those who lack the confidence initially to go it alone and it will allow us to take responsibility once again rather than try to pass it to someone else.

When it comes to family and community we are also better at one than the other and we will bounce between them repeatedly. In doing so we enable the intellectual concepts and understanding to be revised and reviewed. We may also review bias and prejudice as they bombard our awareness, allowing us to determine if our beliefs are important or not – if they are we can hold them as a priority and if they are not we can release them.

Consider the following questions:

1) Do you find yourself hoping against hope that things will be different?
2) Do you constantly review the past and try to rearrange circumstances?
3) Do you think about the needs of others or yourself or both?
4) Can you envisage a life without suffering?

Conformity

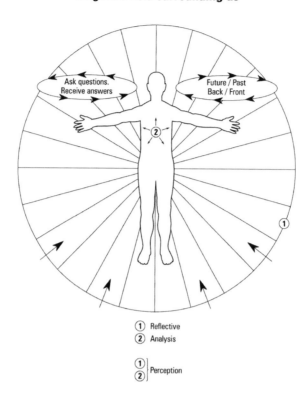

Magnetic field surrounding us

(1) Reflective
(2) Analysis

(1)
(2) Perception

Allows opportunity of specification
Work and application

Although we do not all like to admit it, the truth of the matter is that more often than not we try very hard to be accepted by those we trust, or those we want to trust us. However, if we have been dominated or ignored previously then the end result may be that we are now timid or rebellious, or sometimes both. This then presents a problem: do we try self-help or turn to others? Or do we just pretend everything is fine and ignore it, hoping it will either resolve itself or vow to give it attention at a later date? These options are all fine so long as they work, but if they do not, or when they reach the point where they stop working, then we are left with no alternative but to counsel ourselves, and at this point we must learn to be content with the knowledge that we have integrity, despite the fact the events in our environment may be unsatisfactory.

Only when we surrender ourselves to a higher level, with the knowledge that we do not know it all and need external help, will Nature's Law free us, maybe even providing us with tools to help us. Although we are creatures of space we have Earthly bodies, and so while we are occupying the planet we belong here. Whether we like or loathe our lives, the fact remains that we are alive and must plough forward. We all want to be accepted and trusted, and in order for that to happen we must prove ourselves acceptable and trustworthy, and most of all we must be disciplined to the time and space we occupy, which will reward us with natural authority. However, if we get too close to other people or situations our feelings may block our affinity to the higher standard we surrendered to. We must be careful to get out of the way and let the natural path unfold.

The Future in Motion

Any actions we take in the present will help shape the future and start the wheels turning to create those future events. However, it is difficult if not impossible to understand something we have no experience of, and so we must work to align with constructive suffering instead of being destructive in how we perceive things. This is done by slowly finding the slot that starts things off gently; we must remember that life is trying to heal itself and, as integrated parts of life, we must be both accommodating and accommodated. As with most things, this is best done over a period of time rather than too quickly otherwise we risk disturbing others.

An essential lesson of life is that people are not all the same. A sensitive person will be instinctive and reflective, concentrating on survival only, including the possibilities and memories it contains, whereas a higher visionary intuition will be perception, asking the higher power what it requires through meditation.

This instinct and the vision we possess are both coordinated by our ability to analyse the next step and to tie up loose ends on the previous step before advancing to the next one. However, this requires awareness that much is happening beyond our capacity so we must work in the area we currently find ourselves in.

Love can use the intuition responsibly because there already exists within the brain a parallel intention, meaning there is a recognisable affinity – when the heart opens, wisdom will enter, so both work in tandem. We are only able to start the next step when we accept self-responsibility, instead of trying to manipulate others. What this means is acknowledging by accepting responsibility of ourselves, we can leave other people to accept their own responsibility and determine the best course of action for themselves, and that course may be different, but just as valid, as our own. So we must choose to love for the sake of loving, rather than in the hope of getting something in return.

Consider the following questions on adequacy:

1) Do you feel safe in your situation?
2) Do you feel able to express yourself or do you suppress your thoughts because you cannot verbalise them accurately?
3) Can you trust yourself to behave in a socially acceptable manner?
4) Can you accept that others must also express their needs as well as you doing so?

Spiritual Attraction

The diagram below is a visual representation of self-work. Although we surrender to higher power, we must not be fooled into thinking that this negates the need for hard work; the higher power neither replaces our own effort nor excuses its absence. If nothing else, we require the parallel experience and that is only gained by working for it; if we ask the Management Upstairs to cover our complacency we will be ignored or receive a karmic slap on the wrist.

Thanks to the chakra system we start to increase the purity of each centre, allowing us to safely attract power, secure each centre and find a focus for life. Before this can happen, though, the two supporting channels to the sides of the spine will need to be adjusted, which in turn can cause aches in our back or front from past pain, so do not be alarmed if you experience this. If you had acute pain in this area in the past then it may become chronic now, serving as a memory from the past, because the negative is being changed into a positive rather than the change occurring from scratch.

Once this change has been made a new seed can grow from the base, and this is where the exciting change happens. Growing ideas raises the consciousness; the ideas are combustible and waiting to be released so new life can enter, the new life being creative and expanding life, trust, courage, integrity and will power. The joining of the abstract and the actual showcases a union of energy, but it is a blind path for us to follow because we are completely ignorant of what is happening or where we are going; all we know is that something amazing is taking place.

Our next step is to feel enthused about our new direction. This involves convincing ourselves that everything is good; while this is a fact of all evolution we tend to forget it when we feel stress or pressure.

Nonetheless, we are fully able to choose to enjoy what we want to or have to, and this choice is what anchors us in a constructive manner in the work we must undertake.

Centres of spiritual attraction

This process is about empowering ourselves and reconnecting with a higher power. We will have nothing to be concerned with if we have expressed love and displayed the highest standards we can produce, just as we need do no more if are cooperative and willing to listen and learn. At this point, all we can do is wait for further instruction.

Consider the following questions on flexibility:

1) What do you feel you are letting go of?
2) What do you feel you are connecting to?

3) What is the next step?
4) Can you be in the space and wait through time until you know what to do next?

When Change is Inevitable, Choose to Enjoy it

Encouragement is a positive, sometimes even necessary, means of support, and we must be aware that we need not wait for someone else to provide it: we can encourage ourselves by learning how to strip down and understand previous states of mind and then override the message as we await a new experience, in a similar way as one may reformat the hard drive of their computer. When only we ourselves are involved the situation may be tense; when it involves a friend we find it easier; but if it involves a whole group, such as family or work, then collective factors that have held us in good stead over the years need to be found.

It can prove difficult trying to inspire certain people until we find a way into their inner clock. First will be spiritual introduction, closely followed by facing up to the challenge as well as the emotional, intellectual and social structures which will try to keep things stagnant, because it is easier to cope with what is already known. Following this will be re-education and then, finally, the new manifestation.

Consider the following questions on direction:

1) What within your life is confusing you right now?
2) What is the new direction you desire to go in?
3) Is it logically possible at this time?
4) Can you convert chaos into order anywhere in your life, even if it is just a filing cabinet or wardrobe? This will indicate to the mind that the inner and outer can be harmonious.

Chapter 12: Healthy Stress

Motivation

Various things can motivate us in life, and change finding us is a motivation as much as us actively seeking change anyway. If we choose to make changes then we will be aware, content and happy; on the other hand, if changes are forced on us then we will not be quite so graceful or accommodating.

Consider the following questions on unchosen change:

1) Do you feel irritable and do not know why?
2) Do you feel anxiety and anger against someone or something?
3) Do you feel persecuted or that others are against you?
4) Do you feel neglected, abandoned or left out?
5) Do you dislike being touched physically?
6) Does the unfamiliar make you afraid?
7) Do you feel unhappy with how you look?
8) Do you dislike yourself?
9) Do you have a sense of failure or lack confidence?
10) Do you feel unable to cope or trapped?
11) Is it hard to concentrate and difficult to make decisions?
12) Do you feel dizzy, suffer persistent headaches or neck aches or bite your nails?
13) Do you feel tired, inert and lacking energy?
14) Do you sleep badly or too much?
15) Do you fidget and feel the need to escape your current life?

These symptoms are indicating that unchosen changes seem to be taking place and the memory is reminding the body of the negative consequences that occurred the last time similar circumstances were encountered. At this point we will require time and space as we enter, willingly, the negotiation that will permit us to find peaceful coexistence with those we encounter. We need internal communication here so we can combine the ideal abstract with the actual potential, for the coming together of the past and future involves a complicated procedure and we must ask the question, "Are we naturally cooperative or are we usually rebellious?" Most importantly though, must we always be in control or are we willing to trust enough to let life lead us?

The last question is most important because to say we will obey an instruction is not enough; we must be willing to actively collaborate because before any action can be taken by anyone on our behalf we must go through the stages of research, discussion and/or negotiation. As stated previously, this means we must rid ourselves of any existing bias, prejudice or inherited predispositions. We must be aware that during this stage the difficulties we faced in the past will become apparent to us once again as we adjust our capacities and tolerance levels to what they are now instead of what they used to be. To do this we must have a quiet and still mind; if we do not, we will try to control the situation and then we run the risk of pushing away those people we want to associate with.

In order to repair past misconceptions and improve our being to the state we should be we will require time so that we can put the past firmly behind us and be prepared for the future without the shackles and weights of what has already happened. For the space to be clean and clear we must shed selfishness, competitiveness or self-indulgence so that all can benefit, not some benefiting at the expense of others, because the sacred union can only bear fruit when it is ready. We cannot force it along, rather we must surrender and do what is required of us.

Hold on tightly – let go lightly

Surrender, forgive and accept the past is past.
Trust the future as you meet it gently

The seat of power. Must take and use essence and release effluent — **Anus** — Let go of resentment

Balances — **Spleen Solar Plexus** — Digests life to date

Having loved and given – contracts. Frees unconditionally — **Heart** — Lets go of hatred. Bitterness at obstructions on journey

Prepares for new expression — **Throat** — Lets go of authoritarian fears

Old pressure releases in favour of update — **Brain** — Lets go of non co-operation with light body

Keeping Our Balance

We cannot and must not rely only on our five physical senses of touch, sight, taste, smell and hearing; we also need corrective balance because we respond faster than the brain's immediate reflex speed.

The brain's spine is linked to everything else but in particular the main glands. Each one of our nerve and gland centres are connected to a wheel of energy, referred to as the 'chakra'. Often heard but less often understood, the chakra is the central hub of thinking and awareness of thought, ability and sensitivity which has to align with all the other centres of awareness and energy. For obvious reasons, the state of total awareness must be unified. Guidance is registered not only at the perimeter but also at the centre, and both these fields must also unify before we can safely move forward. The intuitive instruction enters the glandular system from the chakra and hormones are then released into the bloodstream, which we recognise as being prepared for impending danger. This is the process of awaking to new possibilities.

Initially we will attempt to analyse and contemplate action within inaction. We will learn reason and as we progress and try to update our truth we will become wiser as we make sense of things that make none. We will receive much advice from both the inner realm and outer realms, but it will be difficult to decipher which is good and which is bad, especially if we do not trust ourselves to know the difference at this point.

We will try to remain as detached and impersonal as possible as we move further forward, because we are unaware of what the end result is going to be or supposed to be. What we need at this point is more knowledge, and we acquire it by getting into communion/communication inside and outside. Although this will cause a struggle, from that struggle goodwill emerges; we may not know how goodwill will come of it, but it is possible that this clash is in order for us to be able to love others more every time we make an attempt to connect to the collective awareness.

As we ask questions such as 'What can come of this?' the whole state of being will be awoken, and this is where we need to make sure our approach is as loving as it can possibly be. Once we reach this point we will be able to utilise the confidence we have acquired from the past and we will be humble, modest, patient and wiser than before. This wisdom aids us in our increased tolerance towards others, for we are now able to let others see things and learn for themselves instead of us trying to take control and telling them what they should be seeing.

Perform the following visualisation exercise about future potential.
Relax as you push thoughts hindered by negativity out of your mind.
Connect to the 'feel good' factor – whatever it may be – and concentrate on it. Be as unanimous and inclusive as is possible while you ponder what is happening inside you and around you. What must you discard before proceeding?
Imagine the possibilities and reflect on them. Visualise them as completed successfully and see yourself content, enjoying the process. Energise them and affirm them so you are excited at the prospect of future possibilities, but without neglecting your current responsibilities.

Colour Dynamics

Aside from colour psychology, colour dynamics is divided into two main groups of study: physics and chemistry. The physics of colour consists of light and light use, while chemistry involves the study and use of pigments, materials and compounds.

The physics of colour starts with white light, which is the sum of three major light rays: red, green and blue-violet. When red is added to green yellow is created; when green is added to blue-violet turquoise is produced; and when red is added to blue-violet it makes magenta. If yellow, turquoise and magenta are mixed they create white light, otherwise known as a 'full spectrum ray'. This light maintains health and balance within a unified field.

The chemistry of colour studies action and practical use, consisting of the main colours of red, yellow and blue. These are referred to as 'subtractive colour' because when mixed they create new colours – for example, yellow and blue make the new colour of green, with no hint of either of the original colours.
The colour pigment spectrum is often referred to as the colour wheel. The final combination of mixing creates black, removing all traces of pure colour; however, when a pure colour mixes with white the strength

of that colour is lost and a pastel colour is created. When this pastel is mixed with a complementary colour the result is grey.

Thus, we can understand that if we are in light for too long we will crave for darkness so we may rest, but if we are enveloped in darkness for too long we will crave light so we may grow and develop. As such, it is important that we balance light and dark to a level that suits us, so we may rest and grow as needed, but without affecting the balance of others.

Colour self-portrait

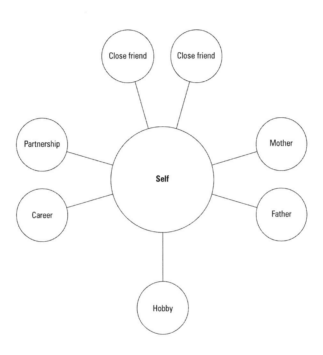

Name a colour for the above associations

Psychic Health and Hygiene

Like chakra, 'psychic' is a word often heard and often misunderstood. Quite simply it is when a change occurs such as the invisible becoming visible or the unfelt becoming tangible. The beliefs that we hold may have been influenced or instilled from our environment, what we watch and read, and those around us. While these influences may have been good for us in the past, there might come a point in the future where we update or release them altogether and take a new approach. Indeed, this is a natural part of growth and development and for this spiritual journey in particular many beliefs, especially prejudices, will need to be shed. In order to do so, as with anything, the decision to do it must first be made and we must then adopt an attitude that supports the transition from one belief or state of mind to another.

The Pathway

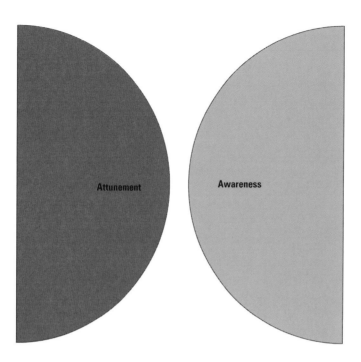

As we start the transition we examine the group dynamic surrounding us and quite often so early on we decide it is too difficult to undertake. Worse still, if we mention this to those in our group they will invariably all offer their own nuggets of advice – which is of course very kind and appreciated, but because we are all on our own paths the advice differs from person to person, leaving us with an overload of options and we become overwhelmed, then finding it easier to flee. Or, worse still, the options offered may be met with resentment by us and this can conjure up painful memories, which can in turn make us feel angry, rebellious or uncooperative as we try to alleviate and distribute the pain to ease the burden on our own backs. An equal possibility is that we may find ourselves becoming selfish and acting as if we do not care, or turning back to old vices in an attempt to dull the pain or avoid facing up to what we need to change.

In order for us to begin a new chapter, we need to be a friend of the Earth and have faith in the Heavens, the total care system, the Management Upstairs, the abstract, whatever it is we believe is coming into actualisation. Attuning in this manner allows us to filter our past, taking what we need and rejecting what is hindering us, as well as providing us time to be realistic about the marketing of our ideal as we try to secure it to the Earth in the best interests not only of ourselves but as many people as possible.

This process is like opening a portal, on the other side of which we will find a series of clues – they may not seem to follow any sequential order and some may even seem irrelevant, but we must notice and follow each one until a bigger picture and a clear space emerges, which is when we will be able to understand the mechanics of what we once considered unknown and unknowable. This allows a new way to gently come into fruition.

Having digested the old meal of life we create an atmosphere that we can tolerate, and only when we reach this point are we inspired to have the strength to gain an insight into a suitable next step. We then create a rhythm that suits everyone, catering to the old, young, able and disabled in equal measure. In the process of this everyone's needs are assessed on their current state, not what they used to be or what we think they could or should be. At this stage in the journey we are able to reflect and look inside ourselves, remembering how complicated and daunting it seemed to find our own path; using this vision we can be empathetic to others.

A true mystic can eventually become a shaman, because it is only these people whose work integrates so tightly into the everyday that the seam joining Heaven and Earth is invisible. Upon reaching this stage they are aware of the fact that neither learning, observation nor practice ever cease – the maintenance of them all are the essence of life itself.

Stressors From the Past

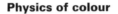

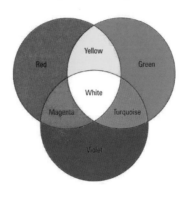

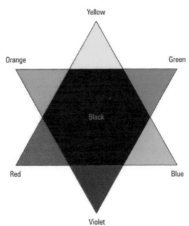

Throughout our lives we will have found a path that allows us to live without holding our breath or suffocating as well as fulfil our desires enough to satisfy us but without drowning in them; we have embraced support without allowing so much input we forget who we really are. There is much we have learnt that we have used to balance ourselves, but now these lessons are breaking and changing as we feel prompts from our past once again. Now in order to be comfortable the inner and outer must reach a harmonious resolution.

To do this we must go back to former pain so we may settle it once and for all, no longer running from it or avoiding but facing it head on and neutralising it so it causes no future disruptions. There is no need for us to defend ourselves or vie for others' attention; all we need to do is include all those we can and love both ourselves and those we meet. We must also learn that applying wisdom means attending to the person or people in greatest need at any given moment and that we need to create coverage for all, though not necessarily all at once, rather than being ambitious or competing to come out on top. It is of particular importance for these lessons to be learned if we have any feelings of betrayal, abandonment or rejection from the past, which are all insecurities we need to be rid of.

The experiences that can cause such emotions have a negative impact not only on our relationships with others but our inner selves as well. Instead of drawing awareness to our being incapable of dealing with situations that make us uncomfortable we armour our outer selves, stifling the ego at the same time, but because the ego and physical awareness try to exist peacefully together we cause a struggle between them.

Moreover, any tension in the relationships we have – be it with family members, friends, new people we meet or our partners – can cause fear and anxiety to the point that we cannot express ourselves. Instead we are paralysed by our own emotions of either inferiority or superiority. This in turn can make us feel isolated and lonely, which may make us conform to things we do not want to or frustrate or deprive us. Many negative things can be experienced at this point, causing problems internally and externally through our interactions with others.

To reverse this agonising process we must start slowly, in our thoughts and intentions and words. We must first make an affirmation, believe in it, be gracious and accommodating to others and this will create a new foundation for us, from which we can proceed safely into the next chapter of life.

Preparation and Development

Known ideal

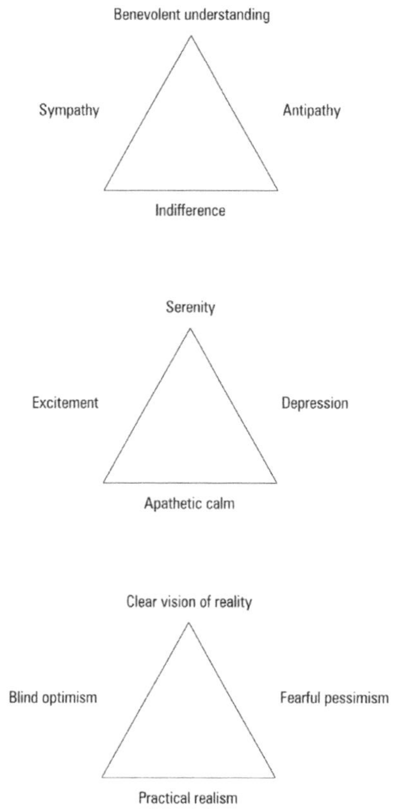

Benevolent understanding

Sympathy   Antipathy

Indifference

Serenity

Excitement   Depression

Apathetic calm

Clear vision of reality

Blind optimism   Fearful pessimism

Practical realism

Before reading the rest of this section perform the following visualisation exercise:

Relax as much as you can and then concentrate on the most pure and abstract. State the aim of unanimity and goodwill until you can feel it radiating from your centre, filling first your heart and mind, then lift this feeling into your head.

Imagine yourself as motivated and valued, with a part to play even if you are currently unsure what that part is. Express your willingness as you contemplate the best part you could have with your skill set.

Make a choice and affirm it. Energise your segment, concentrate and refrain from telling others how to be or how to live, only prompt the next step rather than dictating it and persist with this until all can see the path ahead. Be aware that this is not particularly easy at this stage because you will be remembering past experiences and emotions and there may be confusion as to whether they are remembered for you to take responsibility and continue with them or if you should release them. Time will help you decide, though.

Events such as these will help you determine if your old reactions have been cleansed or not. If we feel that someone is invading our space, or imposed upon by someone demanding we do something, we may become angry. If this proves to be true then we are presented with the opportunity to find out if we have been 'cured' of old emotions or if we need to remain at a distance until consistent behaviour is displayed – by us as well as those we interact with.

It is possible that we will want to feel secure in the presence of specific people or that we want to be trusted and accepted immediately, without earning the acceptance or trust of others. This attitude may see us looking for numerous spiritual fixes as an attempt at being reassured or feeling protected without us realising that we are actually going about finding security in the wrong manner.

If we decide to be humble and modest then we must rid ourselves of pride and the desire to control or manipulate people and/or situations. Nor can we afford to be competitive, because if we are then we do not believe in equality – if we do then we will recognise that there is no need to try to get a bigger piece of any pie because in time all will be rewarded equally, so we must be patient and gracious and be willing to help those who need it. It is at this point that we must join with the soul force and allow ourselves to be informed of what we agreed to and also what we may need reminding of in case we have forgotten. In order for us to coexist peacefully it is important that we neither expect nor assume anything, because we still do not know what is required of us. Instead, for now we will be comforted by honesty, loving care and those with wisdom or abilities that complement our own, and we will enjoy uniting energies. When we make mature, developed responses to everyone, not just those we agree with, and show consideration to all forms of life on Earth we will be guaranteed flexibility and interaction.

Once this is completed the ideal will be realised inside our self as well as in the family and our environment. However, it is realised but not yet demonstrated and until the latter has occurred the ideal is not yet being applied. To make that so, we must surge forward.

Guardians and Stewards
Colour, a Brain Stimulus

The sun is the Earth's source of light and heat, its rays travelling ninety-three million miles of space in just over eight minutes to reach our planet. Light travels at one-hundred-and-eighty-six-thousand miles per second and forty per cent of light can be seen by humans as the visible spectrum. In this spectrum we see seven major colours, which are found in nature in a rainbow: red, orange, yellow, green, blue, indigo and violet. Each of the colours has a different wavelength and vibration and when they are used as pigment or light fractures each of the colours causes a different reaction and effect in us. For example, certain colours such as red raise blood pressure and increase pulse and breathing rates. Blue has the opposite effect and various studies have demonstrated that variations in the amount of colour have effects on our nervous activity, ability to concentrate and muscular control.

Light spectrum

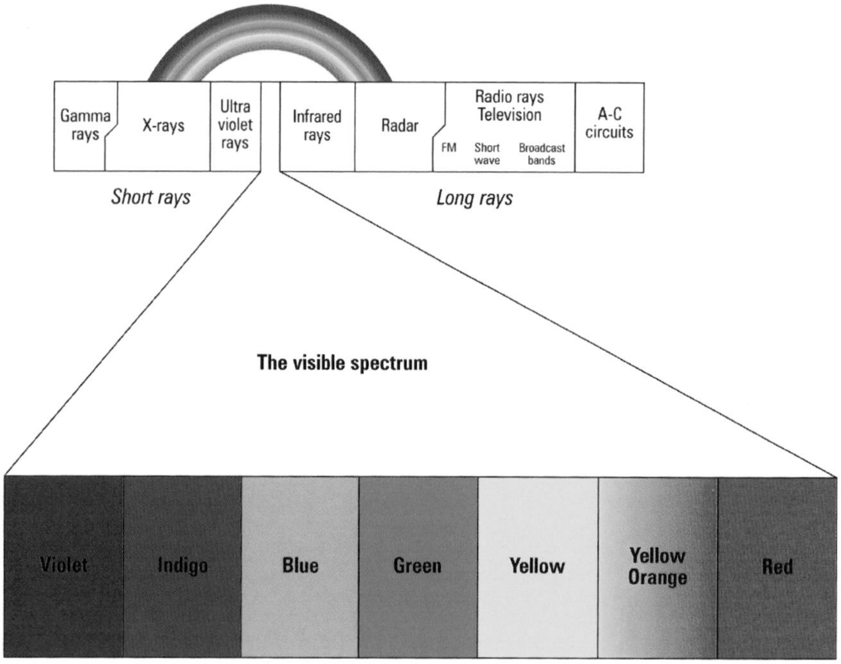

| Gamma rays | X-rays | Ultra violet rays | Infrared rays | Radar | Radio rays Television | A-C circuits |

Short rays   *Long rays*

The visible spectrum

| Violet | Indigo | Blue | Green | Yellow | Yellow Orange | Red |

As humans we require both guardians of space and stewards of time. We require supervision at the levels of thoughts, words and actions. Consider the mouth as a metaphor: the teeth guard the space and steward the tongue's ability to flick and make sound against them – the tongue is active, the mouth passive, and together they create a union with specific capabilities and capacities.

Confusion will arise when expanding capacities cause a change of direction, which will bring chaos, insecurity and vulnerability our way. To make the transition gentle and smooth we must slow down and borrow energy from the physical, giving the intellectual the required time to understand the changes. As part of this we need to sedate our emotions and focus on creating order again.

As we create a new space we must also provide as much time as necessary to heal. Although it is stress that motivates us it is distress that we must discharge, being careful not to negatively impact on anyone around us. To make this so, we might isolate ourselves from most people so we can prepare for the forthcoming new placement, taking time to mingle with others occasionally to check how well we are coping with our new order. We can also use this time to let go of some people and celebrate moving forward with others, but also acknowledging that no one is in a better or worse position than anyone else, just a different one. Also during this time we will close off what we no longer need and our progress may be a motivating factor to those who can use our experience to progress themselves. We will also be able to assess how long it will take us as we create objectives and goals, letting ourselves be carried forward by instinctive desires. On the quest of finding out what it is we do want we may go back and visit the past to be sure of what we do *not* want, as this gives us flexibility and the ability to cooperate with others, allowing all to feel safe, cared for and just as important as our own self.

Much hard work is undertaken, internally and externally, to enable us to free people to fulfil their own potential regardless of the situation(s) they find themselves in. However, it is only when the inner work unifies with the outer work, providing clear results over time, that we are able to move on. When such a point arises we will be an embodiment of compassion, tolerance and universal service to all around us.

We will be stressed, as this pushes us forward, but not distressed; filled with wonder not dread; grateful rather than greedy. When we find ourselves being gracious it will be because we genuinely feel that emotion and not because we have an ulterior motive. We will have forgiven and let go of previous grudges and resentful feelings. When we think of the past it will be as a key experience that allowed us to cleanse unnecessary things and create new space. Ultimately, though, we will be now willing to surrender to the higher power as we ask for opposites, such as being ill so we can transform it to health.

PART 4:
LOVING LEARNING

Chapter 13: Stress Management

A Free Choice: Release or Repeat

Release can cause us frustration and exhaustion as well as the feeling that we are being cheated and led astray rather than in the right direction. It must be remembered though that anything that holds any real value frees things rather than restrains them, and encourages without interfering or domineering. This generous backdrop to our lives is independent and free-flowing – it can give and take and do and be, as well as allowing a return to the beginning so we can complete the circuit.

Having survived all the problems that were encountered already, we now have the capability to adjust any difficulties we may face in the future. We can create something and become united with it and reproduce it repeatedly until such a time comes when we rid ourselves of skins and personas that are out-dated and we simply stand in our own light source. By being willing to create things we can experience whatever is necessary without worry, for we can overcome difficulties. At this stage of the journey we are aware the collective was born free from interference; we know we strive to make the most for the collective rather than just ourselves; intellectually we now have charisma and of top priority is learning to lead without harming others; spiritually we only learn through actions to develop wisdom and connect the abstract with the actual. It is only as we complete these steps that we understand what was required of us in order to make that completion.

With the newly acquired knowledge of what was required of us previously we are now much more open and unreserved about doing things in the future that need to be done without knowing why or what is required of us for it to take place. Instead, we do for doing's own sake. Indeed, for us to rid ourselves of the stress and strain acquired just from living then it is crucial we completely surrender to our soul path. This is now easier because we are well aware that we can trust ourselves to work not for our own gain but in the best interests of everyone around us. So we will be content to be confused as we move forward and wait for the new direction to become clear as life unfolds before us. We can now relinquish control and allow chaos to surround and envelop us so that new, refreshed order will establish itself.

Consider the following questions:

1) Did you try to be popular or gain publicity by fighting or running, thus selling others out?
2) Did you maintain a quiet mind and be dedicated to the task at hand?
3) Do people feel safe enough to be open and honest around you?
4) Have you proved your trustworthiness?
5) Do you give people the time they need to accept, or do you assume you are correct?
6) Do you ask the correct question and make the appropriate comments for people to be gently encouraged to make the right decision or do you demand and manipulate them into it?

Authority Issues

Both life and death are constants. We are born to experience things and once we have we release that experience as we die to it, although this process may be met willingly or with much resistance.

As has been mentioned throughout this book, our being tested and observed is an unavoidable fact. While we struggle with our process we may be seen as cruel, torturous or one who enslaves others to our own regime. Alternatively we may think these things of another until we become willing and cooperative with everyone without it being a conscious effort or decision – it will, in time, be a natural reflex. However, to reach this state of mind we need to overcome the desires for:

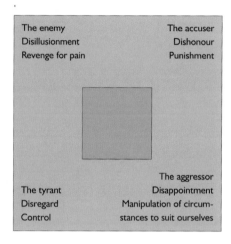

Quite often we as humans will resist cooperating because we lack trust. If this is the case then it may be advantageous to build a new team with carefully selected members, each practising their own skill and not one they are uncomfortable with. In such a team the members will be happy and content, willing to share and consult with others, support, encourage and care for others as much as possible, and negotiations are carried out with the majority being catered for rather than a loud minority.

In order to achieve this many personal issues will need to be addressed, including but not limited to: ignorance, arrogance, envy, revenge, spite, scorn, sneering, monopolisation, disregard, hostility, division, frustration, exclusion, belittlement and lying.

Consider the following questions on the application of the intention:

1) Did you bastardise any because of your need to be loved?
2) Did you hold true despite how others judged you?
3) Did you sell out in order to avoid the collective challenge?
4) Did you see the job through to a logical conclusion and from where you could not take it further?
5) Did you use others in the process?

Right Use of Power

Only we can decide what is justified and unjustified in our lives; the decision is down to the individual not any others, including us when it involves other people. That being said, though, we may find that if we do something immoral then outside forces might aid us. Nonetheless, it is us, and only us, who can decide how we should progress and if we are willing to allow ourselves be guided by our soul and release previous pain and distress in order to embrace the present stress, which will facilitate our moving on.

Applying the vision

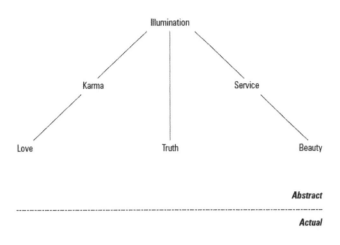

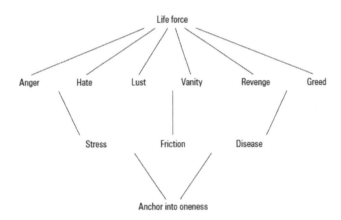

The diagram below shows what we all have all experienced and which have led us to cower, but interacting with others can allow us to soften the rough edges posed by these situations providing we trust our inner guidance and the Management Upstairs.

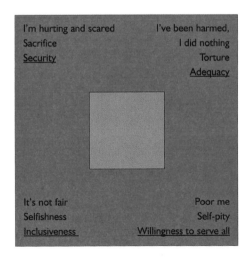

The question at this point is not 'can' we trust the Greater Power to apply both a standard and ethic that includes us, because it will, but 'will' we trust it to do so? This involves us having the stamina and persistence to keep up the daily disciplines required of us, much like we either do or do not have the persistence to exercise or floss our teeth daily. We must have the stamina and persistence to continue even when the standards and disciplines are challenged by outside forces and when we feel physically exhausted, especially when we are forced to make choices.

We must bear in mind that if we take no action then our inaction will result in further dividing the community and that in turn will exacerbate the inequality issue, which does not allow for unity. We will care for and share with others, doing our utmost to cater for all we can.

In our environment will be multiple and varied circumstances, from which we need to distinguish the bad, which we must discard, and the good, which we must focus on. We will need to reassess the following:

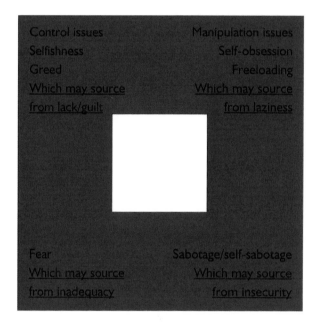

We must, then, create a new framework and look inside ourselves to determine if we are yet ready to let go of past issues; if we decide that we are, then we can become 'markers' for others who are in similar situations to the one we are in so they may do it for themselves rather than trying to pass the responsibility onto others. If the unknown fills us with dread or our current situation makes us angry or frustrated then we may not be able to move on. Our grief will either internalise or externalise until the pressure between the two can coexist peacefully. This pressure serves as a bridge for us to move from the past into the future, so we must state our wishes clearly in the hope that they will come to fruition.

When faced with a problem we can reduce it by choosing goodwill, or we can choose not to care because we think it is too difficult to solve; our head hurts from trying to deal with it and our heart feels hurt or damaged. To make matters worse, we cannot make sense of what is going on in either of them. So we must ask, or even instruct, the head to honour instead of judge and forgive instead of blame so the pressure can be released. We can reassure ourselves that attacking or neglecting responsibility is unnecessary, because if we let go of the past then we give the future a chance to present itself and this will cause big changes in our present.

If our heart feels hurt or heavy – which is entirely natural and normal – then it is neither wise nor prudent to push others away or try to use them, even if acting in a defensive manner feels like the right thing to do. Rather, if we have proven ourselves as being able to contribute and willing to look after others then we have nothing to fear.

We should appoint the Light and wait; it will show itself when the time is right. In the meantime we need to love those in our community and be happy to wait until they are provided opportunities or situations that are similar to our own, at which point they will find their newfound personal space as it should be now rather than how it used to be. And remember, what everyone else goes through is no less stressful than it was for us; the changes happen to us all.

Chapter 14: Freedom

Breaking Through To Break Free

**The stress of the past
gives way to the future**

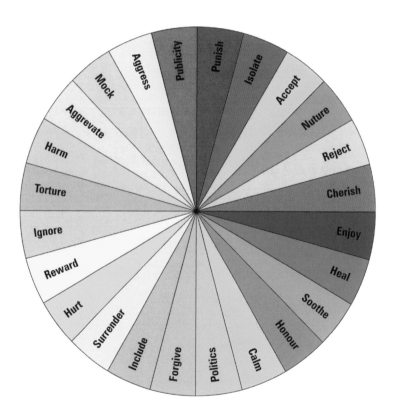

If we feel that we have lost face with our peers, that we will lose our security and thus lose the ability to deal with life's challenges, or we find it difficult to trust when we do not know all the details, then we may not be ready to forgive – ourselves or others. We can often think that although things are not perfect, it is better to make do with the bad you are used to instead of dive into a potentially worse situation, regardless of the fact that the new situation could be, and often is, far better. Complacency holds us back from progressing and traps us in our negative situation.

It is possible that we feel let down or misguided by pursuing clues and leads that only make things more confusing and so think we should have followed a different path. If this is the case then we may feel used or abused, that we have been conned into going somewhere we should not have gone; this can lead to behaviours from us that make those around us feel used or abused also, all of which has the capacity to break down relationships or cause setbacks in previous advancements and developments.

Before we focus on changing ourselves we can feel a range of emotions including jealously, competitiveness, resentfulness or just having relentless ambition to succeed. During this time we will have no problem in punishing or enslaving others while judging and justifying how others perform. We are happy to blame others in our group while we pass our own responsibility onto them, or we may blame ourselves for not performing better than we did.

Look at the diagram on the previous page, which reviews and revises what our hopes were but we did not receive. Some people will be trapped between 'self-indulgence' and 'guilt', scared to enjoy something through fear of being tortured and similarly incapable of cherishing or ignoring, rewarding or ejecting, because we are unable to surrender to the Management Upstairs. At this juncture we may have much difficulty in knowing who to include or exclude. This might be a tumultuous time because we are in the dark as to what is required of us.

Why Wait?

The Kingdom of God

Present on Earth   Perfection

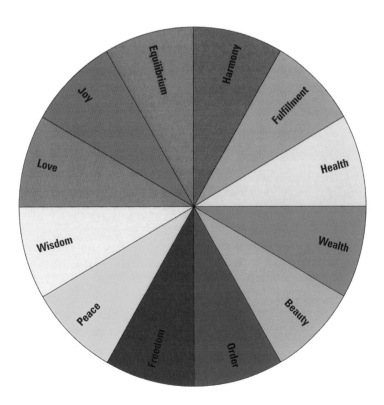

We may have had our faith in the Kingdom of God shaken, especially if we have encountered authorities that have abused their power, such as parents or teachers. Negative encounters with such people may lead us to doubt the effectiveness or purpose of meditation or prayer, so it would be prudent to review this as we relinquish the desire to cling to the past and instead let go of it lightly. In spite of the aforementioned encounters, this can be relatively easy if we acknowledge that we have done our best.

If we make the conscious choice to hold on to bitter feelings then we are refusing to experience sweetness, which sets us on a path of self-indulgence and the urge to steal from others so we may enjoy what we have not earned. We may notice a change in behaviour, such as being suspicious of others or thinking that they have it easier in life than we do. In having such an attitude, though, all we are doing is inflicting guilt upon others and dismissing all who seem to have more than us, whether that be talent, humour or money. It is a poor habit that many possess to judge others on their current worth without taking the time or effort to find out how they got to their position.

Take the time now to answer the following questions on coping with the learning process:

1) In what manner do you think you are self-indulgent?
2) Where do you feel guilt – in your behaviour, your body, or both?
3) What do you enjoy now? Is it different to what you enjoyed previously?
4) Do you trust in your capacity to be held secure, having everything you need to enjoy good health?
5) Do you accept that you have been gifted with learning through being shown rather than just being told?
6) Can you forgive yourself for your resentment during the learning process?
7) Can you forgive those who have acted as stewards for you even though you felt their guardianship was unsafe?

It can sometimes be beneficial to take a step back and wait in the newly created space for time to pass. This allows us to review the changes and see where we are now instead of lamenting on where they used to be. By taking one step back we gather the facilities to advance two steps, instead of stagnating on the spot as we may do if we insist on struggling forward rather than taking time to breathe.

Updating Truth Will Set Us Free

As stated above, it can be beneficial to take a step back at time. The changes that are afoot happen not because of us but in spite of us, so while we can make the journey easier on ourselves we cannot halt proceedings – this is why it is important for us to relinquish control and let ourselves be guided.

At any given point in life it is easy to feel vulnerable, insecure or deprived and thus easy to succumb to the will of someone else. This is a particularly difficult time to wrap up loose ends and attend to unfinished business, and we may find it problematic to find the motivation to attend to our own needs without the burden of including others with compassion.

In addition to trying to aid others we also want to be aided ourselves. This leads us to asking if we want to save or be saved, but we must remember that nothing is broken and so nothing needs to be fixed; rather nature cares universally and so we are not in need of saving – we are already taken care of. Certainly we may need to be better at redistribution so more people can benefit from us, but this is a learning curve to managing efficiency and minimising waste, which is not the same as needing to be fixed. We may be burdened with guilt at not having done more, either at doing less than someone else or less than we wanted to, but we can only do our best – which varies from person to person – and so long as we did that we can be content with our efforts. Similarly, as long as we have good intentions then the odd mistake or negative outcome is forgivable, and we will always learn from such mistakes so they are not repeated in the future.

It is possible that our desire to continue moving forward has waned somewhat. In such times we must not despair but rather wait it out, for the truth will be forthcoming when the time is right and this will get us back on track again, complete with the rewards of our hard work in the past. No matter how bad the current situation is, either physically or emotionally, the love of nature and the Heavens are open to us; if we open to them in return that love will blossom when we state our interest in progressing and releasing past pain. If we remain honourable and patient, the path will make itself known and balance will be restored.

At this point it is worth answering the following questions about your internal state:

1) What was the last war you were engaged in and is it still ongoing?
2) What do you feel hostile about?
3) Do you lash out and attack or retire and defend?
4) Are you aggressive towards others?
5) Are you aggressive towards yourself?
6) Do you look within yourself as well as your environment?
7) Are you filled with fear or dread, terrorised or saddened by pain or being hurt? Do you feel apprehensive at your ability to be brave, courageous and joyful in case you lose it again?
8) Are you ready to live in peace yet?

Staying Still

We need to continue working within our own area of expertise and skill as we work with those whose skills are complementary to our own rather than at direct odds or carbon copies. The standard is set through prayer and meditation, asking our soul to override decisions that are not conducive to what we need. During our meditation we are free to ask questions if we have any uncertainties, such as 'Who With?' 'How?' 'When?' and 'Why?'. We can do this as many times as we need to until we are sure where we should be headed. As always, we need to have trust for this as we will be blind to the long term; only the next step will be visible. This should not be cause for concern, though; not only does the Management Upstairs have our very best interests at heart, but once we have been successful once we will be more trusting and willing to be faithful next time without feeling oppressed or forced.

The next step for us is contemplating needs – of the market, our family and ourselves. It is important that we do not confuse our interests with those of others, so we must be clear and concise as to our aims and needs, create a plan that we stick to and monitor regularly to ensure the best outcome for all.

Tests such as these come along once in a while and they are always subtle. While the tests force us to speak honestly yet diplomatically, we must also permit free choice for all as well as room for others to experiment. There is a warning here, too: such an attitude will attract people to rub up against us, including those who are out only for themselves and who will boast of their own superiority and our weaknesses to others while simultaneously being nice to us so as not to face confrontation. We must therefore be well prepared and equipped for such people because they will be opportunists trying to undermine us. We can either do nothing and take the moral high ground, or act in such a way that lends energy, rather than removes it, as the latter will only magnify the situation.

Having knowledge can cause grief and we must learn how to cope with it. Many people lack this ability and these people often refuse to believe other people have it. As such, we must learn the skill of silence, not telling people what we know unless we are specifically asked, because telling them without invitation will not impress or interest them, so we will be wasting our breath. We must also refrain from handing over our power to those people who propagandise to meet their own selfish needs. While our path may seem difficult, we must be loyal to it and not lose our soul connection because someone tells us they know a better way. We are surrounded by temptation and it is always harder to resist when we walk a difficult path, but it is the difficult one that is the most rewarding and we must retain our integrity. When people offer kind words or other incentives to distract us or divert us from our course we must be strong and remember that it is the people who remain by our side through our difficult moments, that remain dedicated to us, who demonstrate the way.

Chapter 15: Positive Thought

Heading For the Best

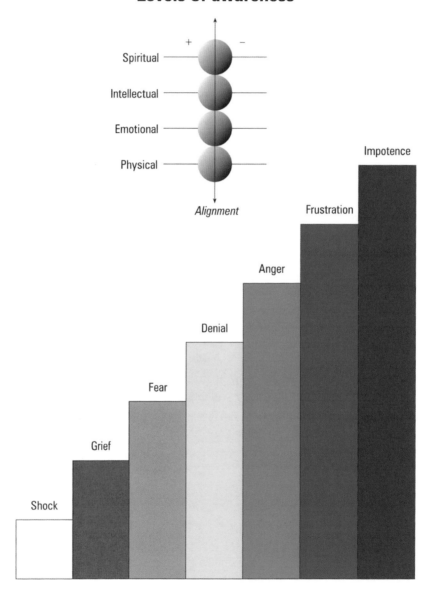

Levels of awareness

Spiritual

Intellectual

Emotional

Physical

Alignment

Shock

Grief

Fear

Denial

Anger

Frustration

Impotence

All these are experienced at all levels

We are able to remain positive despite being in a negative situation, but only if our attitude is of trust, truth and genuine interaction and if we are always striving to do the best by everyone and not just ourselves. It is when we can do this – and *only* when we can do this – that we are living within our integrity.

When we experience trauma the body's energetic field suffers a shockwave, which comes in stages. At first we have the shock of the trauma, which is followed by the grief of having suffered the trauma. Then we feel fear as we wonder if we are strong enough to cope with the impact of picking up the pieces and moving forward again, and then we enter the stage of denial, where we try to avoid the situation and hope it will fix itself. These feelings stir up emotions within us and although we are not deliberately setting out to be nasty to others we may find ourselves being angry – at others or ourselves – and frustrated at our inability to change the bad situation, which in turn leads to us feeling worthless.

Trauma is not confined to something physical, rather it can also happen emotionally, intellectually or spiritually. Needless to say, this can affect our attitudes, behaviour, understanding and any current prejudices or biases. When trauma does occur on a physical level it can appear as an illness; when it happens emotionally our sensitivities are questioned as we express and release hurt and pain so we may become peaceful. Intellectually the trauma can make itself known through mental pressure, losing old skills or disappointment as we witness old theories letting us down in a situation they could not possibly work in. Finally, on a spiritual level, we can lose faith and hope and trust. Having spiritual trauma can cause us to temporarily lose our way.

To overcome trauma we need to overcome the feelings of anger, denial, grief, frustration and shock by experiencing them again. As with phobias, they can only be overcome by facing them head on. Once we have confronted them we will complete the circuit and our space will be clearer than before. At this point we can pursue a new way.

Despite the fact this process will feel negative at the time it happens, it has the very positive effect of releasing our baggage and giving us release from what has been holding us back, so the negative is only a short-term event with long-term consequences.

Walking Our Talk

A new form is created by forgiving the past and releasing the pain that we acquired from it. Rather than dwell on the past, we can thank the Heavens for guiding us through it safely to emerge on the other side, and this will put us in a better position to identify what we do not want to experience again, from which we can learn what we need next.

At this point you need to assess which level you habitually work through: spiritual, physical, emotional or intellectual. By identifying which levels are more difficult we can strengthen them.
The first exercise explores the physical level of awareness, which works through verbal communication such as talking, walking and generally being who you are. Are you in your own light or are you influenced by the wants and needs of others?

This influence can be reduced by surrounding yourself in a golden white light. Build it into the form of an egg and erect mirrors facing outwards so anyone attempting to give you grief only sees themselves, so they cannot influence you without your invitation. Inside the egg ensure you have a sacred space on Earth that you are rooted to, such as a garden. Visualise the air and sky which can be warmed by the sun, or a night of rest, depending on your mood.

The second exercise explores the emotional level of awareness which is shown through body language. Are your feelings derived from yourself or those around you? Do you agree with them or not?
Observe both yourself and others. In what situations do you find yourself closing your body off by crossing your arms or legs or turning away? When do you feel trapped, want to leave or enjoy the situation so much you want to stay longer? What is the body language of others when you are nice, nasty, or you say something they do not agree with?

The third exercise explores the intellectual level of awareness, which works with historical understanding, i.e. based on things we have experienced in the past. Are you ready and willing to find the knowledge you now require and to relinquish knowledge you have but is no longer relevant? Suppressed emotions may make their way to the surface at this point and make you feel depressed, at which point you will need empathetic support to reach through the struggle and find a new way to relax. It is wise to take a step back from events and do something fun that requires no effort. When a balance is found again, you will know what help you require as you will know what it is you do not want.

The fourth and final exercise explores your spiritual awareness. The spiritual body blossoms as you become aware of hidden messages that will aid you on the journey. The messages can come in many shapes and forms, such as people, places, a picture or book or even a conversation you overhear. On an unconscious level you will filter out everything except what is necessary.

You may also be inspired by noticing things you previously would not have observed, such as taking note of when pack animals support each other or walk away; or witnessing something convert into something else, known as shape shifting, which is similar to noticing smoke rising and being used as communicative tools by tribes.

Perceptions of Reality

**Communication proficiency –
past, present and future**

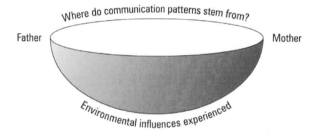

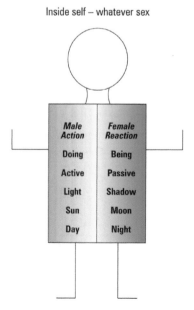

When the four levels of awareness – physical, spiritual, emotional and intellectual – are aligned the areas 'bleed' into each other, so we can move between them all without any difficulty, which leads to us having accurate internal communication. This in turn allows us to express ourselves to others in a clear manner, although this in itself can cause an array of new problems for those we talk to may feel threatened or confronted. Fear not, though, for this is not our problem but theirs and they must embark on the journey we are on, and we have no obligation to remain at their sides while they do so – we can if we choose to, but it is not a requirement.

The trouble is that everyone has a different perspective on the same circumstance. No one is right or wrong, so we may all defensively protect our stance; the viewpoints are just different in much the same way as changing channel on the television still results in watching the same physical set. If, however, we wish to communicate with someone then it is our responsibility to 'change to their channel', in other words we must adapt how we come across. We should listen more than we talk so we become aware of how to communicate with someone we want to deal with. This includes paying attention when we have said something so we recognise how they respond, whether it is positively or negatively. If they respond with the words "I see what you mean" then we can learn they are mostly visual, so it would be wise for us to describe things as pictures when talking to them. Conversely, if they say "I hear what you say" then they are primarily aural people and so the best way to talk to them is with a harmonious rhythm and by presenting the words logically. If the person says "that feels right" then they are kinaesthetically oriented, meaning they use touch and feelings to relate to something. We can communicate best with these people by asking them questions, such as how they felt when something happened, and follow it up by telling them how we felt. When we hear someone say something does not taste right, we get a glimpse of their ability to digest life's experiences. To communicate with them effectively we should gently say what we have to say and then stand back, patiently awaiting them to make the next move.

By analysing how people respond to communication we will develop skills that enable us to talk to different types of people in a concise and effective manner.

PART 5:
LEARNING TO UNITE MORE EFFECTIVELY

Chapter 16: Planting New Seeds

Evolution Potential

Evolution potential

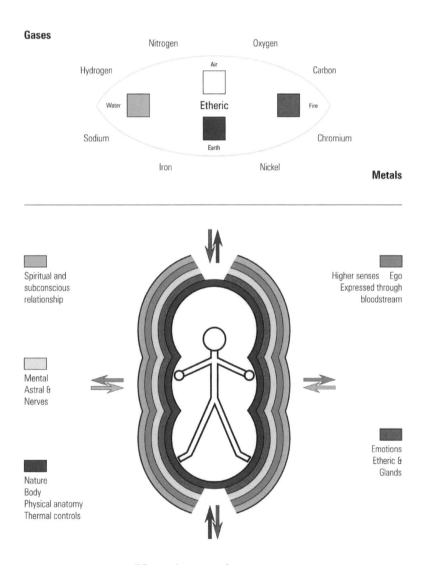

While they may not be immediately apparent, there are parallels between human beings and the planet Earth. For instance, Earth is comprised of gases and metals, which provide us air, sustaining life and purity, water, which controls flow, fire, which keeps us warm and cooks our food, and earth, which nurtures and allows things to grow.

Certainly we are mostly composed of water and require air to survive, but there are numerous other aspects that make up the body. Modern thinking is that the cerebral spinal fluid houses the spiritual purpose. Our soul carries the desires to help all others, to remain safe and ensure we look after ourselves as much as possible without harming others. Our blood is where information from the past is housed, information which can carry us to deeper levels of consciousness, not limited just to our own genealogy but also historical administrations on which our social and geographical structures were organised.

As the blood circulates the nervous system gets involved and this is what permits us the choice of refining, repeating or releasing. Our ability to define how much we can adjust old understanding will be dependent on our individual tolerance, but it is here that we refine instinctive reactions and change our attitudes as necessary. It is this process that allows us to shed ourselves of antiquated fear from our glands. These processes are not always easy but, just as going through illness and being restored to health, as we progress through and realign our physical body supports us on Earth. The Earth contains everything that we require for safe growth, within Nature itself and also within ourselves.

The upper section of the above diagram represents the mouth, which is the womb space into which everything can be placed. The degree to how effective and efficient it is depends on the individual's ability to align everything and practise repeatedly until a united effort is achieved, where everyone contributes what they can without any individual dominating. Within the mouth the tongue is the active element and the teeth guard the space. Unlike our genitals, which can only be completed with another person, the individual completely controls the mouth.

By laying down a standard we are creating our next abstract, the blueprint we must work within to idealise that abstract. In order for the etheric blueprint to be correct we require a supportive flow ratio (water) and an infrastructure that can hold our weight (Earth). We will require air to purify us to ensure old patterns remain cleaned from our system, and the fire of love and enthusiasm will warm us. The abstract can only become idealised when the four elements work together. However, some of the gases and metals that comprise our planet need to be adjusted for us to do this and so it is common for people during these times to have their minerals out of balance, in which case it is a good idea to seek the help of a nutritionist.

For us to have a circuit optimising potential we need to receive from the invisible and give to the visible, meaning we have to receive from the Earth and give that to the Heaven. Thus, we need to be both transmitters and receivers, and this requires us to remove old disciplines and replace them with new, updated ones.

To proceed properly we need to analyse the outer band of our learning remit to check it is defined. Then we must look at our spiritual and subconscious as the spiritual and physical need to be in agreement. Agreement at this stage may lead to feelings of anxiety and irritability, shown as the green band on the diagram above; this is nothing to worry about and is merely everything returning to the bloodstream and our ego stating its concerns about its ability to process everything.

Following this is the red band, or the emotional part of us that reminds us we have been here before and it did not work and now we must face old feelings once again. It is important to stay still at this point and review what has come before and make a decision about the identity they desire. These must be established before moving on again. It is common in this phase for the glandular system to protest, which will manifest itself through tenderness in the groin, armpits or neck.

As you move forward step by step you may notice aches in various areas of the body or notice changes in body temperature. Again, this is nothing to worry about and you require time for everything to settle down and find balance.

Peace In Our Time

When we have the complete circuit from receiving and transmitting as mentioned above we are defining our new shape, which accommodates both internal and external pressures equally. The diagram above shows the base, spleen, solar plexus and heart equate to earth, water, fire and air, respectively. This is a natural and inherent part of being an inhabitant of the Earth and it is up to the owners of those organs to keep the four centres as clear as possible.

The holistic picture

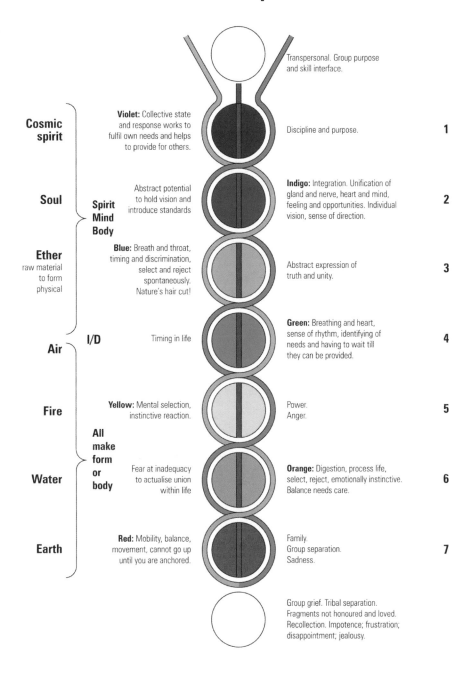

There are two channels of energy that support the spine and they work on either side, crossing diagonally as shown.

There is a masculine energy, called "ida", and a feminine energy, called "pingala". When the two channels are harmonious in their purpose, the kundalini, or energy of the consciousness, will rise straight through the centre with no more distinction.

For this to happen, however, depends on how well we cope as part of a group, which refers not only to a group of people but also groups of cells and organs within our body. As with any group, the one we find ourselves in may consist of people we do not particularly care for, and so the challenge presented to us is to love as much as we can, remain consistent and progress one step at a time.

There is no guarantee that the Heaven will ignite our light, and for that to happen we must have the 'will to good'. As the light enters our third eye we will require a review to update our sense of direction, but we must refrain from trying to achieve that vision immediately. As always, we must be patient and demonstrate love and kindness in the meantime. Again we must release old knowledge that is no longer relevant, and as it happens now we may find it hard to concentrate or we may forget things entirely. It may be a somewhat difficult process but by keeping hold of the total vision we will succeed.

It has been mentioned already that the pineal gland is linked to our Spirit, and as this pushes us forward the energy centres on the spine affect our glands. As toxins are released the glands will release their chemical and hormonal balance, which can be erratic until everything finds a balance again.

The glands in control

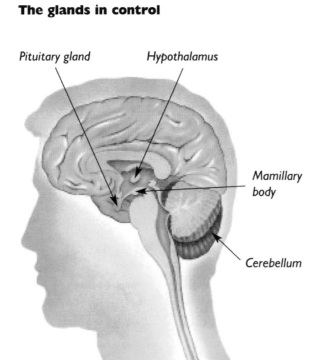

Pituitary gland Hypothalamus

Mamillary body

Cerebellum

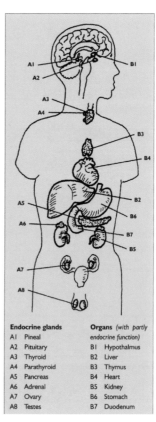

Endocrine glands		Organs (with partly endocrine function)	
A1	Pineal	B1	Hypothalmus
A2	Pituitary	B2	Liver
A3	Thyroid	B3	Thymus
A4	Parathyroid	B4	Heart
A5	Pancreas	B5	Kidney
A6	Adrenal	B6	Stomach
A7	Ovary	B7	Duodenum
A8	Testes		

As an overview of the glands, the pineal tells the pituitary gland which relays the message to the solar plexus. It is the pituitary gland, or the body brain, which discharges. The pineal and pituitary glands work in tandem to strike the balance between the abstract and the actual, and this information reaches the physical body by way of the immune system. If the immune system is not performing at its optimal level we may become ill, so it is important to eat, sleep and exercise well.

The diagram above visualises the locations of the glands.

Body Cycles

24 hour body clock

Each section = 6 hours   Subdivided into 3 x 2 hours

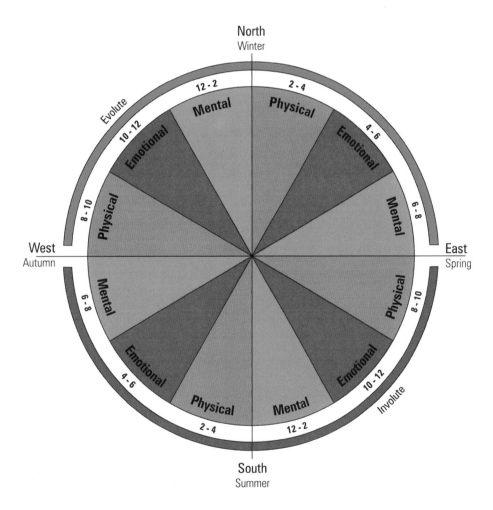

Day.   Night.   A.M.   P.M.

Base scale – Daily
Physical   2 - 4   and   8 - 10
Emotional   4 - 6   and   10 - 12
Mental   6 - 8   and   12 - 2

High scale – Life
Baby: Child: Teenager: Adult

Each day the body goes through a cycle, although the cycle varies from individual to individual. You will no doubt be aware that at different times of the day you tend to be more awake and alert than at other times, in the same way that some people categorise themselves 'morning' people while others 'night' people. By acknowledging our own patterns of lethargy and energy we are able to work with them so we can be most productive, rather than trying to battle through the times where we have no energy which can sometimes result in getting less done than had we simply waited to perk up. Furthermore, by knowing the cycles we will come to understand ourselves better. For instance, if we feel depleted physically then we should turn our attention to something else so we can recuperate; if we are depleted intellectually we should do something that requires no mental effort, such as listening to music or watching television. By being aware we are able to feed our emotional, intellectual and physical self.

We have similar cycles at night but these are yet to be fully understood, although advancements are being made such as the knowledge that dreams occur more in certain stages of sleep. When we travel to a different time zone our body clock is thrown off course; what should be day is night and vice versa, and we are thus able to see how quickly we are able to adjust and how well we stabilise within forced change i.e. we have no control over the time and so we have no choice but to adapt to it.

Now answer the following questions and write the answers down:
At what times of the day are you:

- Most physically active or at your peak?
- Most physically inactive or low?
- Emotionally at your peak?
- Emotionally low?
- Intellectually at your peak?
- Intellectually low?

Having determined the times of day you are at your peak or low points, you can plan your day in the way that best suits you, taking into consideration your group dynamic and consulting the diagram.

Chapter 17: Harvesting

Concentration of Energy

Many great new theories in operation

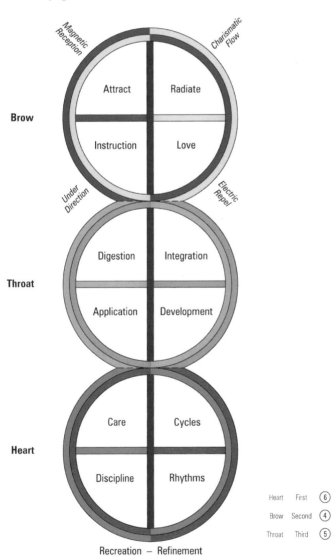

Although we have never been separated from our soul, the transitional period may have led us to think that we have been because we may have believed that, with the difficult path we are walking, it does not care for us anymore. So as it calls to us the relationship between our soul and us begins to be healed. Nonetheless, this imagined detachment may have caused us to feel ostracised, and in this state we are untouchable because we will not let others in. So our hearts need to create a purity of vibration where love is a standard that is acceptable, and as this new discipline becomes integrated with the cycle it will attract purity of intention.

As this cycle develops we integrate new things that happen to us and then express this as our new standard. As the highest possible common denominator now becomes our lowest common denominator, recreation is a direct result of the process of refinement. People involved in metaphysics or healing often feel themselves compelled to give to others rather than take from them, because they are aware that by giving they have much more control over life's drama. People who always want to try to help others need to learn to move at a pace and within a structure that will neither threaten nor challenge them at a level more than is required at that moment in time, otherwise they will hurt others instead of help them. The reason for this is that as we act to a higher standard the last thing we want is to be provoked too quickly by hostile reactions; instead we need to wait for our environment to settle down. As we recognise this, our heart will open and we will want to help everyone; however, it is essential at this time that we recognise there is very little differentiation between care and control – it is all too easy to try to care for someone but end up trying to control them instead.

Energy and Vitality

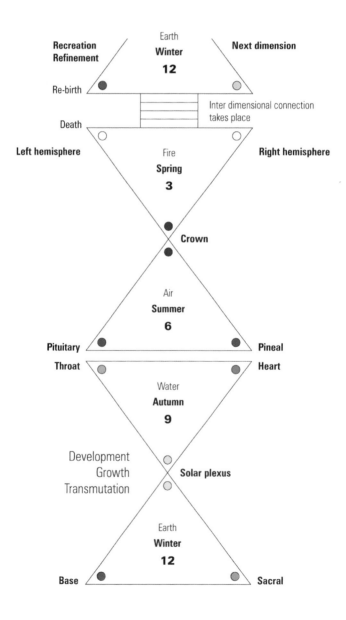

The Earth's pull is centred in the solar plexus and this guides us overtly, but we harbour subtler guidance in our heart and we process it with our head, which is why people often talk of their heart saying one thing and their head another. Finding a balance between these two areas affects all others and accordingly each must go through its own 'season'. For instance, when it feels like winter in one area we may forget that it will be summer in another area. Thus we go through each season at each level so we may grow safely and proportionately. We therefore attract the refinements that are required for us to develop new potentials and evolve to a level that is deeper and richer than we are currently able to fathom.

In order to move on, as stated previously, we need to let go of old emotions and feelings, despite possibly not wanting to remember the experiences they provided us nor wanting to face the truth that they offer. Nonetheless, we must face them and release them so we will be free to create a new space, a more solid foundation from which we can grow and develop at an elevated rate.

It is the hips that facilitate physical movement and the solar plexus works within this environment. As our integration of experiences at a physical level takes place the solar plexus is put under pressure because it will be trying to express the invisible visibly, to release old memories and move us on.

Negotiation will commence between the crown centre and the solar plexus, because the crown centre works with balancing the internal and external. The crown centre is in charge of stabilising the pineal gland – the soul-purpose gland – and the pituitary, which translates it into the body. This balance between the intuitive and the logical, the inner and outer, will be centred within the crown centre and solar plexus centre, which will be experienced through the throat, which is the gateway of the soul, and the pelvic girdle, which is the gateway to movement. During this time we may notice imbalance on one side and this will rectify itself over time as the balance is found.

If the bottom part of the above diagram is turned ninety degrees and placed on the one above a Maltese cross emerges. When this change takes place within us our life will become a light force and we will once again start to move forward. The continuous movement we will encounter, of recreation, refinement, then recreation again, will slowly diminish our fear of birth and death, despite their being one and the same thing: as we die to Heaven we are born on Earth and vice versa. Nonetheless, because we are somewhat ignorant of this process it is extremely difficult, if not impossible, to relinquish the fear we possess. Therefore, in order to release it, it is vital for us to study the areas further.

Motion Sickness

When we physically experience something we receive the capacity to understand the inner and outer to the highest level of our ability. By doing so we anchor ourselves to the Earth firmly, helped along by touch which in itself is not only a great comfort but also makes taste more pleasing. Thus, we have the capacity to connect to clearer vibrations, sweeter smells and, therefore, a more beautiful vision.

Perceiving beauty is to want to make it a reality, so we reverse our direction and experience the new beauty, cleanse our old patterns and revisit old areas that we would prefer to leave alone. We then make certain that our vibration can be maintained at a constant level no matter what situation or condition we find ourselves in. It is only at this point that theory and practice meet, merge and change direction.

The way to bring the inner and outer together is by establishing the outer workings and viewing it from every possible angle. Looking at something from the top will provide a different view than that of the side or bottom, so we need to mark the boundary of our new territory, working from the edges to the centre. When we reach the middle we have to cope with the events of our everyday lives, which we can only achieve by having accurately set the boundaries and worked correctly from edges to middle. The next step from this is slowing everything down in order to make a connection between Heaven and Earth.

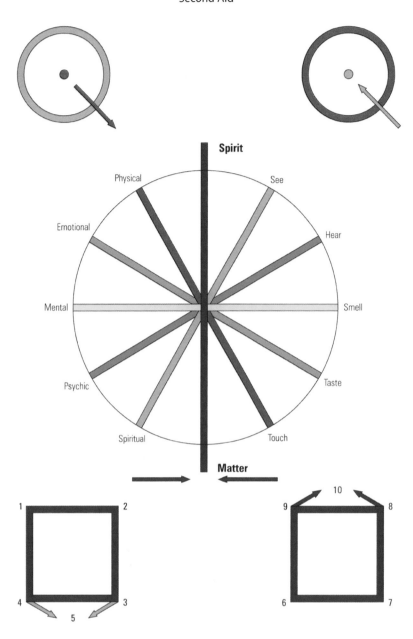

In the diagram above, the square in the bottom left corner shows the framework of uniting Heaven and Earth. To achieve this we must review everything that has taken place and return it to Heaven, because it is a varied representation of the same thing and it is our unique contribution towards the entity as a whole. The diagram shows housing at one, self-work at two, family at three, friends at four and our anchor into the Earth at five. However, we can only anchor at the rate of the slowest group member so we may need to slow down to accommodate everyone.

To have the willingness to serve we work unconditionally within the present, so we need to be anchored to the Earth at the point we can do the most good rather than just where we think we should be – these two points are not always one and the same. To be within the present completely we must be completely involved and willing to undertake any task regardless of what it is, from working an unsatisfactory job to vacuuming the house.

We will not reflect information until we have been tested in this way, and such tests can make us feel as though we have gone back in time. However, as you will be aware at this stage of the journey and book, this is necessary so we may review and update information so we can move forward. This puts us in the position to walk in the same direction as Heaven, which is shown in the above diagram as the square in the bottom right corner. We are now able to walk in two directions with ease: we have the ability to walk into the Heavens and turn around to walk back to Earth. We will be comfortable in visible and invisible realms because we will have unified vibration and sound, and we will know that all is equal spiritually.

When we reach this point we will become instruments, where the invisible world will be able to give light to the Earth and it will be used where required without worry because our shape will not change and people will only benefit, not suffer, from our presence. This is absolutely necessary because the invisible world is only able to send light into an individual that possesses a shape strong and developed enough as to not change its form, and it is up to us individually to create this form. Knowing this, we accept our role gracefully and gratefully.

The centre of the diagram highlights that the alignment between Heaven and Earth needs to be checked out; we may be able to see this spiritual vision but not be able to bring it to action. Moving across the wheel we will be able to hear the invisible becoming visible by its vibration, but the question is whether we have the courage to wait exactly where we are while we become part of the Greater Power.

When we have released those parts of our past that no longer serve us well we will recognise what the concept of the spiritual abstract means to us. We will try to aid the light rather than be the light because we recognise we do not know everything.

We will now have completed the entire circle: the slowing down and revision is complete and we do nothing but wait for God to give us the next step. We are now moving into a new position, and it is possible to feel somewhat motion sick at this point.

Life Force

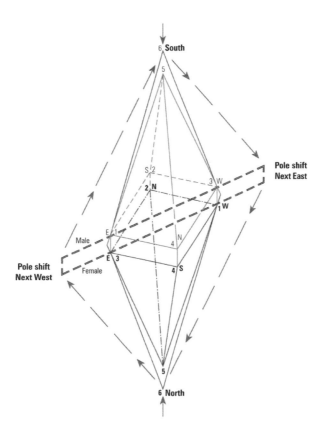

Cellular extension one joins another, 4 becomes collective 5th and is extended to 6th
6 + 6 = 12 after which we get a pole shift or North-South becomes East-West
and the cycle starts again so the hologram becomes an instrument of the greater
and harmony with all life forms

Cellular extension 1 joins another, 4 becomes collective 5th and extends to 6th. $6 + 6 = 12$, at which point a pole shift occurs e.g. north-south becomes east-west and the cycle starts over. The hologram is an instrument of the greater and harmony with all life forms.

Accepting the possibility to work to a greater plan means that we will be living to a level of such intensity and expectancy that we are constantly challenged. Completing the invisible form and constructing the building to a design that has emerged from our inner guidance and guidance of our peers means that we have lived both dangerously and profoundly. Trusting this process means we are both warmed and worn by it; it is living, loving and lightening in such a manner that it helps direct others to wherever they need to be going.

The diagram above shows that the east, where the sun rises, is where the child is born and the sun then moves clockwise over the course of the day. At the southern point the sun is at its strongest point in the twenty-four-hour period, and by point three, the west, the sun is setting. North, the fourth section, is where we return to the sunrise the following day.

Chapter 18: Fertilising

The Path Of Return

The Spiritual impulse alerts us to its presence through the conscious mind. Our subconscious desire to link to the path of unity encourages the soul to a point that the air is purified and the person is permitted to rediscover the hope of uniting all.

This impulse is not confined to the subconscious, though; rather it passes through each of the body's systems. For example, the muscles may feel dislocated or disconnected from their usual cooperative state, or one may feel emotionally indifferent with no strong feelings positively or negatively.

The body's systems communicate in their own language and this allows a decision to be made of which one has more need over the others. When this identification is made the other systems support the weaker one until it is able to stabilise; then attention is turned to the others individually starting with the next weakest first and the strongest last. When people start working with others before they have cleared their own field they often cannot sustain the new extended level of awareness and so they fade away or suffer an illness. The problem is that they did not work to clear their own unprocessed materials before trying to handle that of others, so it is important to move forward slowly to ensure we are making the right changes and accommodations.

The light stabilises within us when we are between twenty-eight and thirty-five, and this is when we try to become centred upon the Earth and begin to root. It is at this point that we are able to work in everyone's best interests because we know that everything is a part of the Spirit and nothing is really as detached as people often perceive. Of course, as this energy is concentrated into us it is possible that we will feel trapped and/or nervous, and this is a repeating pattern. Once we have analysed it horizontally we will attempt to do the same vertically but at a different level. For instance, we may ask "Can I bring the Heaven to Earth?" but this solely depends on our spiritual intent: to be of use to the invisible world we should at some stage in the future be quite equipped to create Heaven on Earth.

To do this consciously we need to, at an intellectual level, have to cooperate and learn the connection the physical body has to have a shape upon the Earth that can be used by the invisible world. Regardless of any process or transformation, we are still part of the everyday life on Earth in every capacity – physically, emotionally and intellectually – but in an increasingly detached way as our spirituality is incorporated. Emotionally we need to clear old memories from our muscular, digestive and glandular systems so they can be aligned, creating a purity that the invisible world can trust.

The aforementioned disconnection then becomes a reconnection and our universal compassion becomes harmless in action not just abstract. We acknowledge that our limited vision does not provide enough scope for us to see the goings-on within the bigger picture and so we act as instruments of the invisible world, concentrating within the present knowing that we are pure, because we are also aware that we are simply obediently obeying the instructions handed down by the Management Upstairs.

Spirit	Water	Subconscious	Fire
Dislocate	Soul body	Genetic Muscles	Disconnect
Dispassion	Physical Emotions	Digestive	Compassion
Love	Emotions Mental	Circulation	Care
Embracive Non fragmentation	Mental Soul	Glands	Group orientation
Light	Soul Spirit	Nerves	Concentrated
Earth	**Conscious**	**Soul**	**Air**

0 – 7 Nourished
7 – 14 Etheric
14 – 21 Astral
21 – 28 Ego (Connection to life path)
28 – 35 Expansion of self-centred side
35 – 42 Crisis of values
42 – 49 Spiritual initiation
49 – 56 Leadership role
56 – 63 Spiritual attunement. Wise perspective
63 – 70 Freedom to voluntarily contribute
Time expands

A crisis of values has to happen to reach this level of evolution and typically this happens when we are between thirty-five and forty-nine. There is usually a spiritual initiation when we have encountered the seven stages of growth seven times, and then we begin from scratch in an arena where our ego has been reduced to nothing and then rebuilt as a tool for others to utilise. Although we are put into a leadership role we are being trained how to lead and whether to be dictatorial or democratic, allowing each group member to practise their own skill without being lambasted by others.

Naturally, it will take time to fine-tune the wisdom we are striving for and this will again be handled by the Management Upstairs. However, be careful not to reach the quoted ages and expect these changes to occur; they are stated as guidelines only for people to have a reference in accordance with their own experiences. In reality the ages can be much younger, before the age of thirty, and indeed for those who are evolving in a different direction it may never occur at all, because some only reach physical optimisation while others stabilise emotionally or intellectually instead. Because we are all different, it is crucial that we learn to both accommodate and interact with everyone, for growth is a natural occurrence at any age and it is not for us to force.

Perform the following self-reflection exercise on personal experiences:

1) If you review the pressures that you have found difficult in life what comes to mind?
2) Do you anticipate a re-enactment of the past every time a new pressure occurs?
3) Are you prepared to release it by letting go of resentment and forgiving everything?
4) Would you describe your instinctive reactions to be of dread, grief or aggravation when someone behaves in a manner that you do not anticipate?
5) Are you willing to change these reactions and anticipate an improved state?
6) What area of your body do you feel is under pressure? Direct your attention on it with love, tolerance and empathy and then wait until it softens and release is experienced.

Repeat the above until you feel at ease.

Centring

Going from the inner to the outer requires courage and persistence, as well as being able to maintain focus on our ideals and apply these in our day to day lives. Because our potential is linked to our vision – in that we can achieve only what we can envision – we attract a flow of experience which will allow us to relax to the point that we can immerse ourselves in the required task. Moreover, we are aware that our being able to concentrate and stabilise ourselves is essential if we are to be able to reach subtler, more refined vibrations. Until that point we focus on making life as pleasant as we can for ourselves and others.

As each of the energy centres activate we will be granted many practice opportunities. We will be granted the space and support to clear these energy centres and our body systems one at a time and, although at times we may feel as though we are moving too quickly, we will attract a flow that we have the capacity to work within. This will, in turn, reward us with the required potential to become clear in both vision and insight so we can cleanse on every level without overexertion.

During this time we will need to be fully rested and ensure we sleep well, primarily because we will not be physically active but active on another level, and just as with physical activity sleep will be necessary to recuperate. Our energy will be redistributed, so it is our task to notice the change in order to facilitate the change with sleep.

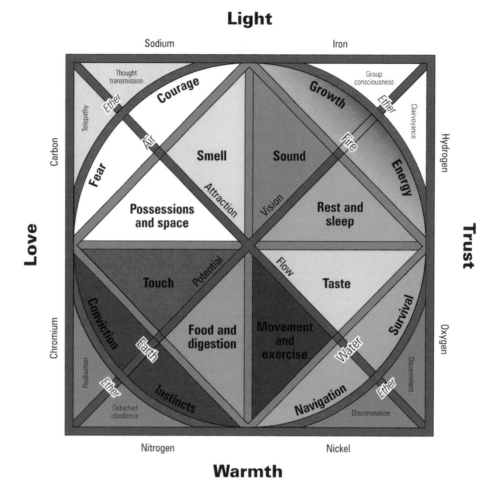

In times like this we will need to take the material that we require to regenerate from the Earth. Changing times like this can cause changes to our body, too, and we may notice that we are gassier than usual and it is worth keeping an eye on vitamin and mineral levels so we can supplement as necessary, thus undertaking Heaven's work. These steps will mean we are taking one step back to take two forwards, so do not worry if you feel you are stepping back to a prior place.

It needs to be remembered that it is our choice to proceed or not, and help is always available if we choose to ask for it. The question, though, is whether we will display our trust by following the advice given, even if we do not agree with it at the outset. A good metaphor at this point is the carrot dangling on a stick in front of a donkey: the opportunity is presented but in order to keep going requires commitment, stamina and the acknowledgement that we are on a journey where each step marks progress.

By obeying the instructions handed down to us, even if they transcend our current level of understanding, the atmosphere around us will clear and our sense of smell will become acute. At this stage of the journey we can say that we want to work and remain in this atmosphere, others are encouraged and invited to join but it is ultimately their choice that we cannot influence.

As the light and love merge warmth will radiate from us that will encourage trust towards us from others, and this will allow us to trust the invisible world more than we have been able to up to this point. The circle of eternity will at this stage start operating and we will interact and dramatise to smooth out any rough patches. Then, and only then, we will be available for the invisible world, but it will take repeated practice runs for this to occur.

Blueprints, Plans and Circuits

Physical changes can take up to seven years from beginning to end and emotional changes can take eight. Our mental flexibility, which is our ability to assimilate new concepts, can take nine years, while spiritual changes occur over twelve years. The so-called midlife crisis is a common occurrence that comes about because all these areas are changing at the same time. These cycles all contain a structure of breathing in and out, taking a rest in and out, refining and repeating. If we are able to relate to this structure then we can constructively work within it, in just the same way as swimming with the tide is easier and more constructive than attempting to swim against it.

The reason that it takes up to seven years for physical changes from start to finish is that energy does not move in a straight line. Rather, the body's cellular structure is renewed every seven years and this is when changes will be solidified and previous states or actions flushed out. The diagram below shows body changes start with red, orange, yellow and green; emotional changes start with the spleen energy and are orange, yellow, green and pale blue; intellectual changes begin at the solar plexus and are yellow, green, pale blue and indigo; finally, spiritual changes begin at the heart and are green, pale blue, indigo and purple.

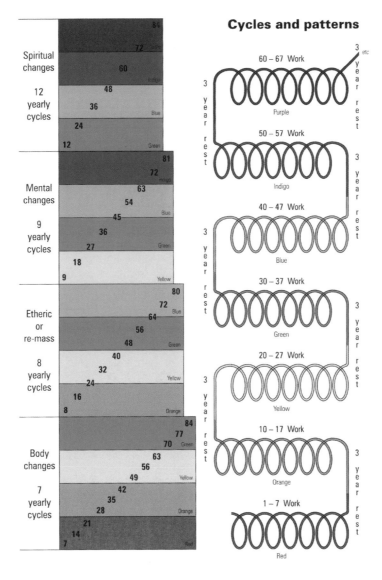

This process has us working with colour-coded movement, which can be translated if the physical recreation and regeneration occurs. If it does we will need to find an updated balance and this will require the courage to not only change but change by interacting with others and having good will throughout.

As stated previously, the journey requires discipline, which means we must be able to both administer it and adhere to it. This will lead to us acquiring deeper levels of awareness, but in order to maintain this character expansion we will have to contract so we may cleanse deeper inside the body. We will slowly develop an awareness of the impressions we have stored within our body, what they restrict and why they do so. We then must consider whether it is our whole body that is involved in this or just a particular part, and we must bring any weak areas to the same strength as our most developed part. This does not forbid illness or disability, and indeed it is possible that we may need to sacrifice some strength in a given area to ensure that all the energy is evenly distributed throughout the body rather than having pockets of strengths and weaknesses.

PART 6:
LIVING THE DREAM

Chapter 19: Group Dynamics

When To Let Go

A possibility in anyone's life is that they have been so inclusive they cannot bear to entertain the possibility of trying another project. Alternatively, we might find ourselves trying to be overly nice to someone instead of showing our true feelings and emotions; it is a common trait in today's society to drop integrity for the sake of popularity. At this stage, then, we must make a list of priorities in a strict order and a realistic rhythm. We need to learn that it is not possible to be all things to all people, and trying to make this possible will diminish our Earthly use to zero.

Take the following items and relist them in your own order of priority of who you want to be popular with, with most important at the top and least important at the bottom. Once you have made the list, focus on number one for a period of time that you define in advance, after which time you can review and update the list.

- The Heavens
- Your soul
- Yourself
- Your family
- Your partner
- Your friends
- Your boss
- Your colleagues
- Your acquaintances

Sometimes, to try and remain in control, we will assume we know the wants and needs of others. Not only is this abusing a situation and another individual, but it also results in us losing the control we so desperately want. If and when we give, we do so unconditionally and do not do so in the hope we will gain something back – to do so is to manipulate a situation for our own needs. If we do have something that we know could benefit another, and we believe in them and their plans, we give to them, but we then leave to their personal judgement what to do with it and we must never linger to try to maintain control.

There is no shortage of people who are desperate to be needed because chronic insecurity means they are unsure of their own personality, instead living vicariously through others. Such people are typically needy and often expect others to provide for them rather than shouldering the responsibility and undertaking the task themselves. Aside from the fact that these people will not grow with such characteristics, such an attitude breeds cynicism especially from those who have been burned in the past; as the saying goes, 'once bitten twice shy'. Before they can be helped, though, they must be willing to admit they need to change their characteristics, and before entry can be made by another they need to cleanse their own space.

Have I Done Well Enough?

At times we will think that we currently know nothing other than what we have been doing is not what we will continue doing, and this seems of little use because what we really want to know is what the next step will be before leaving the one we are residing on. We hate uncertainty, and some may take particular exception to a higher power than themselves being in control.

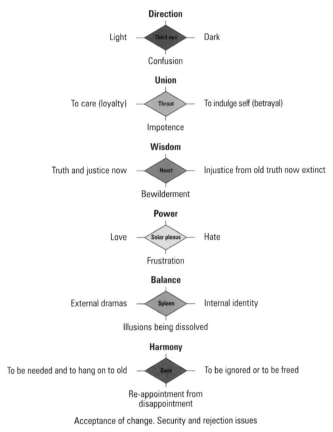

Good direction – having the courage of your convictions to trust higher instructions
(Authority issues together with right use of entrusted power)

Direction
Light — Third eye — Dark
Confusion

Union
To care (loyalty) — Throat — To indulge self (betrayal)
Impotence

Wisdom
Truth and justice now — Heart — Injustice from old truth now extinct
Bewilderment

Power
Love — Solar plexus — Hate
Frustration

Balance
External dramas — Spleen — Internal identity
Illusions being dissolved

Harmony
To be needed and to hang on to old — Base — To be ignored or to be freed
Re-appointment from disappointment

Acceptance of change. Security and rejection issues

Male – Active – Wine – Overriding past / Female passive / Reactions stored in body's framework

The chaos that ensues is confusing and the truth is now separated from the previous truths that we clung to. At this stage we will attract wisdom if we wait and if we have been as wise as our development allowed, but we may have difficulty in knowing how to wait. The answer is in creating a new balance. By acknowledging our disappointments and not ignoring them we make it possible to have a reappointment. Evolution is all about progressing and moving forward, so there is no justification in retaining the old for the sake of it, especially as the new, while daunting, will improve things.

Chapter 20: Colour

The Foundation

The light spectrum

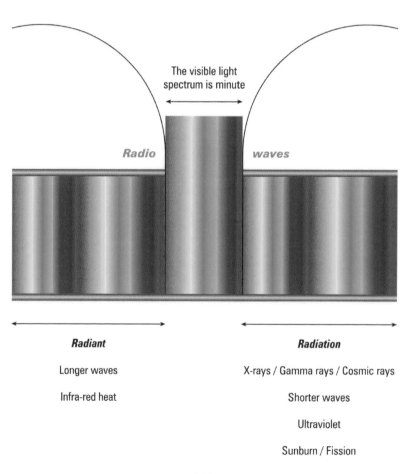

The visible light spectrum is minute

Radio   waves

Radiant

Longer waves

Infra-red heat

Radiation

X-rays / Gamma rays / Cosmic rays

Shorter waves

Ultraviolet

Sunburn / Fission

Our personal points of view are how we test new things; they are utilised as a possible way forward but we must remain humble enough to remember they are not necessarily *the* way. As with anything, we test the waters and if we do not have success we try another method before making a decision about the viability of the new project.

The spectrum that we receive into our eye to be able to see is minute when compared with the breadth of the spectrum in its entirety, but we often forget that light penetrates the body directly and so we receive much more than just what our eyes receive. Despite the apparent paradox, the faster we go the more we can see. For example, if we are on a train that has stopped by a hedge we cannot see through it for the small holes disappear, but when the train gathers enough speed the holes become more apparent so we can see beyond it. This same principle allows us to see that we receive and absorb colour without realising it.

We only see a colour that an object does not absorb, but we typically see combinations of colours. Seven of the colours – red, orange, yellow, green, blue, indigo and purple – link to the Chakras, which are themselves situated atop the spine and linked to the endocrine system. Although the body's multiple systems link to this, they do not show the big picture in its entirety.

A Way Forward

The impulses of growth

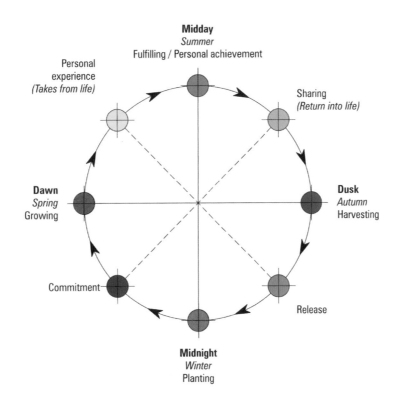

Red: The foundation to expand provides the personal courage that we require to acknowledge it, and prompts commitment from us while also allowing us to make choices. At this point, it is not God's will but our willingness to follow God's will. Red is the colour of decisiveness, the one that says to relate your idea to life and apply it so that the theory can be applied to practice. It is in this way that we, with little knowledge, grow in the same way that a child grows and develops without knowing how it is happening. Red is a link to creative energy and sexual instinct. Throughout life we make conscious and natural relationships to physical form, making use of opportunities that present themselves.

The Pivotal Balance

Orange: Because we must keep our balance we have to digest the experiences life has taught us so far before we can eat another of life's meals, just as we must digest breakfast before tackling lunch. This task is processed at the spleen or navel, and rather than just being about ensuring survival it allows us to build everything we have acquired into our own form. There is no set instruction for this, though, because each individual's path is unique and so each must find their own way. Such practices as martial arts and complementary therapy provide an external reflection that makes it easier for us to sift through the information and channel our focus to the next step, so they can be considered a kind of do-it-yourself approach. It is possible that we may require the assistance of a spiritual director at this point to avoid being overwhelmed by fear of the unknown or experiences that we have already encountered.

With faith we acquire an updated insight which in turn leads to a broader mind, and this allows us to be more tolerant of other people. Following this we will develop better knowledge of what is needed by whom and when.

The pivotal point

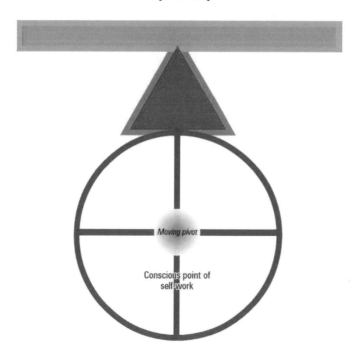

A Design For Living

**Silver – the mental stimulant
towards complement**

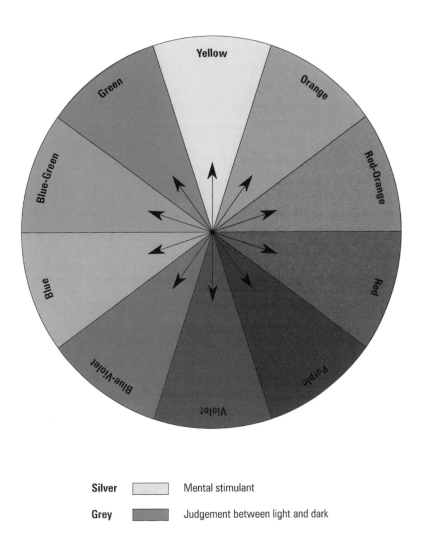

| Silver | | Mental stimulant |
| Grey | | Judgement between light and dark |

Yellow: It is important that we take only what is useful and ditch what is useless. We must build on what we already know, which may be "I know now so I want to educate" or "I believe now so I want to know". It may be something entirely different, as education is personal and unique to each individual and we make the decision to carry things out in our own way, thus declaring our personal democracy. The impulse of yellow casts more light, revealing more of the big picture and the colour serves as a mental stimulant, opposite the physical stimulant offered by red.

When we toil in the garden we know that creating fertile ground from solid dirt is difficult, and digging the ground over only conceals the weeds rather than removing them. As such, we need persistence, stamina and motivation to complete the job fully and successfully, and the same is true of the journey we embark on in life.

Following the Guidelines

Green: At this stage we must make the commitment to update our self-work and we must be our own mediators to balance everything we know, which is called the "inter-dimensional line". On one side of the line is everything we know and are used to, and the other side is unknown. Knowing this, our aim is to complete what we already know as we meld our inner knowledge and outer environment, because in doing so the foundational layer is given to something else; so long as we are not too spiritually ambitious or materially grasping we will progress safely.

Balancing out

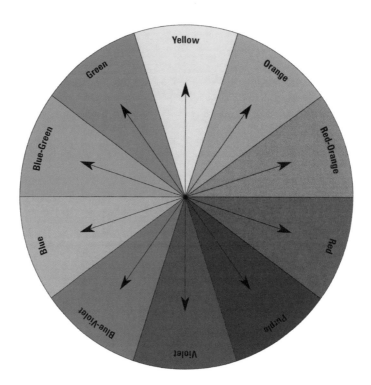

Once the rebuilding work is completed we will have something worthwhile to give to the higher powers. As time goes on we realise that we are representing great forces with transformative values, but the fragile balance is difficult to apply to life; it is tough to do so continuously for others but even more so when trying to include ourselves. Nonetheless, we must at least start, and work on balancing the head and heart so they move forward in unison and to the best of our abilities as they stand at the present moment.

Meditation will allow us to transcend our current level and move to a higher plane. By remaining committed to it and describing our existing experience as simply as we are able to, the seemingly impossible experience before us will become a natural integration of life.

Improvements

Blue: As we learn to help others free past emotions from their bodies it is imperative that we work to the letter of the laws of the Spirit and Earth. Our presence will heal, whether through our eyes, hands or voice. Others will look upon us a benchmark or resource point as they try to balance themselves and unite the inner with the outer experiences of their own lives. We learn increased awareness from colours and shapes, which helps us to free enough space to retain our faith and speak our truth. We all draw support from somewhere and while for many this is religion or spirituality in some form or another, others among us are supported through music or cultural values and traditions, any or all of which allow us to reinstate our own law. Thus, all that is required of us is to live the best we can within the laws of nature and God ('God' in this context being the name applied to the director of the subtle worlds).

It is in this area that we need to learn the language of communication so that all who are attracted will have their requirements met. Because we need to be shown we must be willing to be taught by a living demonstration that is relevant to each stage of understanding. Indigo is the area of abstract thought, and blue is connected to the throat and links to our ability to know what to say or not to say, as well as what we should retain and reject from our life experiences. If we choose to leave blue too early we will make an attempt to jump a step ahead, which will lead to an avoidable crisis. This marks an important lesson that we must only progress one step at a time and not try to overexert ourselves by moving ahead too quickly. Each step is a progression of its own from which we learn important lessons and acquire new skills and knowledge. Therefore, by trying to skip a step we will be missing out on vital information and will only hinder our progress.

Creating free space

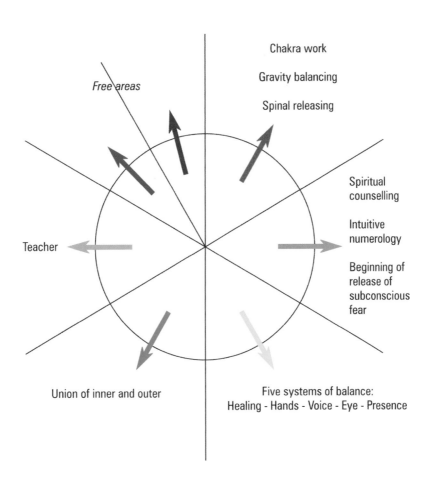

We are all dealt with at our own level of need and understanding. As with anything, the mysterious only remains a mystery until our knowledge increases and we understand the process, at which point it becomes a reflex or an unconscious movement. Relating to this specific journey, then, as we understand the subtle realms more comprehensively we will be able to keep up to date with our progressions rather than try to fight the process for fear of what may await us next.

Discipline and Obedience

Overshadowing

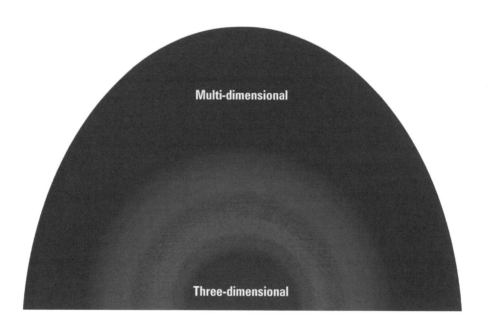

Indigo: Indigo is the psychic cleanser and although we feel no pain when going, it can cause some hurt to no longer feel important within the balance of things. This is a transfiguration experience when we are overshadowed with the consciousness of love, working to transform all things. During this time we transcend ourselves and instead are so in tune with our soul that we make clear and understandable decisions based on the timeless wisdom that our soul possesses.

Once our awakening reaches a certain intensity we stop wondering and begin knowing, acquiring knowledge and wisdom that we did not have previously and the next step from this is unconditional acceptance. At this point we become overshadowed by past experiences and we then feel a surge of reinstatement, much like feeling dejected and low following a relationship break-up followed by the feeling of ecstasy and joy when we enter a new one, which gives us confidence with a greater intensity than we had before.

Having reached this stage we start restating traditional systems that we learned at some point in the past, perhaps a long time ago. We know that these systems are no longer necessary, rather they need revising and updating to be relevant to us in our new and updated state of existence.

Light aims into life

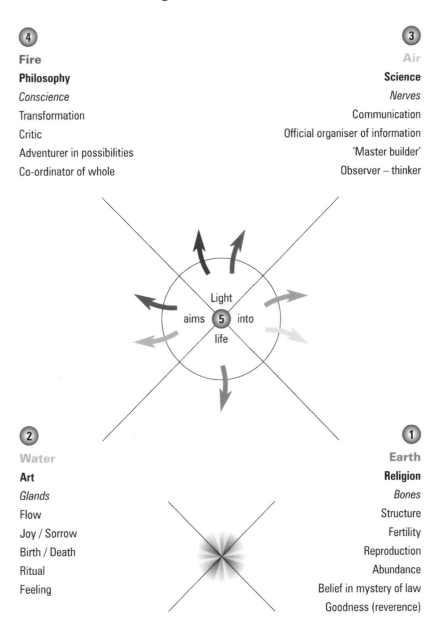

4

Fire

Philosophy

Conscience

Transformation

Critic

Adventurer in possibilities

Co-ordinator of whole

3

Air

Science

Nerves

Communication

Official organiser of information

'Master builder'

Observer – thinker

Light

aims **5** into

life

2

Water

Art

Glands

Flow

Joy / Sorrow

Birth / Death

Ritual

Feeling

1

Earth

Religion

Bones

Structure

Fertility

Reproduction

Abundance

Belief in mystery of law

Goodness (reverence)

Once we start to recollect our personal vision we merge both ends of the spectrum, with indigo being our view and once we combine it with red our life is recreated from scratch. When blue and red are mixed purple or indigo is the result, and when we are working in a disciplined manner the lower ego is released. In the third eye area is the pineal, which links to both the pituitary and hypothalamus, which together produce endorphins that create an effect equal to that of even the most powerful external drugs, which helps relieve tension and promote our awareness.

This step stimulates the mind and brain, which may lead to us experiencing pain in the bones because we are focusing extra strength into the abstract spiritual realms to allow for a union of feelings and thoughts as well as assistance from both our soul and the spiritual realms. The parathyroid restricts the pace of the thyroid and how calcium is used within the body, which in turn slows down the metabolic rate, so do not be surprised if you notice a period of weight gain. The upshot of this is that our physical body is rid of psychotic, obsessive and/or addictive behaviour so not only ourselves but those around us will benefit – and the extra pounds can be shed, too. The result of this cleanse is we will feel less fear and inhibitions, in the same way that orange helps us but at a higher vibration. Indigo suppresses the heart palpitations that can occur from the changes in the thyroid's pattern, and it also helps us to rest and release frustration and fear. This allows us to notice that we have no intolerance to life, we are free within it, and we can then move forward.

The Anchor

Co-ordinating invisible states – parallel experiences

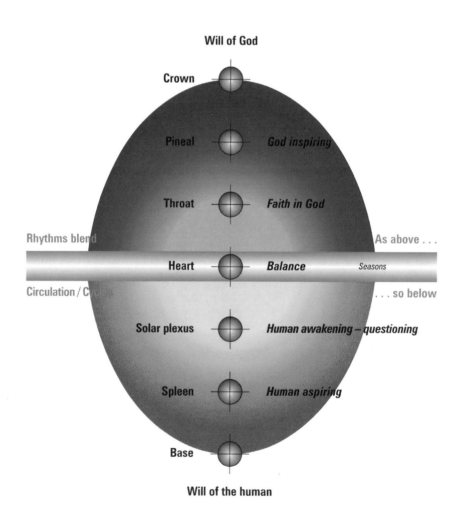

Violet: We are who we are today because of our past experiences, and our new updated self is anchored to the Earth through the crown of the head and the pituitary gland conducts it through the body. The will of the greater needs to align with our own will, and we aspire to reach our true full potential, although this will not always be easy.

We all have some self-destructive tendencies which make us try to avoid our responsibilities, needs and motives. This has the result of us being unable to commit to anything, which makes us think that attuning with the whole and realising the spiritual dimensions are too difficult. After all, it is easier to turn to vices than it is to try something new, especially something that may not be particularly easy. At the red level this may mean turning to sex or drugs, and on the orange level it can mean being addicted to a group instead of having enough faith and innocence to have a non-denominational approach. The yellow level encourages us to pursue our own actions with no regard for the feelings of others so we can acquire what we want regardless of the cost. At the green level we may be materialistic, desperately wanting to acquire things we really do not need. At the blue level we are very self-assured and have the arrogance to believe we do not make mistakes, which can result in us selfishly pursuing our own pleasure at the expense of others'. At the indigo level we can mistakenly have a sense of grandeur and superiority and both we and others can feel persecuted because of this. At the violet level we may challenge those with addictions and feelings of guilt regardless of the feelings of those surrounding them. Such responses must be eradicated until we feel content with a sense of self that is in harmony with life where we can adapt to our situation as the need arises.

Physical work and exercise clean the kidneys and liver, purify the blood and detoxify shocks from the past, as well as promoting the immune system. Violet helps rid mental and nervous diseases because of its properties as a sedative for our artistic temperament.

Before we are able to progress on the journey we must first look back over the spectrum and check that we are applying the life principles. The chart below shows how the body systems are both independent and interdependent.

New rules

Colour	Life nourishment	Body system	Action	Spiritual principle	Domain
Red Base	Food	Muscles	Will	Life	Physical. War / Military
Orange Hara Spleen	Medicine	Digestion. Assimilation	Acceptance. Construction	Holiness	Medicine. Holy path. Seeker
Yellow Solar plexus / adrenals Pancreas	Reason	Nerves	Understanding	Wisdom	Science. Research. Analysis. Psychology
Green Heart Thymus	Economy	Circulation	Self-control. Renewal	Eternity. Evolution	Agriculture. Economics
Blue Throat	Faith	Respiration	Discrimination	Truth	Religion. Ethics; morality. Music. Healing
Indigo Pineal Third eye	Metaphysical abstract	Bones	Integration	Strength	Abstract thought. Intuition
Violet Crown Pituitary	Spiritual	Glands	Transformation	Sacrifice. Spiritual power	Inspiration
Collective	Cosmic	Atomic	Demonstration	Love	Care for all. Balance. Creation

Rising Up

Extension

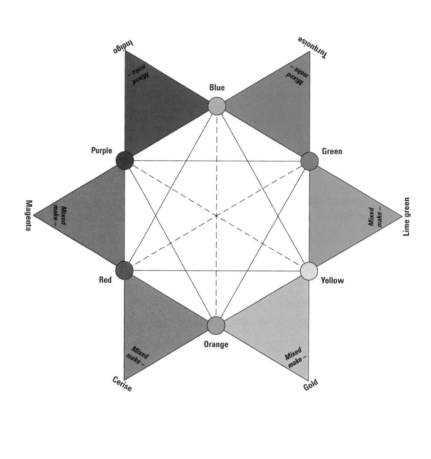

Earth primary colours

Womb. Female wider at hips.

Action. Male wider at shoulders
– together, the male and the female,
internal and androgenous.

White light: White light, containing each colour, is the centre point of our being. Colour is invisible to us unless reflected against an object, and whether colour is absorbed or reflected depends on the object in question. The collective human becomes an organ within the mind of greater humanity, which absorbs the collective pattern or radiations as the output reflects greater light. If we imagine a colour and then step into its essence we feel the colour's intention, which is a reminder and serves as a reference; it is not energy in and of itself.

Light affects all levels and it can influence all of them, including, but not limited to, our spiritual beliefs, physical attitudes and emotional responses. The Earth's form is reflected in our own physicality. For instance, females represent the Earth's womb and so have wider hips, which allow them to be disciplined, responsive and have the stamina required for birthing offspring. By contrast, males have broad shoulders which create an ethic where childbirth is possible. When the male and female are placed together there is an infinite potential of extension, as shown in the diagram above. The male and female relate to us internally via our state of being (female) and what we do (masculine) they must unite in common purpose within us.

PART 7:
LEARNING TO GROW MORE EFFECTIVELY

Chapter 21: Releasing History

Deepening Awareness

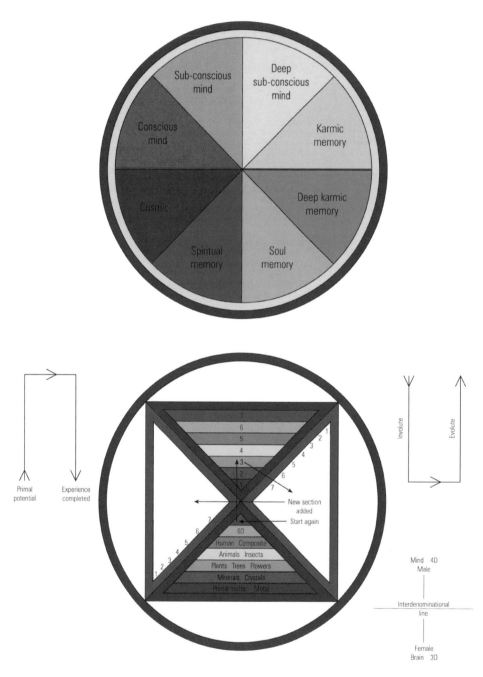

**Union of male and female gives possibility
of bringing forward next section**

As we reach the limits of one stage, that ceiling becomes the floor for the next stage. We grow as we progress and each step is a progression of its own. Instead of only using the tools in our conscious mind, we also utilise what is stored in our subconscious.

In the top diagram above the conscious mind is located to the west because that is the past, and anything in the conscious mind is something we have already completed and so understand it as much as we need to. The subconscious mind is located behind that and is where we store such things as phone numbers – things we can draw on when we need them but do not think over all the time. Beyond the subconscious mind is the deep subconscious, from which we experience déjà vu or knowing that we have met someone previously but cannot remember when or where. It is in the deep subconscious that we embrace holistic concepts that may be useful to us, and so it is sometimes a requirement for us to forget the familiar so we can remember more. In doing so we are able to separate essence and effluence and unite everything we think we need. Finally, located behind the subconscious memory is the karmic memory, which comprises the things we have agreed to undertake in this life at this time. These things make up the half circle, from the diagram above, in which people tend to live.

The world is contained in a grain of sand and each chakra holds a memory of the whole. Because it is both the microcosm and macrocosm we can go as deep as we are capable of, and the anchor of life, swinging from positive to negative, will go halfway around as most of us only live in one half. When it swings we try to find a point of peace, at which point we swing from the light into darkness and then darkness into light, meaning we experience both highs and lows. When the pendulum, or anchor, swings halfway through a cycle it either slows down and stops until we repeat the pattern or it will turn over thanks to gathered momentum and this will allow us to link to memories stored at deeper levels.

Beyond the karmic memory is another, deeper memory called the deep karmic memory. This memory goes by such varied names as 'many lives', 'simultaneous reality' and 'multidimensional reality', but essentially it is where we are directed on the soul level. Crucially, though, we only need the one memory we require to work to the benefit of ourselves and those around us, rather than trying to use too many memories at once.

The spiritual memory lies behind the soul memory, and this is the memory that tells us to work to the point of need and have no fear because there is divine discipline that will look after us. This rests in front of us the cosmic order, which is the discipline that allows the universe to run without our intervention. If we are able to drop our old memories then we will be able to meet the Heavenly mother and father, which are the Earth and invisible God figure, respectively.

Input and Output

The following table explains the functions of the body parts and the effects of shock to those particular areas:

Functions	Effects of Shock
Head – consciousness of extension, psychic development, brain relationship with body.	Loss of mental balance, cerebral congestion, migraine, concussion, fluid conditions.
Pineal – third eye, motor power of nerves. Linked with pituitary.	Loss of motive power, neuroses.
Pituitary – master regulator of the body, glands, synchronises all fluids, controls balancing power.	Glandular diseases, diabetes, dropsy, urinary, lymphs.
Eye – linked to pineal.	Loss of vision.

Ear – linked to throat.	Loss of sensitivity to tone.
Throat – larynx, speech, mouth, gullet, breathing, ear ducts.	Laryngitis, tonsillitis, quinsy, speech difficulties.
Heart – circulation, charges blood with vital forces.	Paralysis, stroke, circulatory diseases, rheumatism.
Hand – servant of the mind, means of physical creation, transmitter of healing power.	Loss of sensitivity or memory.
Solar plexus – digestive functions, bowels, abdomen, procreative functions, hormones, a master gland, child birth.	Diseases of the stomach, ulceration, constipation, malnutrition, acidosis, hernias.
Base of Spine – spiritual and coordinating centre, sex function, vital forces to nerve ends.	Sex malformations, bowel complaints.
Knee – linked to base of spine and feet.	Excess fluids, immobility, mineralisation.
Feet – magnetic centre to earth. Helps balance fluids.	Immobility, inflexibility, deformities, excess fluids, mineralisation.

Expansion

From our new position at the centre of a circle emerges a new area which covers the diameter of yet another circle. In order to investigate a circle the centre must be contained, and so we create a square around our own centre in order to examine our situation from every possible angle. Acknowledging that misshapen areas are at risk we must hold the shape until it is smooth, at which point it will regain its buoyancy and a new shape will be allowed to appear.

Changes must all take place slowly over a period of time rather than as quickly as possible so that the different areas have time to align. It also takes time to be able to understand and continue our examination, which again is reason for moving slowly and also for the importance of double checking all areas have the strength to withstand the shock that change causes. We must also ensure that the areas are flexible enough to be able to adapt to the changes. Moreover, we must have the ability to pick and choose what is useful and what is not, and it is only when we have acquired this skill that we will be able to move forward once more.

In the diagram above the bottom circle is the person who has succumbed to being a servant, while the top circle is the will of God providing necessary information. Within the centre square is everything we need. In numerology the top circle is 'zero' and the bottom circle 'nine' when we return to eternity. Within that we then have the seven rays which are coloured red to purple in the diagram.

7 stages of growth

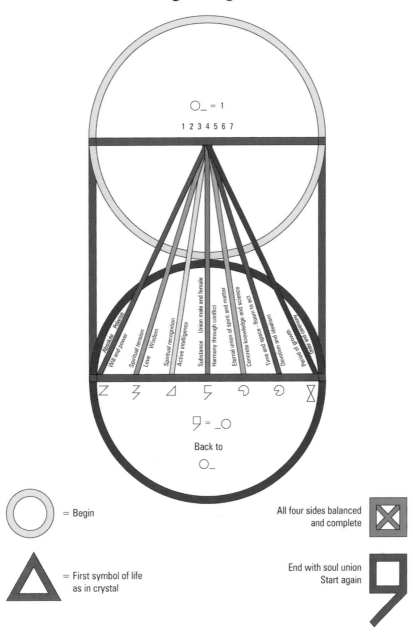

The first ray is Will and the power we have at our disposal, which allows us to unite the mother and father. The second ray is Spiritual Tension, Love and Wisdom. We need to unite light with love and wisdom and until we do so we will not be serving the light at all, either giving too much love or not enough in a disciplined form. Thus, there will be an experiment for us to find our place.

The third ray is Spiritual Recognition. We must understand that perfection is actualised upstairs, but downstairs, where we dwell, we must take the next step.

The fourth ray is Harmony Through Conflict. As we start to unite masculine and feminine we must go through a small battle before reaching peace, and so the harmony comes as a result of the conflict.

To do this we must learn to utilise the fifth ray, which is the Union of Spirit and Matter. This lesson is using the knowledge of those who precede us; to get to the future we must first visit the past and determine what equipment exists to support us. As God only starts where humans stop, we need to learn the mechanics of our skill remit so that we can work at any level.

The sixth ray is Time and Space, which is essentially the lesson that we need time to learn and space to act. It is also important here to remember this is a journey not a single step, which means using the past to move into the future. The invisible world is well aware that we live in eternity and by simply taking a step forward we will have worked to improve our imperfections and mistakes from the past, and this is good enough for the invisible world.

However, because we are inherently impatient we may resent the fact that this all takes time, and so the seventh ray is Discipline, which is where we learn to relax and surrender and understand that all processes take time, that the journey cannot be completed overnight and if we aim for that we will only hurt ourselves.

Chapter 22: Laying a New Foundation

Repatterning

Message	Reaction	Development area	Stage of motivation		
Be perfect	**Shock**	Planetary ingredients	Potential Experimental Start Birth		
Be strong	**Denial**	Mineral	Physical Infancy Experiment	Sex	
Please me	**Fear**	Plant	Emotional Childhood Investigation	Drugs Drink	
Try hard	**Anger Frustration**	Animal	Mental Adolescence Courage	Education Delinquency	
Hurry up	**Bargaining**	Human	Composite Adult Responsibility	Law Penal system Gambling	
Disorientation	**Confusion**	I/D Soul added	Harmonic Commitment Persistence	Service	
Balance	**Positive contribution**	Spirit	Relationships Group potential Original creativity		

New cycle – higher octave

It is important that we are aware of our response in each stage of growth as we move into higher vibrations. We receive a shock when we experience a situation we want to be perfect and it is not, so we make an attempt to be strong enough to withstand a negative challenge. Whenever we are dealt a blow we may reinforce old patterns rather than create a new pattern with the possibility of complementing others instead of competing with them. This requires that we know how to interact. In many circumstances the situation will be reversed and this may well happen again in the future, and this is working with illusion and disillusion, which helps us discern where our boundaries now lie.

This is not easy and in this time old fears rear their heads once again and new ones are also thrown into the mix, so we look to blame others. We may encounter anger and frustration, and sometimes we will try to fight this while other times we will make an attempt to ignore them, and it is this that sets the information boundary we have available.

Progressing beyond this point and refraining from slipping back into old patterns and habits requires much courage because this is the point in time where we release everything that has happened already. It is here that we stop blaming others and commit to finding things out for ourselves, setting out to create a world filled with experiences that we choose to have. All we take on this next step is the essence of the past, rather than the past itself. Naturally, then, it is imperative that we learn the difference between what is allowed and what is forbidden, and that we learn it for ourselves instead of taking the words of others.

As we take the next step we will find ourselves in a space where we can serve others but simultaneously feel confused and disoriented because we are unsure of what is happening. If, however, we manage to find the balance and slowly move forward we can allow the intuitive to work with and complement the linear activities, from which we can find our place and make a valuable contribution to our surroundings. We then find ourselves in a position where we are able to make a choice on how to move forward and what standards to apply.

What this new freedom means is that we need to truly work with ourselves, which entails recognising that things are perfect on a spiritual level and we want to bring that to Earth, too. The problem, though, is that because the Earth is so polluted we cannot bring that spiritual level to it, and if we do not accept the Earth's toxicity it is possible that we will never recover from the shock of entry, which in turn means we will not even properly utilise the ingredients that are here. We may have forgotten that everything is spiritual, so we may never accept that the Earth and our bodies are spiritual places also. If, indeed, we have not been able to accept that then perhaps we tried to live with strength only, and in the times it failed us we may have resigned ourselves to being classified as weak or wimpy. If that shock was not handled well in childhood, such as when we came off worse in a physical challenge or we broke a bone or two, then the discrepancy between absolute and partial strength may make itself known later in our sex life. On the other hand, if we have managed to resolve that discrepancy then our sex life will be fine.

The plant kingdom is a huge help when it comes to dealing with fear that we store in the glandular system. The glandular system may say that in order to take responsibility for ourselves we need some external help, which may come in the form of alcohol, sex or drugs. In reality, meditation is the best, albeit slowest, way to deal with things, but all too often people try to take a shortcut using vices. In fact, an interesting figure is that half of all people in clinics for solvent abuse were looking for a shortcut to spirituality.

The process beyond that is the anger and resentment at being told from all sides that we need to try hard, which aggravates us because we see people all over the place getting things for free and landing on their feet time after time without hard work or applying themselves. These emotions link to our animal instinct and our ability to interact positively with others. It also links to courage, in that we have been educated and having come through the other side find that, actually, it was not sufficient to carry us through. Indeed, the point at which we declare the education to be insufficient is a crucial one because it is the exact mid-point, with three vibrations above it and a further three below it. Being the mid-point, we have the choice of which way to move and in this position we can move back through what we have experienced and already know or we can progress forward and acquire new knowledge and information. In this particular instance either choice is fine, but the most beneficial would be to embrace both.

In the following stage we may try to negotiate with the invisible world in a bid to speed up proceedings. At this point in time we will probably find ourselves feeling tired and doubting whether we have the capacity to keep going. It is in this stage that we will find ourselves haggling or trying to increase our rewards, such as asking employers for increased salary or holiday time. We have all gone through this particular stage in the past, too, when we moved from pampered youth into adulthood and suddenly had to be responsible for ourselves and be equipped enough to express ourselves on every level.

After this comes disorientation, in which, as may be expected, we will find ourselves in a state of confusion. In this stage we may struggle to remember why we are enduring this process at all and we will feel lethargic. The reason is we are at the transition point between one chapter and another in life's book and the invisible world is now actively inputting, which will affect us directly. Of course, as with all the preceding stages that knock us out of whack for a while, once we overcome this balance will be restored and we can make active contributions because the spiritual levels can work with us directly. We will be able to work in our groups without upsetting the other members, and we will find ourselves with more responsibilities within the subtle realms.

Arrival On Planet Earth

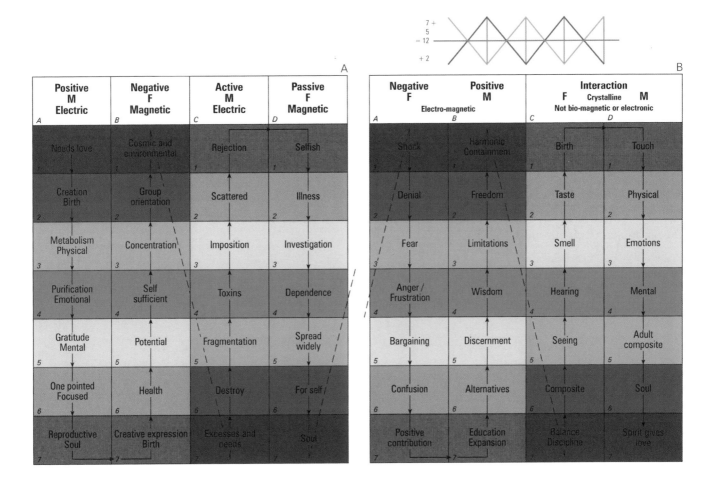

The universe is held together by love, and for us to learn to give it we must also recognise the need for it. In order to do this, we take birth and undergo experiences that affect us mentally, physically and emotionally.

This chain of events holds the potential to help us reach our highest standards, which are intrinsically within us even if the life experiences rely on our strength and those around us.

Our personal proximity to others is a form of measurement through which we can observe what we need and what we do not need, for ourselves and for others. This requires dividing experiences and finding what our toxin and pain thresholds are in internal and external parts of the body; it is in this way that we deduce how far we can look after ourselves and what we should expect from others, although as with many things we must perform the experiment multiple times before we can reach a firm conclusion.

The diagram above demonstrates how the negative female magnetic impulses and the positive male electric unite, and they are the feminine gravitational pull of the Earth which shows us the necessary requirement. We can regard this as stage one. When we come to Earth we know that we will need love of spirit to manage and to anchor both to the Earth and our environment. We know that life is not just to save ourselves but rather will be a group effort, and we must concentrate everything – creation, group feeling, macrocosm and microcosm – into our physical body as we learn our role and how to enact it effectively.

To do this we must become self-sufficient so we can properly serve the spirit. We must be grateful for everything that we have experienced in the past because it is from what is on Earth that we are able to endure. We also require a point of focus on staying healthy because in a healthy state we work with ourselves, and in demonstrating that we can attract spirit to Earth, which will then allow us to reproduce the spiritual field.

When we arrive on Earth we are held down by, and work with, the active electric spiritual requirement of our life and the Earth's passive magnetic pull. It is this pull that informs us to reject the Earth's selfishness so we can operate in a clear space to attract the spirit instead. It will also be what says that we feel confused by the genetic and environmental conditioning that we operate with, that we feel trapped by the investigation and all these negatives are feeding us toxins and we fear that we will become dependent on these toxins, thus ignoring the spirit. What this really is is the negative and positive, or masculine and female, in action and we try to bond things together electro-magnetically.

Within us is a feeling that says we must listen to the higher vibration at all times and use our mental body to take the next opportunity, that emotions must be handled properly and physical responsibilities fulfilled so we do not move on at the expense of someone else. This feeling tells us that we can expand and increase our knowledge, and that when this is done we will be entitled to the spirit's love – and that is why we are here.

The seven chakras and the five bands of the aura are at this time in a supporting shape and they unite with a common purpose. They extend capacities to create a strong, solid foundation that will be able to serve all equally. When we are willing to both change and be changed the intuition and rational mind are activated, so we can instinctively be encouraged to create a holistic state.

PART 8:
LEARN IT OR LIVE IT

Chapter 23: Reformation

Types of Stress

Stress type	Locations of stress and symptoms	Cause	Second aid
Environmental	Head and feet e.g. aching head and feet	Birth trauma	Protection
Internal	Head e.g. eye ache; ear infections	Childhood / Parenting	Body awareness
Deprivation	Throat e.g. coughs; sore throat	Relationship pressure	Ego awareness
Overload Doing everything oneself	Head and breathing e.g. thick head; breathing difficulties	Anxiety	Rhythm of life
Conformity	Digestion e.g. gut ache; indigestion	Fear	Self-image
Frustration	Digestion – Bowels, kidneys e.g. constipation/diarrhoea; kidney infection	Tension	Relaxation and space
Loneliness	Lower back – Legs, feet e.g. back ache; heavy legs	Isolation	Exercise
Note: It is recommended to take an inventory of body and symptoms at least once a month			

Personal assessment

There are several types of stress that can be experienced on any given day and because stress can occur frequently it is a good idea to learn what feelings can be associated with the different types of stress, mainly because they will occur either in isolation or together during transition. During these times we will recollect unprocessed material from the past and be prompted to act immediately, and it is essential that we work with the symptoms in addition to making an attempt to alleviate the factor(s) causing the stress in the first place.

Pain in the lower back may be felt if we feel isolated or lonely, and this pain will affect the legs and feet. If you experience such symptoms then certain types of exercise can alleviate the pain or get rid of it altogether. When we feel frustrated or resentful our bodies will be tense, which can have a negative impact on our ability to make choices on adapting and committing to what we need to eliminate. Our kidneys and bowels can be affected by this, which can be rectified by relaxing and taking the time to adjust and absorb the causes of the stress before we try to take on new knowledge or experiences.

If fear prevents us from doing so then our next step of action may instead be to conform to the environment we find ourselves in, even if we find it hostile. This may cause aches in the solar plexus and, worse, massage previous fears that question our ability to fit in with others.

When we find ourselves in an overwhelming situation we may try to do everything ourselves if we are unable to find others to help us. If we are unable to handle it we may notice pain in the brain or difficulty in breathing as we feel pulled in various directions, simultaneously trying to please everybody at the same time. Such behaviour is liable to cause anxiety on the issue of whether we think others will find us acceptable and this in turn makes us doubt our personal contribution to the whole. To combat this we must change our rhythm to that of the requirements of the Heavens.

If relationships have made us think that our contributions have been ignored or undervalued then we may find expressing ourselves difficult, which has a knock-on effect of feeling deprived. The upshot of this is that we will have a sense of inadequacy and insecurity, which may cause a persistent cough as our throats try to clear the issues, but ultimately we will need to confront them head on.

If we are unsure of what is required of us and are straining hard to see then our eyes may ache. For those who were neglected in childhood or whose parents were less than doting, the problems may have been internalised which will cause general discomfort in the body. The remedy for this is to take the time to be interested in our own health and appearance until we are satisfied with ourselves, rather than putting the satisfaction of others first.

There is also the possibility of being born into a hostile environment, such as a war, local crisis or even domestic problems at home. This means that we were not fully protected in our infancy, which can make us feel off balance mentally or emotionally, or cause aches and pains in the lower body. Such trauma resurfaces in transition phases and it can only be resolved by centring ourselves and accepting all equally.

What To Do

The chart below shows how we can reach a state of wholeness by embracing self-knowledge, responsibility, expression, love, worth, respect and awareness. It is daunting to accomplish all this, and there is the question of in what order it should be approached. The lesson here is just as it has been up to this point, though: listen to intuition, for it will guide us if we allow it. It is possible we will have dreams of things changing and more often than not they will, but not always in the way we had thought or hoped. Nonetheless, we have full choice over our attitude towards it but it is up to us to create a rational sequence to bridge the extremes. Nobody else but ourselves is able to inform us what the best next step is from our current position, so we must work this out for ourselves and then stabilise it before others can look up to us for guidance, and we must create a rhythm that all others can connect to.

Before moving on to the next section, answer the following questions on a balanced understanding:

What do you feel you have learned about yourself through contact with others?
What do you feel yourself to be responsible for at present?
What do you consider to be the responsibility of others?

A whole scenario

	Crown	Third eye	Throat	Heart	Solar plexus	Sacral	Base
Chakra name	Crown	Third eye	Throat	Heart	Solar plexus	Sacral	Base
Chakra position	Top of head	Between eyes	Lower neck	Centre of chest	Over stomach	Lower abdomen	Base of spine
Colour							
Related illnesses	Depression. Epilepsy. Alzheimer's disease	Tension headaches. Migraine. Glaucoma	Tinnitus. Hypothyroidism. Asthma	Heart disease. Cancer. M.E. (CFS)	Gall stones. Allergies. Gastric ulcer	Lower back pain. Fibroids. Irritable bowel syndrome	Hypertension. Osteoarthrosis of hips. Cystitis
Negative emotions	Despair	Confusion	Frustration	Hurt	Guilt. Resentment. Anger	Possessiveness	Fear. Anxiety
Positive emotions	Peace	Clarity	Freedom	Joy	Confidence	Nurture	Courage
Basic needs	Acceptance	Purpose	Ability to change	Unconditional love	A healthy self-esteem	Independence	Security
Endocrine gland	Pineal	Pituitary	Thyroid	Thymus	Pancreas	Sex glands	Adrenals
Spiritual aspect	Self-knowing	Self-responsibility	Self-expression	Self-love	Self-worth	Self-respect	Self-awareness
Musical key	B	A	G	F	E	D	C
Musical tone	EE	AY	I	AH	OH	OO	UH

154

Fourth, do you feel others have discharged their responsibilities towards you as best they could?

Fifth, are you willing to forgive those who did not match up to your criteria?

Sixth, do you express your feelings easily to those you are grateful to?

Seventh, do you express your displeasure equally easily without bottling things up or blowing up?

Eighth, who do you care for and who is no longer a part of your remit as far as you are aware?

Ninth, do you feel guilty or do you trust the process?

Tenth, do you value your own worth?

Eleventh, do you respect yourself?

Twelfth, what attributes do you respect others for?

Thirteenth, are you aware that you have done all that you can and that it is now time to let go trying so hard to allow yourself to be led?

The Flow of Living

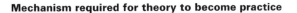

Mechanism required for theory to become practice

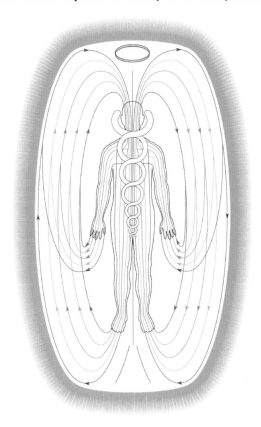

We are now starting to understand that in order to serve humanity the theory we need to respond to must be made practical within our potential. Our thumbs link to the programmes in our brain that represent higher authority, which means issues that we have no direct control over. Our index fingers point the way to respond to that authority on Earth, and this might mean we see a vision that others do not, and so we will need to modify and represent this vision in various ways before we can respond to it. This will require patience, but so long as we work the vision then we will be supported by life. On the other hand, if we modify the vision to suit our own needs then life will not support us. A permanent rule is that if we are working towards a universal good then we will receive support and overcome any obstacles that stand in our way. An important lesson is learning that we will be in trouble if we put our well-being above that of others; this is not the same as not helping ourselves or putting others above us either, but rather it means knowing that neither we nor they are more important than anyone else.

When we reach the stage of attempting to unite the abstract of what is required and what is not and apply it to those surrounding us we notice the fourth, or ring, finger. This is where we must ask if the active and passive are balanced within us and whether or not we will strive to complement others or instead bustle for pole position in the social hierarchy.

Our little fingers remind us to look at the past and also show us areas that need our attention so we do not become overwhelmed by undertaking too much at once. We must release guilt, grief and regrets and acknowledge instead that things are the way they are; all we can do now is make the most of them. By the same token, we cannot dwell too much on what we want or expect from the future, because new scenarios can and will appear in the meantime which may mean that those anticipated future events never materialise. So at this stage we take what is useful and let go of what is not needed, being realistic about our ideal scenario until balance is acquired. We then will become more stable and content, organising and administering to the best of our ability.

The feet bear the same messages as the hands but in application, and when the theory and practical meet we can move forward once again. Although at times we may want to slow things down and repeat what has gone before to improve on it, we must recognise that we changed and so have those in our company, so we must let go and move on, rather than holding ourselves and others back.

The Current Identity

The eight colours of the spectrum

Violet ●●●●●○○○○
Very fine chemical changes in the body / Value; hope / Respect; divinity / Honour / Dignity

Blue ●●○○○○○○○
Decrease of blood pressure / Expanding / Anti-stress / Sleep / Slowing / Relaxation / Peace

Turquoise ●●●●○○○○○
Anti-inflammatory / Body building / Calming nerves / Cooling

Green ●●●○○○○○○
Cancer control / Consistency / Neutrality / Cleansing / Balance

Yellow ○○○○○○○○○
Calcium related / Criticism / Intellect / Thinking / Detachment

Orange ●●●○○○○○○
Anti-depressant / Submission / Carelessness / Uplift / Dance / Joy

Red ●●●●●○○○○
Increase of blood pressure / Misusing power / Contracting / High vitality / Challenge / Strength

Magenta ●●●●○○○○○
Fine chemical changes / Meditation promoting / State of perfection / Spirit / Release / Let go

The spine
– energies expressed through colour

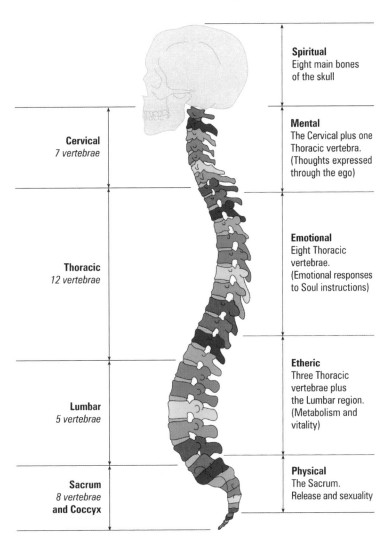

Cervical
7 vertebrae

Thoracic
12 vertebrae

Lumbar
5 vertebrae

Sacrum
8 vertebrae
and Coccyx

Spiritual
Eight main bones
of the skull

Mental
The Cervical plus one
Thoracic vertebra.
(Thoughts expressed
through the ego)

Emotional
Eight Thoracic
vertebrae.
(Emotional responses
to Soul instructions)

Etheric
Three Thoracic
vertebrae plus
the Lumbar region.
(Metabolism and
vitality)

Physical
The Sacrum.
Release and sexuality

We will notice a growth in our sensitivity, and while we should welcome this with open arms quite often we do not. Our ability to respond to this growth depends on many factors and if we do not honour ourselves as much as possible we can experience loneliness, in which we can imagine many things and go to comfortable places or places of fear and boredom – and either one will affect us and those in our company.

This space can be considered akin to a gap year between school and university – a place in which we can unwind, reflect and contemplate the forthcoming life. This also provides the time required for vitality to return, and we must slow down and make sure we are in a neutral zone so that our thoughts can settle. This prevents problems arising through carelessness because we will no longer be doing things from habit as we are used to. As we slow down our rhythm will also slow, and this will allow our baseline to be established. Things that cause fear or aggravate a situation will recede and we will stop providing energy to the old or critical judgement of ourselves and others. Finally we will view things for what they are, no more and no less. In the establishment of new values we will once again find hope in the fact that something new is coming along and this will allow us to be stable enough that we can confidently express our needs in a way that everyone can understand. However, the chemical changes that will occur in this period can affect our backbone: both the metaphor for our backbone in life and our physical spine.

Our thoughts, emotional reactions and body valuation must all be monitored until such a time as we are as comfortable as possible. If our body needs treatment we are free to provide it, whether it be a massage, acupuncture or anything else. Our life's new shape is again finding a colour and rhythm that will over time produce a revised form. Stamina has been bestowed upon us and by this point it will be at a pace we find comfortable, rather than too fast with us playing catch up. So for now we must be patient, taking time for ourselves instead of actively and anxiously searching for results.

And Now?

Ready for renewed service

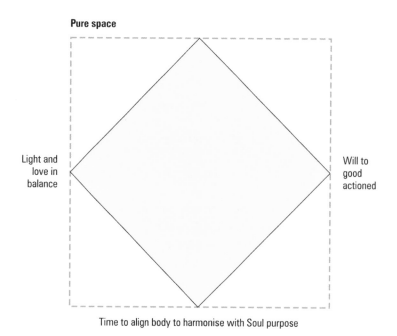

Pure space

Light and love in balance

Will to good actioned

Time to align body to harmonise with Soul purpose

In this present moment we will find ourselves in the space we need to be and the will to good is in action. However, it will still be a time of uncertainty because we will not know how the light will shine in or around us, nor will we be certain of whether we will be able to love or be loved in the way we are used to. We will need time for the body to recuperate and the mind to release outdated anxieties.

We may find ourselves becoming somewhat reclusive and feeling lethargic or flat. Exercise and relaxation will help the realignment process and once realignment is finished all will be well. We will only be allowed to proceed when we are harmless to both ourselves and others, and it is fully our choice whether we enjoy the transition or try to fight against it, or try to speed it along. As mentioned already, though, we must be in this for the long haul, partly because trying to take shortcuts will only be detrimental either mentally, physically or both. We must be patient and await the next instruction – it will come quicker than expected and by completing all prior steps properly we will be ready on every level.

Chapter 24: Beyond Revolution

The Whole World Is Contained Within A Grain Of Sand

The eyes

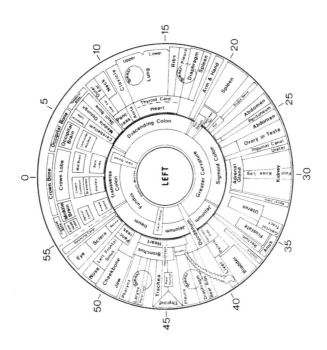

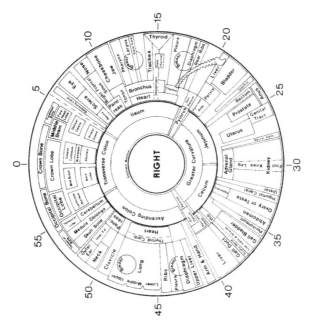

The hands

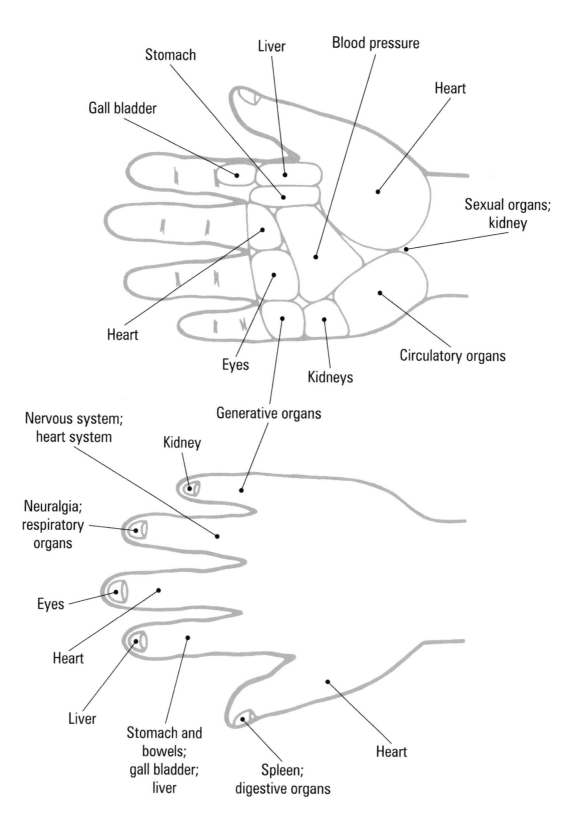

The feet

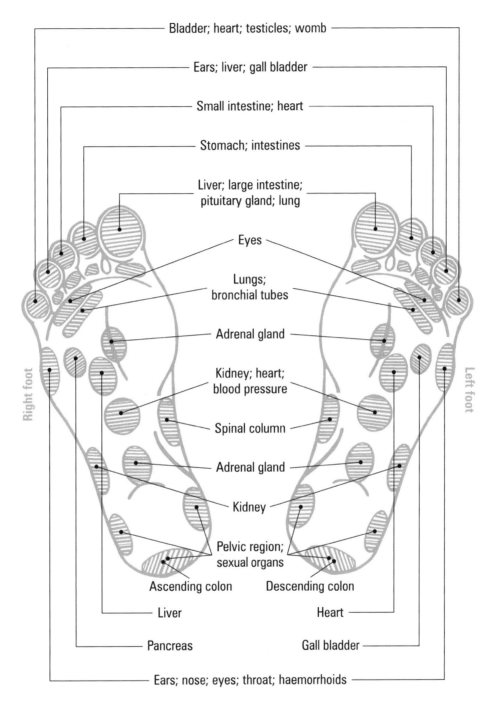

Bladder; heart; testicles; womb

Ears; liver; gall bladder

Small intestine; heart

Stomach; intestines

Liver; large intestine; pituitary gland; lung

Eyes

Lungs; bronchial tubes

Adrenal gland

Kidney; heart; blood pressure

Spinal column

Adrenal gland

Kidney

Pelvic region; sexual organs

Ascending colon

Descending colon

Liver

Heart

Pancreas

Gall bladder

Ears; nose; eyes; throat; haemorrhoids

Right foot

Left foot

Now that we have completed work with the macrocosm we align to it and start work on the microcosm. As the diagrams above show, through studying the eyes, hands and feet we are able to link to multiple other parts of the body. However, our being able to 'see' what is on its way to us can affect the eyes, making them blurry or sore. Maybe we need to divert our focus elsewhere but we are trapped in place, scared of the upcoming changes just as we would have been at the start of this journey.

The irony of this is that staying in the past is difficult and carries its own burdens, but our selective memories will romanticise the past and downplay the negatives, or we may find ourselves in a place – physical or emotional – that is the result of a past event or action that is now no longer needed, such as living alone in a family-sized house for example. The correct thing to do in these instances is to make the necessary changes to meet our current needs, because if we refrain then we will gradually become increasingly uncomfortable. When we open our hands and express that we have the will to give and receive, new options and their supporting structures will be more appealing than they were before. When we give things away that we no longer need we are helping others by providing something they do need, just as we give to charity for the same reason. In return we now have space to receive something more useful to our current state, despite the fact that we have not sought it out. Even though we may not be able to see how, this benefits everyone; with this in mind, we may not always be inviting and accepting of change, but the least we can do is cooperate with it rather than try to stand in its way and prevent its taking place.

With each passing moment we will be walking into the future and in the process finding ways of adapting or acquiring things to suit our immediate needs. Any feelings of inadequacy or insecurity will fall away and in their place will be interest and excitement for the upcoming life, even if we initially feel somewhat lonely. During this time we will trust the flow and perhaps even find a level of contentment that we previously thought impossible.

If our ideas manifest then we must ask whether or not the living process will support us. In order to this, we need to observe body language and human nature and listen to nature's rhythms and our own internal whisper. We will be guided by our eyes, hands and feet and although we may not want any confrontation we may find ourselves in debates regarding our policies. Accordingly, we learn to honour any given situation without interfering with it.

As we grow and develop we are able to handle our own feelings with a more mature version of our own truth, which will come about through trusting ourselves and taking responsibility for our actions, rather than trying to pass it on to others. We will see what is possible and impossible and this in turn will allow us to relax, content in our knowledge, and we will then be able to recover again. We can facilitate this recovery by seeing a specialist, such as a reflexologist or chiropodist, or we may just feel the need to tell our friends what we are now doing in life instead of asking for advice – this is a small step but signifies our newfound strength. As with all the stages that have come before, this period of downtime is where we patiently await the clarification of the spiritual intention.

The Changing Earth

Even something as constant as the Earth changes over time, and its inhabitants must adapt to these changes. Despite the changes, the Earth's history contains much might and power and the lesson we learn is to judge not the merits of it, nor to distrust it, but rather to work without jealousy or trying to fare better than others, but to complement their efforts with our own. As habitual as it may be to blame or keep others at a distance, we must remember that there is nothing to be gained from this. We can only gain positive rewards through acceptance and cooperation.

When we say something, anything, it is either heard or it is not heard. If we speak half as much as we listen then the value of our words may be more worthwhile; on the other hand, if we feel ignored then we are likely saying something that does not warrant listening to. This is often combatted with age because with maturity often comes the practice of not offering up information unless our input is requested, at which time we will say what we think to be true, and if we do not know what is true we will openly state as much, rather than saying something for the sake of saying something and hoping to gain trust and reverence as a result. Indeed, when we act in this mature way for a length of time people will realise we are trustworthy and honest, especially if we combine this with a respect of their trust by not gossiping behind their backs.

Such an act of honour will also allow us to act quietly and wisely, not least because it will stop us from getting involved with things we do not understand or doing things for the sake of reward in some form. We do the right thing for its own sake, not in the hope of receiving something.

Part of this maturity is also realising that we cannot stop change happening, it will occur whether we like it or not. And as we grow older and wiser we learn how to accommodate it even if we wish it was not happening. If we have changed to the point that we are free of anger, fear, resentment and frustration then we are immune to them, meaning it is no less pleasant being around those still harbouring those emotions than if they were not. We must care for all people as children of the Earth regardless of age, perspective or attitude, because we are *all* children of the Earth. It is our role to update the historical structures by keeping open communication with our soul and then communicating with all we encounter as accurately and clearly as we possibly can.

Chapter 25: Placement

Down to Earth

Being children of the sun and moon we are influenced by light and dark, with the former internally relating to good humour irrespective of the situation, and the latter relating to ill humour no matter how good our situation is; this can also be described as optimism and pessimism. Provided we are not in a particular situation weighing us to one end more than the other, the extremes of these emotions allow us to find our self-expression between them.

Besides the sun and moon we may also be similarly influenced by other planets, then any interactions between the positive and negative will provide us with more clarity from which we can make decisions. This aside, though, it is the sun and moon that affect the third eye. Throughout life we can be cheerful or miserable and this depends on our attitude regarding where we are and what we are doing. Effort is required for us to use our skills in a creative manner and as we understand what is required of us we may, on occasion, need to be intelligent and discriminate. Alternatively, we might attempt to rationalise things so they suit our ideals. This may be regarded as an amoral use of our skills, though, and it is important that we find our way to where we are needed, not just where we would like to be. It is at this stage that we learn to maintain clear and concise verbal expression – if we do not then our throats will be affected.

Our heart and capacity to attract or repel others are affected by Venus. We learn to give, take and share with a generosity of Spirit, or we may be greedy, selfish, self-indulgent and make emotional demands of others. This is true for many of us and for those people this space must be repeatedly cleansed until it is pure.

The fire in our belly is influenced by Mars and in turn influences the solar plexus; it is connected to the courage that we have when we try to reach a specific goal (although if we are impatient then we will try to arrive without travelling, which cannot happen). If we find ourselves being stubborn for no apparent reason then we may also become hostile and/or violent in a misguided bid to relieve our frustrations.

Jupiter influences both the lower abdomen and the capacity to unite the highest potential into life, although in order to do this we must have faith and be reliant on the higher powers that will guide us to our place and role in the overall plan. These areas have an impact on the reproductive area, where we will either acknowledge our own need to improve and be optimistic and gracious, or we may be lazy, over-confident and irresponsible. As such, we must plan and work diligently and with focus so that we expand without negatively affecting others.

Elements and senses

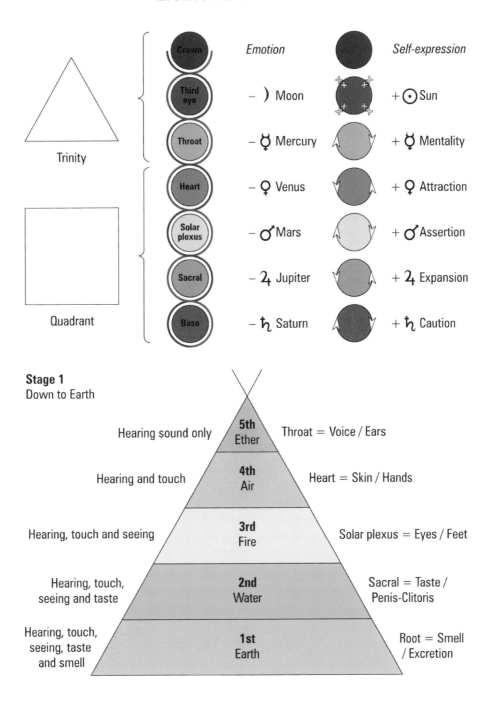

Saturn has influence on the base of the spine and makes the request for us to be disciplined in our efforts as we accept our duties and responsibilities without harbouring resentment towards either ourselves or others. With patience and organisation we will progress inclusively and steadily. On the other hand, we must be aware that by being too reliant on ourselves or by lacking faith in others we can restrict ourselves, making both mind and body rigid, which will in turn make us cold and defensive to others and suffer from crippling inhibitions, fear and negativity.

We will be assisted if we commit to this way of being, and we will know from the outset that something in our atmosphere needs fixing. At first we will not know what to do so we will lose our taste for life, resisting its flow which may have an effect on the reproductive organs. We will look but be unable to see and will not hear what is required; as a result, we will have no desire to touch or taste the quality of life that we are used to. Worse still, we feel a sense of impotence when it comes to changing the situation.

When we reach this point we will know it is time to 'let go and let God', to surrender to the Greater because the fire in our belly has been extinguished. It is time to purify, release the assumption that nobody cares about us and also the feeling of persecution. The feeling of suffering is now outdated and serves no purpose, so it must be shed.

Once we do this we will find our voice and be able to hear and express ourselves appropriately. What has gone before remains in the past and we acknowledge that people have changed as time has gone on. The superfluous excess that we carried has fallen by the wayside and we are protected by our own space, once again reachable by others.

Consider the following self-reflection questions on others:

1) Who do you know that you do not want to associate with and why?
2) Does this source from imagination, past deeds or current issues?
3) Can you commune internally about this matter?
4) Can you communicate with others about this matter?
5) Are you ready to forgive yourself and the others concerned?
6) Redefine your identity and update it to where you are now.

New Growth

Growth is a natural state but we must be sure not to omit anything; we need to be as thorough as we possibly can and progress one step at a time, careful not to try and rush, because it is only by doing it this way that we create a safe and solid foundation from which to work. The experience from being in darkness will have now been converted into light in the body and this is safe: no one can take it from us. Our skills are now an innate part of us, woven tightly into our fabric and they simply become a fact of life.

We are now ready to grow again, focusing on universal goodwill, which reacts on the energy centres and applies the required pressure to reflect the past and move into the future. By being intelligent in our administration everyone will be ready to transmute what is no longer needed, transform past experiences, invest what is needed for the future and release what is left over with happiness not resentment.

Transformation

Safe progress

Unsafe progress

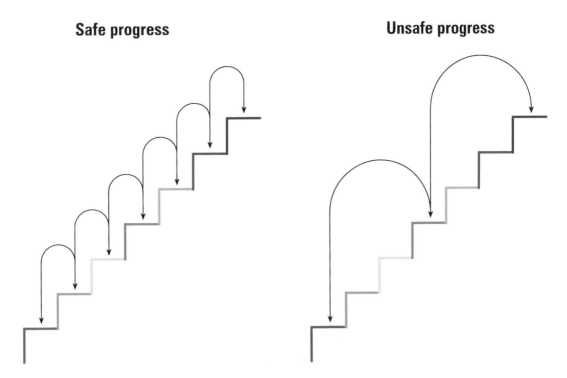

Growth is a natural state. Taken step by step we enjoy and
consolidate safe and steady progress as we absorb light into body

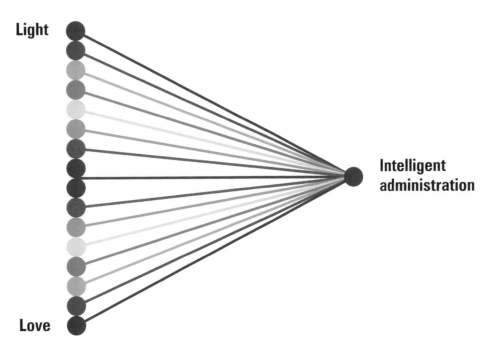

Light acts on will to commune with body. Love reacts within the energy centres
reflecting past and applying pressure to move into future.
Now transmute and transform

Soundform circle

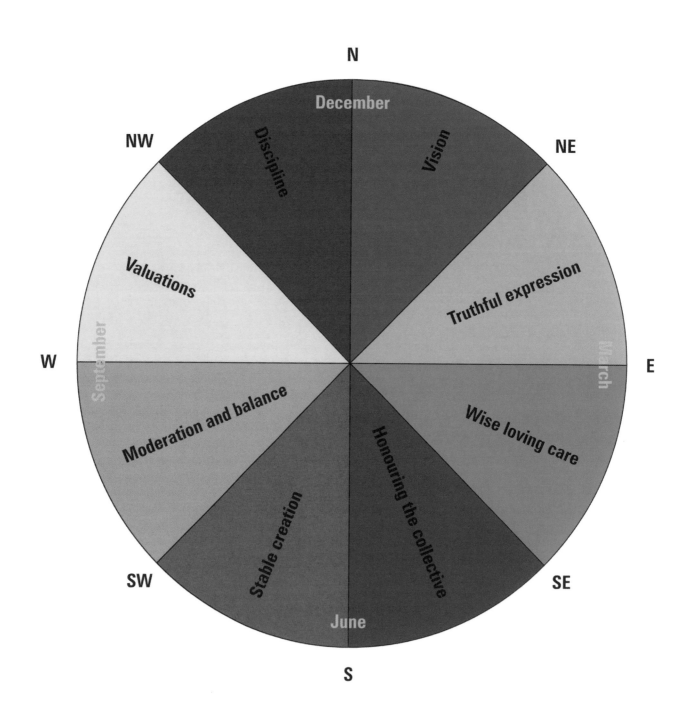

A diamond in the making

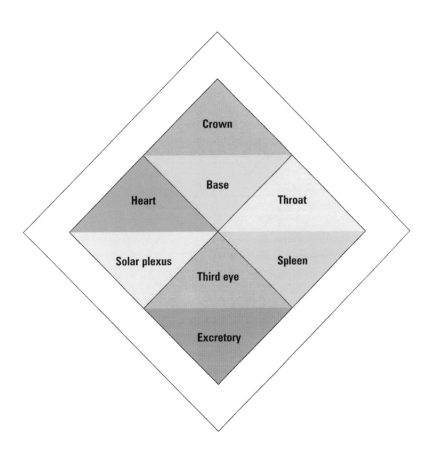

Everyone must be aware that the discipline they have been within throughout their lives has permitted a vision where anyone can express themselves truthfully without worrying about reprisals. So long as wise and loving care has been apparent – without individuals being able to escape punishment for wrong or inappropriate behaviour – then the creative foundation will be stable for all concerned. However it must also be remembered that the collective's balance is delicate because every individual is precisely that: individual, therefore independent and inter-dependent. This means that everyone needs to be responsible for themselves and moderate in both input and demand. Each and every situation will be assessed independently on its own merit, which means that everyone is valued but must take turns. This discipline may not always be enjoyable, depending on when your turn is due, but it is fair.

If all the group members are self-monitoring but under discipline by the group then a solid foundation will be formed. This is the union experienced at the top of the head and base of the spine. Provided the two ends are stable then the components between them will rectify any issues. The capability to express oneself with honesty will need to meet the spleen or sacrum so everyone will be able to accept the viewpoints of others as valid, even if they do not agree with them. This needs to take place without anyone being dominant or trying to take control, rather everyone needs to be treated equally.

We need to develop trust, from which we learn to honour, content in the knowledge that we endure and survive even in the instances when our training is difficult. When we succeed we feel pleased and often proud of our success and are then able to assist others as they undergo the same process. On the other hand, if we fail in our attempt then we will either repeat the process for another go or we will be directed somewhere suitable.

What now?

Bodily functions

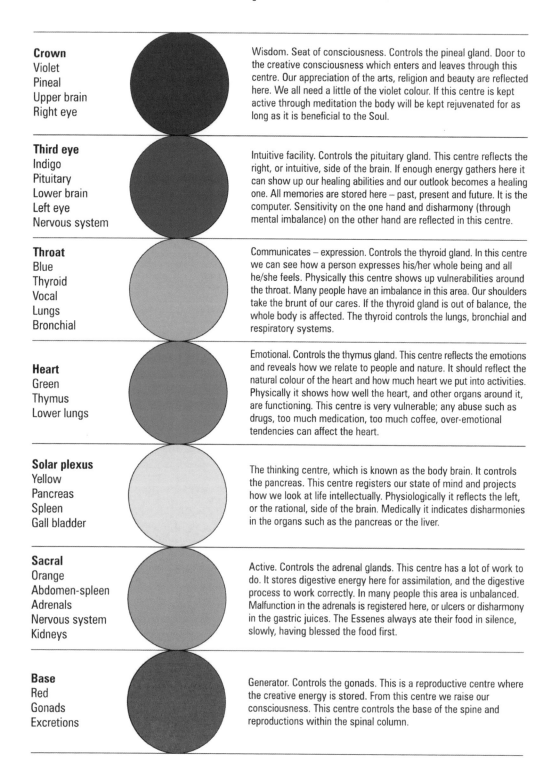

Crown
Violet
Pineal
Upper brain
Right eye

Wisdom. Seat of consciousness. Controls the pineal gland. Door to the creative consciousness which enters and leaves through this centre. Our appreciation of the arts, religion and beauty are reflected here. We all need a little of the violet colour. If this centre is kept active through meditation the body will be kept rejuvenated for as long as it is beneficial to the Soul.

Third eye
Indigo
Pituitary
Lower brain
Left eye
Nervous system

Intuitive facility. Controls the pituitary gland. This centre reflects the right, or intuitive, side of the brain. If enough energy gathers here it can show up our healing abilities and our outlook becomes a healing one. All memories are stored here – past, present and future. It is the computer. Sensitivity on the one hand and disharmony (through mental imbalance) on the other hand are reflected in this centre.

Throat
Blue
Thyroid
Vocal
Lungs
Bronchial

Communicates – expression. Controls the thyroid gland. In this centre we can see how a person expresses his/her whole being and all he/she feels. Physically this centre shows up vulnerabilities around the throat. Many people have an imbalance in this area. Our shoulders take the brunt of our cares. If the thyroid gland is out of balance, the whole body is affected. The thyroid controls the lungs, bronchial and respiratory systems.

Heart
Green
Thymus
Lower lungs

Emotional. Controls the thymus gland. This centre reflects the emotions and reveals how we relate to people and nature. It should reflect the natural colour of the heart and how much heart we put into activities. Physically it shows how well the heart, and other organs around it, are functioning. This centre is very vulnerable; any abuse such as drugs, too much medication, too much coffee, over-emotional tendencies can affect the heart.

Solar plexus
Yellow
Pancreas
Spleen
Gall bladder

The thinking centre, which is known as the body brain. It controls the pancreas. This centre registers our state of mind and projects how we look at life intellectually. Physiologically it reflects the left, or the rational, side of the brain. Medically it indicates disharmonies in the organs such as the pancreas or the liver.

Sacral
Orange
Abdomen-spleen
Adrenals
Nervous system
Kidneys

Active. Controls the adrenal glands. This centre has a lot of work to do. It stores digestive energy here for assimilation, and the digestive process to work correctly. In many people this area is unbalanced. Malfunction in the adrenals is registered here, or ulcers or disharmony in the gastric juices. The Essenes always ate their food in silence, slowly, having blessed the food first.

Base
Red
Gonads
Excretions

Generator. Controls the gonads. This is a reproductive centre where the creative energy is stored. From this centre we raise our consciousness. This centre controls the base of the spine and reproductions within the spinal column.

We can choose to be released or continue suffering. Similarly, we can ask and be aware of what is going on, but we have to be willing to learn to use the new skills that have been bestowed upon us. If we are to become active servers of the Heavens on Earth then we may for a while suffer from headaches or notice a twitch in the right eye, both of which result from extending the consciousness via the pineal gland and becoming released from the past.

In return we will have clearer vision, which is frequently called 'clairvoyance'. The pineal gland redirects the information to the pituitary gland, which impacts the left eye, and we may feel more anxious and emotional than normal.

The throat centre will bypass the emotions from the past, aided by the root centre, so long as we have the intent to serve the Heavens. We will require time to meditate, which will allow us to hear what is required of us – this is often known as 'clairaudience'. When we 'hear' something it needs to find expression within us and this will be felt within the spleen and solar plexus, thus giving us the capacity to express ourselves, as well as working with the pineal gland so that we can see what is required.

The emotional trio is completed by the heart. When the spiritual impulse enters it does so with authority but it also possesses a choice – unless we choose to comply unconditionally then it will cause difficulties for us. As such, we need to be loving, compassionate, tolerant and understanding, because if we make the choice to comply with the Heavens' invitation then we are by default refusing to allow old memories to govern us, so they will break up and make that stored intensity convert into both love and lightness of being. When we are in this stage we will have no information, only that we are on a single step of a path that will take us to higher standards and ethics.

The heart and throat can together be inspired and we may be surprised to hear ourselves say words of wisdom that we were unaware we knew. This may not just be limited to verbal words but also notes or music. This could be a confusing time but there is no need to be fearful, for we are being transformed and in the process working within a wider consciousness than we knew could exist. However, this means that we will need to anchor ourselves into ordinariness and the spleen will assist us in healing. We may feel discouraged, depressed, angry, resentful, scared or jealous, and all of these need to be worked through and released prior to our being able to move forward again.

We can become more detached and discerning because the spleen centre permits it, and from this point we begin to discriminate. We may feel ourselves being apprehensive, confused and insecure but we are also aware that we are in a state of progression and so there is no need to worry. We are now starting to comply and cooperate, and find ourselves grateful for having the opportunity.

Whether we wanted to run and cower or we put up a fight, we know that now we are being freed and we surrender, letting go and letting God. It is not unusual to feel consistently tired at this stage because the cosmic consciousness is taking charge of the body, and this needs to be honoured otherwise it will simply pass. We must now not only trust the Heavens but also the Earth, and have faith in ourselves that we have the ability to see what is required. Nonetheless, despite being able to see what is needed we will remain open to all possibilities and bide our time until all but one close off, and it is that one that will be our next step.

PART 9:
CLAIMING ABUNDANCE

Chapter 26: Power Issues

The Path Forward

We wonder who the 'faceless' people are who exert authority over us, the people who we have no recollection of meeting yet we ask how high when they tell us to jump. We have all been let down in the past but if we are still affected by the event(s) then we must take note of our responses in the present moment in order to find fulfilment in the future.

If we receive a soul call and our work changes us without us instigating it we will wonder how to respond appropriately and of the immediate ones we may feel rebellious, tense, externally dumb but internally insolent. The call is invisible yet so real that we need to try to make sense of it, but because it makes no sense to our inferior minds we become frustrated.

At any given time in our life there will be no shortage of people offering their input, but the problem is that in talking about our problem they try to force their own opinions on us, sometimes apparently forgetting it is our problem at all. This is of course intrusive but at the worst level it is rape of our personal space, and as our emotions run high the pain we experience moves from the head to the heart.

It is neither secret nor surprise that some people who feel they deserve more attention than they are receiving will act out and play up, and if we find ourselves caught up in this theatre then we must learn to identify those issues that are a prompt for us to address without getting mixed in the business of others, which is their own prompt. Of course, it can be a daunting and difficult task to separate the past from the expected, and such factors as boasting and exaggerated body language will come to the surface.

Immense pressure is put on the body as we release negative expectancy, and when the mind calms down the body remains anxious. Often people try to mask by refusing to slow down, instead attempting to take everything on and then finding out that we simply cannot. The other action is the other end of the scale, claiming to be useless. Once we give this area some time we will, as always, see the light. Although it will only be the flicker of a small flame, by remaining determined and giving it a little air, it will soon engulf us.

Ethics and Conduct

We must ensure we have clarity regarding our aims before we are able to demand from others. The first part of doing this is to unify our life so all our actions can be cross referenced and not cause undue stress or strain on those around us. If we are sat on a bus no one can take the seat until we leave it, and in life we may find that we no longer want to be occupying the space we are in but the idea of moving fills us with dread and fear. To get in the right mindset to move, then, we need to analyse our objectives, then our existing commitments and combine the two. While some may consider it selfish to start within ourselves, the opposite is true: we *must* start within ourselves because if we do not and end up involved in something we intensely dislike then we will not be offering anything of any value to others.

Having combined the objectives and commitments we go over the old once again to discover how we can relate to it. At this point in time we will know only what it is we do not want, rather than what we do want, but our task then is to create space so we can work out what we want to do within it. By communing internally and communicating with those around us externally we unite the abstract within the mind with the physical experiences taking place inside us. In parallel to this we will be creating an updated view of what we think should take place next.

During this process we may make others feel guilty for not being good enough or having let us down, but when everyone is ready we can offer the choice of remaining with us or moving on, which will create a discussion for all to be productive. Because we will not have any inclination or will to humiliate or embarrass others we have humility and this is recognised and rewarded with a gentle response.

Unnecessary things we will willingly relinquish, and all our acquired knowledge we will happily share with others. This will allow the change to be a pleasant experience for everyone as well as providing the time and space for others to respond appropriately.

A Modest Balance

A communication network

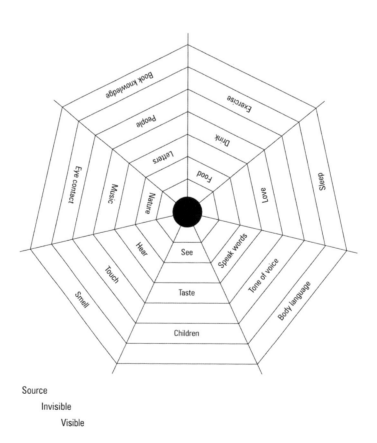

Co-ordination equals balance or absence of dis-ease

Anyone with a keen eye will be able to make the observation that strong leaders are not dictatorial, rather they are able to generate support and followers through strength of character, integrity and conviction, which are traits that people respond positively to. Rather than impose their opinions and beliefs on others, true leaders cooperate genuinely with others and allow people to make up their own minds about following or not. There is no element of deviousness because it is not needed, nor is maliciousness or competitive intent; instead, these leaders live by the same standards and ethics that they preach to others for the simple reason that they know those standards are effective. Most importantly, though, if we feel that their path is not right for us at the time they will not try to restrain us to stay, and if we later decide that it is right for us we will not be rejected out of spite but welcomed with open arms. The reason for this is they have no need to guard their space; it is universal and open to anyone who wants to commit to it.

Well Being

Once we have the ability to commune with ourselves we will also be able to effectively communicate with others, but problems may arise from us working on multiple levels as that can make it difficult at times to maintain alignment. If we feel physically healthy even though we are unwell we can be natural without requiring extraordinary phenomena. If we are emotionally fine then we will not have expectations from others – we will enjoy their company if it is there but we will not crave it. If we want to learn then we will seek education and enjoy the learning process, but there will be no need for more pressure because we will be aware that universal guidelines are in effect. If we are selfish or personally ambitious at the psychic level then we will seek out hidden involvement so we can try to get a step higher on the ladder and achieve something over others or simply out of desire to be a part of something. On the other hand, when we are not selfish or ambitious on the psychic level but rather in tune with our core integrity we are inclusive and want success for everybody.

Perform the following self-reflection exercise to assess your strengths and weaknesses:

1) Write a letter to yourself advising of your strengths, weaknesses, potential skills and established skills – whether they are inherently present or acquired.
2) Considering the above, what would you consider a realistic next step?
3) Does your current situation permit the achievement of your answer to 2?
4) If not, what changes must be made?

Chapter 27: Equality

One World

To dream a bigger dream

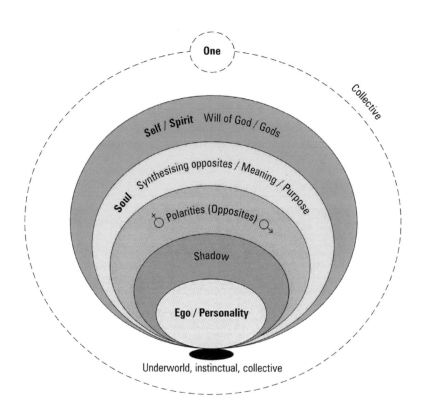

Regardless of the fact that we can all vary by age, gender, race and environmental or religious differences, we are all equal. Although we respect our elders and learn knowledge from those who know things we are ignorant of, our equality is still assured; so long as we have respect and honour towards others and they have the same to us, the occupied space between parties will be sacred. With time, courtesy and care the space will become safe enough for fear, insecurity and instinctive reactions to be explored.

As this is expanded to include more and more people we will become more willing to embark on more challenging adventures and include cultures and customs that we are not already used to without it causing a problem to anyone in our vicinity. In the process we become more helpful and harmless, offering more support and care to all.

To consciously identify with larger groups we need to synthesise opposites, and this process requires two aspects: firstly, the courage of Leo, which will allow us to do the right thing regardless of apparent opposition; and secondly, Virgo's purity of intent, which relinquishes one's idea of perfection to service universal goodwill.

To align with the frequencies of change and now feeling strengthened thanks to our familiarity and experiences, we connect to groups we have chosen through understanding rather than being forced into them. It is our passion to reach our highest potential that now guides us, and our process is at this point to try and balance the higher and lower mental pressures within our experiences.

The first process is to rid ourselves of old, outdated and corrupt forms at every level, which can lead to a clash between the old and new and this can cause some anxiety. The second process is where we focus on the emotional plane and attitudes, which is where we process feelings and make a decision on how to proceed. The third and final process permits the etheric-physical plane of objectives, forms and structures to align with present requirements, and we may notice ourselves feeling unwell at this stage. Indeed, it is not uncommon for people to suffer from serious health issues because the body is dealing with buried emotional trauma in a bid to cleanse. As a result, we must face inwards to sidestep feelings of greed or cynicism and make sure we are taking responsibility for our actions.

Such emotions as pride and arrogance can overtake the personality if it is not integrated. What is required of us is humility and selfless service to the light, happy to give to others without the expectation of receiving anything in return. We must also be content to lead from any position given to us, not only from the front, and our task is to quash pride, arrogance and selfishness, all of which can cause problems and destruction. Strengthening the unity between all life forms requires us to include all, and the key factors for this are simplicity, justice and equality. An unfortunate but certain effect of this process will be disruptions in communication as we learn to compromise and negotiate, so it is imperative that we are flexible and make sure that we do not try to stop updated soul energies from getting through.

If we want a harmonious world, which is what we know the living experience should be, then irrational behaviour must be overcome so that no one is exploited. The ego needs to be subjected to the will to good regardless of the form it takes for us to understand, whether that be God, Allah, Mother Nature or another term entirely; what we need to be absolutely sure of is that the spiritual is the senior partner that has more understanding and wisdom, and that it is the instructions of the spiritual that need to be obeyed.

Naturally, this process can prove difficult and parts of our personality that we do not like will rise to the surface, and this will also mean times that we try to stifle purposeful parts of life. Ultimately, though, the two sides will continue negotiations until a compromise is reached and the aggression subsides. Consider the following questions of good nature:

1) Do you consider yourself to have an open and pure heart regardless of the circumstances?
2) What are you wary of considering past situations?
3) What assumptions do you have about those close to you that are now irrelevant?
4) What expectations do you hold that are negative in relation to those who have hurt you?
5) Are you willing to risk being hurt again now you have changed?

Chapter 28: Parents, Partners and Children

We Love and Hate Them

Each and every individual has expectations about their parents, guardians or any person who took care of them. For many, the standards set by these people are used as a benchmark for 'correct' behaviour and something to aspire to. If the individual agrees with these standards then all is fine, but if they disagree with them then difficulties may arise. It can be confusing to note that while our bodies are relatively young we are actually old souls, and so in some levels we may have more knowledge than our parents or guardians. This can be a troubling point to accept and it can cause guilt and a desire for them to adjust and live by our specifications, and if they choose not to then we may find it difficult to ever forgive them – which will cause ongoing feelings of guilt and disappointment.

Of course, parents set the guidelines on how children should behave and a possibly surprising truth is that children often desire more guidance and care than the parents give; but if they continue to dictate how we should behave then we may feel too controlled or undervalued to make our own decisions. Worse still, we may lack the courage or skills to discuss this with them until we are much older, if we ever do it at all. If we do hold back from discussing it then we will be suppressing resentment and negative feelings, which may lead to depression or physical illness.

There are parents who refuse to let their child go or acknowledge them as grown up; instead they cling to them and behave as though the child is indebted to them. This is, simply put, nothing less than emotional blackmail and it must not be tolerated, for everyone must be free to make the decision of coexisting with another person or not. What makes it even worse is that any issues we have with our parents will recur in our relationships with our partners, children, grandchildren and friends, so we must temper the internal standard with our physical behaviours until the inner and outer unite.

Freeing ourselves involves working within ourselves and demonstrating change externally until the internal and external are united. This is accomplished by negotiating and communing with ourselves repeatedly until resentment and hurt are released. In the process of freeing ourselves we also free those around us and we become a safe space. We are then able to offer opinions to others and leave them free to make their own choices, and this enables them to feel safe in the knowledge that we will accept their choice with unconditional support, and in return they honour our choices.

Answer the following questions to review your interactions with love and hate:

1) Do you want to continue with things remaining as they always have been?
2) In what ways do you consider yourself loveable?
3) In what ways do you consider those around you loveable?
4) What traits do you find easy to accept in yourself?

5) What traits do you find difficult to accept in others?
6) How do these two interact?
7) What kind of person do you want to become?

Connecting With the New

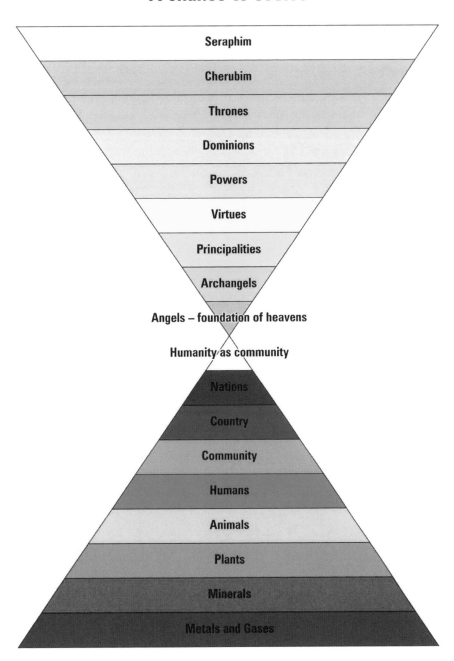

A chance to evolve

Our next step is deducing what our current capacities and skills permit us to do. We must try not to be overly ambitious or greedy so that others also get a fair chance, and now that we have released the past we no longer need to waste energy by being jealous of others who now do what we used to do. We did it, learnt from it and moved on, so now is the time for others to take over the role.

Finding the new direction can be confusing and chaotic, but we must remember that it is through these emotions that the new order is found. Our head must be clear and our mind open as others discuss us and offer us advice even if we feel intruded upon by them doing so. If they become mocking then we must not get defensive or offended but rather excuse ourselves and get back to our priority. If we allow ourselves to be ill-treated then neither we nor they will be served, so if we cannot encourage them to move away then we must move ourselves, for the time being at least – once the new order is found we can welcome them back to our space for inclusion.

As we move along and discover what we are capable of we are then able to find out how long the plan will take to progress. As with the prior processes, though, it is important that we do not try to hurry things along or leave anyone out, but at the same time we cannot drag our feet and try to slow things down; we need to move at the required pace and the Heavens' will anchoring to the Earth must meet seamlessly.

Reflect on the following structure for connecting with the new:

1) What kind of person do you want to be and how do you desire to behave towards yourself?
2) How do you wish to behave towards others, including your partner, parents, children, friends and acquaintances?
3) Ask the above if what you wish is acceptable to them.
4) Listen to them and learn their decisions and needs.
5) Negotiate as good a deal as possible for the collective needs to be met.

Only when this is done can you proceed whilst being considerate to others. By the time that structure is a reality everyone will know they are honoured and they will then be ready to trust that everything is as it should be. The area that has our concentration will need to expand in order to accommodate everyone working within other realms of reality and also contract to incorporate the individual. We need to practise repeatedly until everyone has ceased harbouring suspicious or hostile feelings and we are certain that we do not feel any need to cause harm to others.

Chapter 29: Burnout

Anger and Frustration

Personal reformation

Build up – Break through – Sabotage

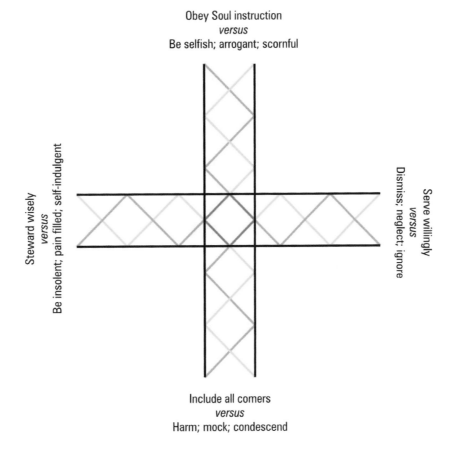

Obey Soul instruction
versus
Be selfish; arrogant; scornful

Steward wisely
versus
Be insolent; pain filled; self-indulgent

Serve willingly
versus
Dismiss; neglect; ignore

Include all comers
versus
Harm; mock; condescend

Co-operate with Mother Nature

Anger and frustration are intertwined, and without both of them existing to inform us that we need to correct an imbalance we would never release the pressure; instead we would just continually suppress negative emotions and be oblivious to them, which can be extremely problematic.

Most people know of the analogy of the human and the volcano, where we suppress our annoyance and work through gritted teeth, hoping the emotions will go away of their own accord. Despite our best efforts, though, our anger continues to grow until it reaches boiling point, when we erupt and take it out on those around us.

The common reaction to this is embarrassment or guilt, but in actual fact we should be grateful for it, because we know that it is healthier to release anger than suppress it. Moreover, by letting our anger reach the point of eruption we put ourselves in a position where we are more likely to lose something, if not in lost time and productivity from brooding then in the disruptions we can cause in our social environment. It is, therefore, much more sensible to work with emotions as they are felt, which negates the erupting altogether.

Frustration is a similar but less intense experience. As an emotion, frustration is what prompts us to look further, question ourselves and others and examine our behaviour. It is through this that we channel our frustration creatively and examine things in a manner that perhaps was not an option previously, and this can help make our growth more pleasurable and less daunting. The key is intuition and insight, both of which entail assessing our circumstances and feelings, and as time goes on and we get better at reading ourselves we will not need to wait for breaking point where we want to scream and shout, rather we can simply ask what any given situation is attempting to show us.

If we are unable to be creatively self-aware when stressed, angry or frustrated, we become sunk in situations of our own creation. Thus, it is important that we do not stop motion, which is life's energy that courses through us, and suppressing anger and frustration will lead to a breakdown of motion. All these emotions need to be confronted and resolved, not least because quite often sudden outbursts are caused by something hanging over us that we have not yet dealt with. One of the best ways of helping ourselves is harnessing our anger and having the energy work in our favour, and by letting others hold their beliefs without being chastised we complete our balance. With a cooperative attitude that we practise frequently, we create a new level of self-discipline that is infinitely valuable. Learning to effectively handle our emotions is a big step forward in the self-awareness process.

Now answer the following self-reflection questions on your relationship to life:

1) Why do you think you are here on the Earth living life as you experience it?
2) Are you willing to explore new experiences?
3) What is your attitude towards adventure?
4) Do you explore experiences internally or are you content with superficial external phenomena?
5) Do you put your learning to work to potentially benefit others or do you keep it to yourself?
6) Are you honest about the difficulties encountered on your journey or do you pretend you are perfect and find all encounters easy?

There is the possibility that we will think a chance exists for our peers to condemn us, and this may make us apprehensive of other people or feel that we will be belittled for having the beliefs that we do. If this is the case, will we still trust the soul guidance to do the best by us and thus follow instructions? Doing so will mean we must take charge and be leaders, but this may prompt us to be scared of being dismissed or ignored by those we care about.

Discernment: Fine Tuning

We are one another

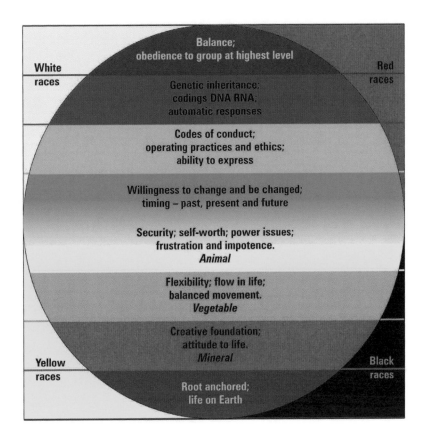

We remain in doubt even as we start to accept the necessity to acquire new information and new rules. To overcome this doubt we need to increase our courage and believe more in our judgement. A good way to facilitate this is to be around someone who can be objective and act as a reflection of ourselves. Such a person can be a wonderful and constructive aide who can help us discern what we should keep and what we should discard, in a similar way to someone helping with a spring cleaning. By reducing the mental clutter we allow our minds to be sharper and work with the ideas that we are either keeping or have recently been acquired. We will then waste less energy on unproductive thoughts and actions and focus more on the areas that facilitate growth.

As our strength becomes organised we start to realise not only how much we have to gain but also how much we can offer others. As we grow we notice a new chain taking place: that we, as students, can suddenly become the teacher to someone else by offering support and advice on something we have already experienced. Beyond this, though, anyone else can also be our teacher, and the lesson learnt is that everyone is linked and inter-dependent.

It is a requirement for us to be exposed to any form of prejudice, bigotry or bias that exposes inequality or is otherwise divisive and learn attitudes that are acceptable to others. The best way of accomplishing this is by spending time with people of various ethnicities and cultures so we can learn how to interact with people and not upset them.

We need to learn flexibility and flow if we are to keep our balance and ensure we honour others. The speed of movement is important: moving too fast will cause fear but moving too slow will lead to boredom, thus learning proper time management will ensure good humour and health. Another positive outcome of this is that we will not feel the need to run away, which means we can rest and recover when we need to.

Such a profound change means that past issues need to be resolved so we can concentrate on the present, and trust that the future will happen as it should. Too many people exert too much effort reliving the days passed that they miss out on what is happening around them currently; others are so focused on the future that they feel isolated because they are the only ones there.

We therefore need to create codes of conduct which are ethical to everyone and in which everyone is able to state what they require. The choice we have to make is to obey the inner calling, which will mean responding to the highest level, or responding to the lowest level.

Perform the following exercise on a plan for the immediate future:

1) Create a plan for the immediate future.
2) Set realistic objectives for the next nine months.
3) Plan to review this in a year's time.
4) Decide on the next step for work, leisure, family, community and yourself.
5) Give yourself permission to adjust this plan after talking it over with others.
6) Tell your plans to a counsellor or close friend and pay attention to their response.
7) Modify the plan if necessary.
8) Take the first step.

Burnout and Balance

We know light because we also know darkness, and we know balance because we also know imbalance. A perhaps seemingly odd fact of life is that experiencing the opposite of our goal helps us measure progress.

Balance is not external, it is internal and so we are all equipped to handle life with inner balance. This allows us to determine how well we will cope before we fail, but if we do lose our balance we just dust ourselves down and try again.

Ironically, inner growth seems to create imbalance – when we are actively experiencing and living life, by taking risks, meeting new people and trying new things, we are at a higher risk of radical swings. By going out and finding ways to challenge ourselves and grow we necessarily wind up in circumstances where shifts and perhaps disasters will take place.

A pitfall to avoid is not getting so caught up in enthusiasm that we are enslaved to our ideals – we do not need to push ourselves to exhaustion just to experience both ends of the spectrum, all we need to make choices is the general overview. We also need to be cautious of burnout, a problem inherent with the modern day where we try to experience everything to the point that we eventually overload ourselves. We can acknowledge the benefits of various activities without trying our hand at all of them; instead we need to find a balance and achieve what we aim for daily, weekly and monthly. The balance must also be sought by helping others and taking care of ourselves, fulfilling our obligations and acquiring new interests. Both are necessary and rewarding and it is simply a case of refining until the blend is correct. There is no need to worry about knowing when that correct blend has been reached, because we will experience new energy and inspiration when it happens. We will eventually reach a point in our growth that we effectively make use of our experiences instead of just being the victims of them, and we can then use this to help others further.

Time management

Past

Future

'Wait nicely' as reorganisation and redistribution are re-administered as you reach for new understanding

Radical distilling of essence. Live don't exist. What still works? Check for – parasites; predators; freeloaders; pimps; leeches – in all aspects of life

Romantic ideal supplanted by contentment with real possibility. Check for – virus and bacteria. Release judgement of success/failure; pleasure/pain. Do not threaten others, prostitute, compromise or settle for less than the best

Take baby steps towards revising intention as you are changed and being changed

Chapter 30: Prosperity

Am I Deserving?

We need to ask whether we are willing to be completely re-involved with life. If we do not then perhaps we would rather shy away and be reclusive in order to remain uninvolved under the assumption this will make us happy. The problem is, we cannot live a vision if we do not tell others what it is. However, if we only take on mechanical tasks we will become bored, so we must find a balance between inner work, regenerative practices and outer exposure to determine if others find our adopted policies acceptable. If we have a vision that is inclusive and required then we will be able to use the Earth's resources, because no one owns material wealth – anyone who does have material wealth has the responsibility to share and promote their possessions, and it does not always stand to reason that just because they have such wealth they also have spiritual abundance; if they did they would be in constant demand by others.

It is not for us to question the Management Upstairs. Instead we should be obedient to the point that if they ask us to use our power to live a miracle on Earth we should say 'yes' with gratitude and humility. If we are able to do this then we will immediately be rid of resentment, frustration, longings and loneliness, although it will be our role to ensure we do not suddenly become too ambitious and expect special treatment as though we are now some sort of superstar.

It is inevitable in life that at times we will be involved in politics or publicity machines, whether on a small scale such as with family or friends or a large scale like a national scandal. It may even happen within us, as our huge collection of cells each try to peacefully coexist with the others; each cell has the hope that the soul advisor will create a loving administration so that any form of threat, like bacteria, can be safely rid from the body to ensure harmony throughout.

Will I Follow My Star?

If you stop to listen and think the way forward will become visible.

1) Do you have the courage to follow your star and obey the soul instruction while continuing meditation and breaking up the bigger picture into manageable chunks?
2) Are you willing to give services within the area of skills, abilities and experiences that are relevant to you or do you wish to do everything and run the world single handed?

The questions above will reveal issues about our capacity to work cooperatively, our attitude to authority and our rebellious history. If we have incorrectly judged ourselves or others or manipulated situations or people to our advantage then these issues will also rear up to be addressed. This process will continue until we can be humble enough to keep our vision of making improvements which prove harmless. The process involves us praying and reporting our observations without embellishing or exaggerating or attempting to make changes in a bid to be politically correct.

As we make an attempt to understand what is happening we need to update our truth and review our life. Doing so allows us to recognise the ignorance and imperfections within ourselves and others and this can cause us grief. Due to this, time is a requirement for healing and the old and new to integrate properly.

Can we obey?

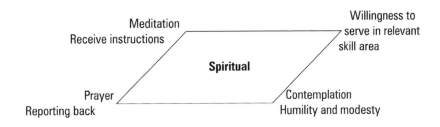

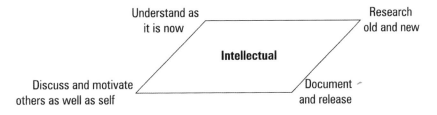

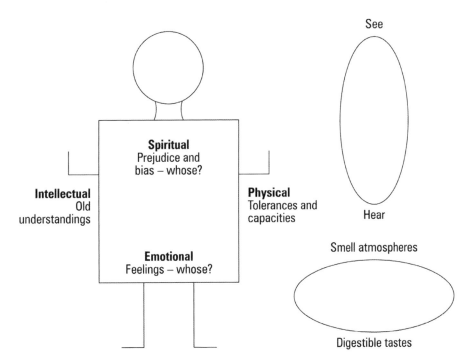

We can fill this period of waiting by helping and encouraging those who are also documenting things; if we cannot locate our own star then we can join with someone who has street credibility and help them, working diligently and learning through action as they have already done what we are learning to do. Our right is earned through selfless input. As we research and document we learn to create a view of where we are, even if we only know where we are by knowing where we are not.

Revising Traditions

At this point we will have ideas about what might or might not work but we know that regardless of the chance of failure we need to do it, or we will regret it forever. It is possible that we lack the knowledge of why we need to do it, instead all we may know is that every way we turn invites opposition, and this can cause us to not care if we realise the idea or not but we do also know that we are starting to awaken a whole new level of awareness. During this awakening we become aware of a new level of prosperity that is so rich in Spirit its material counterpart seems completely insignificant. However, we must still respect the fact that the material is necessary in order for us to achieve anything; therefore we meet in the centre point between Heaven and Earth as we bring the Spirit's richness to Earth, taking what we need from what we want on Earth and combining it with the Spirit. This process pushes us to examine our inner need and experience of union, disappointment and disillusionment regarding partnerships.

As we move on and meet the inner reality, feelings such as ignorance, confusion and the reasons behind our confusion make themselves known and we are then forced to accept that the imperfections in others are not any worse than they are in us. As time passes we learn to trust to the point that we neither divide nor separate the Spirit from life within unfamiliar cultures. We also learn that everything is as it should be and we can accept the vision with the realisation that what we are working towards is freeing everyone, the inner and outer. This may feel uncomfortable but we must recognise this is mainly because it is unfamiliar. We may wonder why we are experiencing difficulty physically, and the answer is because we do not yet know how to apply spiritual answers in life. It is unfair and exclusive to impose our vision on those who cannot get in touch with the answers so easily; we instead need to start where the need lies. In order to do this we need to learn our trade, be tolerant and compassionate as well as inclusive and harmless.

A Channel For Peace

As we connect to our passion we undergo processes and initiations that work out whether we will use, abuse, alienate or monopolise others, so a rigorous test takes place.
At this point it is important to go over your own strengths and weaknesses intellectually, physically, emotionally and spiritually so the weaknesses can be addressed and strengthened.

The first set of questions regards spiritual strengths and weaknesses.
1) Do you pray for the courage to hold the original vision without bastardising its standard in spite of opposition or do you assume it is an automatic function?

2) Do you meditate to see, listen and feel good or to protect yourself and avoid trouble if you can?

3) Do you obey guidance absolutely even if that guidance is challenged by life and you feel it is crucifying you?

4) Do you contemplate the wisdom of administering or organising resources fairly for all, being as selfless as you can?

The second set of questions is on intellectual strengths and weaknesses.

1) Do you research and compare many disciplines, opening all options then waiting for all to close off except the one that will be the next step?

2) Do you document your own impressions along the way so you have a point of reference?

3) Are you able to talk about your own heritage with spiritual directors, teachers, peers and strangers without making excuses or justifying who you are and what you do?

4) Can you present what you have to offer to a receptive market or do you not want to be bothered?

The third set of questions is about emotional strengths and weaknesses.

1) Can you act out who you are and what you represent through interactive dramas in life as you build on your successes without giving energy to failures?

2) Are you attached to knowing what is a failure and what is a success, or do you know that the success of today is the failure of tomorrow and vice versa?

3) Can you create an art form to inspire yourself and be of inspiration to others as well as doing the work to back the project up?

4) Can you dance on the moving carpet of life without losing your breath?

5) Can you publicise who you are now rather than whom you once were?

The fourth and final set of questions regards physical strengths and weaknesses.

1) Can you live and administer the same rules and regulations for all, or do you change them to suit yourself?

2) Can you organise resources to the best of your ability to be of benefit to all?

3) Can you assess capacities in yourself and others to allow for resistance to be worked through?

4) Can you tolerate the negotiations and the balancing out of perfection and imperfection with a good attitude for as long as it takes, which can be up to twelve years?

In Between Worlds

For us to open the door to prosperity we must have patience for the project to come into being, for ourselves and all others wishing to be involved. As we find the direction we should be heading in we will have to overcome the challenges put forth by the greedy, ambitious and those who want to run the show, and we must then pass within ourselves to create a flow that we have the ability to live by. It is possible that our judgement will differ tremendously from the judgement of those guiding us, largely because we have a tendency to think we are much better than we actually are – we all want the end goal but rarely do we want to acknowledge that we are not up to scratch yet. Nonetheless, in this period of time we will develop wisdom as we see the difficulties we have already encountered, and as we begin to lose inspiration and craving for adventure we establish how good and capable we are and see where we went wrong in the past, at which point we cleanse.

The eight paths between the worlds

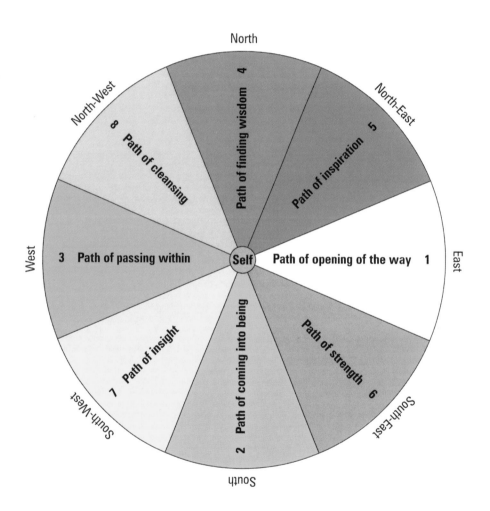

The eightfold way in the diagram above leads to the centre point, or the ninth point; as we review in hindsight past emotions we understand what we romanticised in foresight, and this allows the outer experience to unite with the inner desire and open the path for our next step. Our physical body must align with the next step as the circulatory system develops the ability to cleanse and maintain its actions to allow us to pursue newly available avenues. This also gives the required time for toxins to be released.

The nervous system will at this point respond to the circulatory system's cleansing and this may make us feel anxious, perhaps wondering if we have acted well enough or been empathetic enough.

The parasympathetic nervous system will need an instinct overhaul, at which point we will need to ask if we are habitually gracious and willing, if we have an acceptable attitude and if we take things for granted or not. If we have had a negative attitude then it will take some time for this to be phased out, during which time we may feel either hyperactive or tired.

The abstract meets the actual

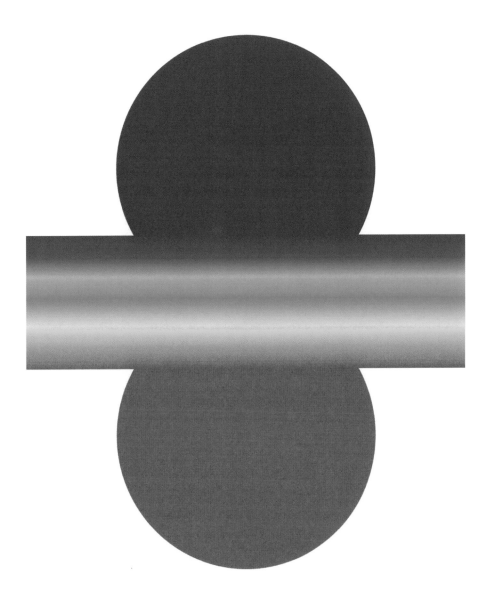

The Future

At this point in the journey we need to look at what we know it is we do not want. Once this is complete we will be able to start the process of deciding what we do want. The future itself is something of an umbrella term, reliant not just on us but the input of others as well. What is needed is to:

1) Review and revise your intention.
2) Create objectives.
3) As best you can, act as if you already have all you need to achieve your objectives.
4) With whatever you decide to do, follow through with delivery of the goods.
5) Identify what the next step is however simple it may appear to be.
6) Make a list of everything you can think of and put them in order of priority.

The eternal cycle

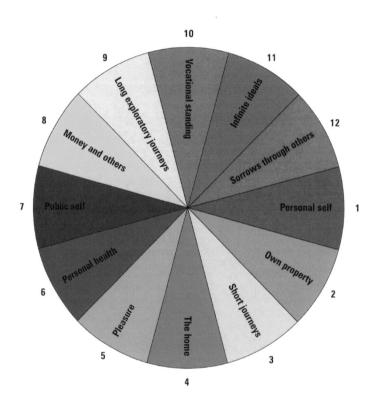

By applying the guidelines listed above we attract abundance, because abundance follows the desire to serve – which we have. Conversely, money has its own rules of being; it is a tool and a dream to many, but if we have it and lack the knowledge of how to use it then it becomes a burden. As money is energy it cannot be owned, and as such it cannot be given away. Due to the fact it is energy it must be allowed to flow, but if we are not able to allow the flow then this is indicative of past disappointments. Similarly, as money cannot be given it cannot really be received, for a monetary gift moves to where it is needed; however, if we are able to clear our view we can have anything necessary to serve the Spirit.

There exist worlds that function perfectly without money. However they work by facilitating emotionally not physically, such as through encouragement and support, or whatever else is required for someone to become more flexible.

In order to analyse our relationship to prosperity we can break things into twelve arenas in life's eternal cycle, which is necessary because the whole is simply too large to contemplate properly. This sequence differs for each person so first we just need to understand the idea. Look at the previous diagram above then read each of the following twelve sections; which section do you feel you are currently at? In each section assess the prosperity levels you are experiencing now and note what changes or improvements you would like to occur.

1) Personal self. How do you see yourself? Now ask selected others what effect you have on them. Is it similar to how you see yourself? In what areas have you gained self-confidence from this interaction?

2) Own property. This focuses on resources (material, intellectual, spiritual and emotional) and the way in which they can be used to shape and consolidate your position. It indicates the avenues through which money will be gained or lost by referring to the money resulting from your labours.

3) Short journeys, routine. This focuses on your relationship with your immediate environment and all the processes by which you determine this. This includes communication, short distance travelling, development of the concrete mind, emotional health conditions and the relationships you have with others.

4) The home. This governs the home and its condition, matters of security and your relationship to your role models. It places a focus on your power to assimilate and your ability to draw on past experiences. It includes a consideration of conditions as we see them in later life, beginnings and endings, issues surrounding the womb and the tomb and the relationship between your animating force and your body.

5) Limited pleasures. This focuses on creation, your abilities of self-expression and exploring your creative talents. This is traditionally the section of pleasure, speculation, love affairs, gambling and children, but it also includes your ability to experience pleasure, enjoy holidays and engage in enterprise.

6) Personal health. This refers to your working conditions and your service to others, including your relationships with co-workers and factors governing your personal health. There is also a focus on your ability to organise and administer your resources, how your health is affected by your efforts to achieve in work and self-improvement and also overcoming your own ideas of perfection in order to serve collective needs.

7) Public self. This refers to partnerships as well as unions with others. This section also includes artistic and social activities and the transitions of consciousness from the subjective (sections 1-6) to the objective realms (sections 7-12).

8) Money associated with others. This investigates the life force and the mystical – death of the old, occult investigation as to making a group dynamic fit, inheritance, sex, financial affairs and so on. This section reveals your ability to share your possessions, transmute your resources and experience a rebirth.

9) Long exploratory journeys. This examines the higher mind, justice, philosophy, science and religion, carried out through higher education, communication and travel. This section includes dreams and spiritual development.

10) Vocational standing. This relates to your standing before the world, such as your social position and career, including your public role in addition to your life's direction.

11) Infinite ideals. This section focuses on friendship, group activities, participation in society and long-term objectives, notably within the society you reside, as well as feeling contented spiritually.

12) Sorrows through others. This looks at the end results and positive and negative accumulated resources. It also includes hidden influences or restraints, self-imposed circumstances and those outside of your control, spiritual life, sorrows, betrayals, limitations and losses.

Balancing the subjective and objective occurs through:

Centering

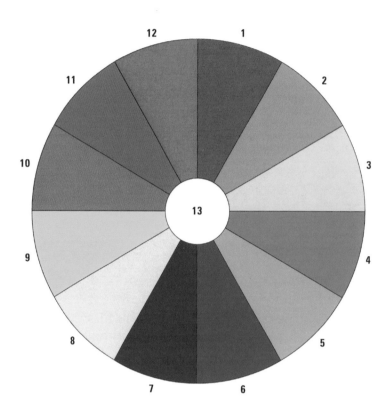

1) Personal self and
7) Public self.
2) Own property and
8) Money associated with others.
3) Short journeys, routine and
9) Long exploratory journeys.
4) Home and
10) Vocational standing.
5) Limited pleasures and
11) Infinite ideals.
6) Personal health and
12) Sorrow through others.
13)

As all of these issues collaborate the opposites are transcended, leaving peace in the thirteenth point, known as the centre of our being. If we try to access the centre of our being, the 13th position prior to experiencing each of the 12 sections thoroughly, we will be spewed out to re-experience those we have missed. Only with experience may we remain at the centre and access any mix of the twelve options required within the moment.

PART 10:
LIVING SPIRITUALITY

Chapter 31: Self-Awareness

Vision

Vision

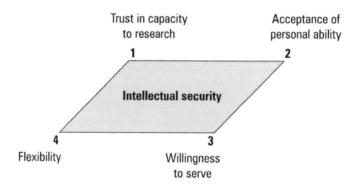

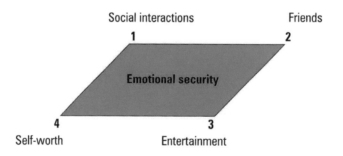

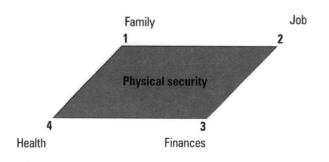

Having a vision is an essential part of life, for without one all will perish. Any individual, group or nation requires a vision otherwise they will have nothing to strive for, and with nothing to work for there is nothing to do but die. We live in eternity, not short-term temporal substance, and so it is our duty to make an attempt to operate on two levels: one of which is within the ideal situation and the other the mechanical cleansing of the past. Our other goal is to come to terms with authority issues and any negativity we have about being told what to do, which is linked to how we feel by not being in total control of our own life.

It is one thing when we have control issues over a benign and benevolent spiritual impulse controlling our lives but another thing entirely when the consequences to others are disregarded as a result of greed. If we have indulged in such behaviour ourselves then we may believe in lack rather than plenty, which can encourage us to take what we can when it is available. Another possibility is that we might be feeling guilty for not helping others as much as we think we should have, and as a result we are suffering the same that was bestowed on them. At this stage we may be feeling too frightened and/or inadequate to cope and this may lead us to sabotage the efforts of others, or we may experience them trying to sabotage our own efforts to make things better for themselves. If we have been manipulated then we may now be self-obsessed, or we might have tried to dump on others because we were too lazy or inert to make any effort. We ourselves may have a hidden agenda or someone else with one may be preying on us, and we may be unwitting to the fact that their actions affect us, and as a result we might have grief or pain that we need to confront.

To try to help ourselves we must clearly define our wishes and hope that they will come to fruition and our behaviour honoured. Of course, simply speaking something is no guarantee that we will suddenly receive support, but if we surge ahead regardless then all will be well as time moves on.

Truth

Can truth be seen as relative rather than absolute? Considering we only ever see a fraction we really have no right to judge, condemn or make decisions for other people, never mind the universe which is completely beyond our current level of understanding. If we do not know or relate to a situation someone is in, who are we to judge on their actions? Nonetheless, what we can do is make the decision for ourselves to release negative expectations. We may have previously had reason to have these negative expectations because things have not been as we would have wanted them, but that is only something to burden us throughout life if we choose it to be. If, on the other hand, we can release the feelings of things being either good or bad or just or unjust we will be able to face the current situation's truth.

If we are the ambitious type then we might have bulldozed other people in an attempt to achieve our goals, and this is unacceptable because we are trying to create a universal care system in which everyone is considered and catered to. We may have lived vicariously through people who were simply trying to survive, and in doing so lacked empathy and compassion towards their difficulties because we were too focused on ours. We might have experienced cruelty and either obeyed or turned a blind eye in a bid to avoid confrontation, or we might have been mocked and downtrodden, causing us to withdraw and become insular. Perhaps we were open and honest and as a result were rejected, which caused us to be wary, always on the lookout for rejection or betrayal. We feel like puppets being manipulated because of our awareness that many things are beyond our understanding and control.

If our self-awareness increases then both our truth and circumstances will change accordingly. If we have had tough times with our peers then we may think we will have similar experiences with the Heavens, and we may attempt to ignore inner guidance. This makes it impossible to move forward faithfully and we will feel punished and unloved or that we are being sacrificed to the benefit of another. As a result we become compulsive, making ourselves indispensable to the point of exhaustion.

Answer the following questions on adaptability:

1) Can you trust others to tell the truth as they know it?
2) Can you trust yourself to tell your truth?
3) Can you accept that no one knows the full story?
4) Can you release all to be judged by themselves and their God?
5) Do you know that having done your best all will be well?

Acceptance

If we find the ability to release the internal war and replace it with acceptance, we will find ourselves to be new people. All too often we hear people say "if my parents had been different" or "if my partner was more compassionate" and so on. These are excuses to pass off our shortcomings or to justify missing our targets; we need to accept that things are the way they are. Our parents show us how something should or should not be done, our siblings offer us new perspectives and we choose our own partners and they can either support us or highlight our areas that need improvement. The world itself is fine, it is the inhabitants that have mis-administered or disorganised things, especially when in a bid for power or money, and so we turn to the Grace of God. It is always easier to criticise or condemn but that does nothing but set the process in motion all over again, so it is a better option to offer a better choice within our expertise and encourage and trust others to do the same.

We should consider the problem and acknowledge that even though we may lack the comprehension of something, our soul understands it just fine, as do the Spiritual beings who care for us. When we are in a time of need we can ask them for advice and give them permission to show us. We must trust, accept and surrender the past and future, working with the next stage in the present moment.

Answer the following questions on goodwill.

1) Do you think you add to problems when you identify them?
2) Do you think you could subtract from the problem, and if so, how?
3) Do you choose not to care because it is just too hard?
4) Can you just let go and give your head a rest?
5) Is your heart hurting so much that you think you are damaging yourself?
6) Do you think you are doing harm to others?

Affinity

In order to develop affinity we need to overcome separation in all forms and become one with every form of life. It is easy to judge and criticise something that we do not understand rather than get involved in something that may prove too difficult, and that is divisive in itself. Or we might just condemn and blame instead of forgive, but whatever we do we will be challenged by these states. As a way of escaping our responsibilities we may pass them onto someone else, which is a type of brainwashing and it damages those around us.

On the other hand, our heart has feelings and is natural if we permit it. Feelings of kindness and caring are natural, as are feelings of sadness and discontent. Ugly feelings may belong to us or those who have influenced us, and we might withdraw as we seek nurturing.

Nourishment will be sought from our reality and we will expect everyone to contribute to our well-being, indeed we might even try to freeload from someone else or use them to serve our own purpose. It is not uncommon to steal ideas, thoughts or even physical interactions, and we are all guilty of playing games between the sexes, races and cultures and we are selectively generous instead of fair.

The challenge we face is moving forward without harming anyone else, the purpose being that if we no longer harbour hostility or aggression then we will not attract any from others, rather we can walk safely into any arena and be welcomed rather than attacked. This will be a refreshing state for us: people will be attracted to us even if we appear to have nothing in common with them, and this can confuse them; animals will accept us even if we do not give them much attention; children will welcome us; trees and plants will flower in order to please us; and minerals will support us and enjoy our passing as we wish them well.

By the same token, sad people will find refuge in our space, just as they will if they are angry, frightened or frustrated, and important people will acknowledge that we are not out to disempower them.

Answer the following questions on acceptability:

1) Who do you seek out when you are unhappy or in trouble?
2) Where do you turn when things are going wrong for you?
3) Do you trust yourself and your inner guidance?
4) Do you get comfort in the service of others?
5) Are you willing to be with those who call you in both good and bad times?
6) Do others seek you out in good and bad times?

Love

Love is something that we can feel and know to be true but we can never understand; the reason for this is that in our physical, emotional and intellectual world 'love' is another word for 'possession'. The lesson for us to learn is to not scorn or hate but to love unselfishly and freely, for love is inclusive of everybody. If the love around us is not abundant then we may doubt or distrust the process.

As most people are aware, there are different types of love, such as the love a parent has towards its child, the love a child has for its parent, the way a husband loves a wife and vice versa, and even the way we love our home, work or environment. The different types of love have been known for centuries, with the Ancient Greeks noting three categories: *Eros* (commonly known as 'erotic love'), *Philos* (the love between two friends) and *Agape* (unconditional love).

If we make no effort to love then we may cause others to feel attacked, which could lead to them trying to shun responsibility. Their pain is contagious, the pressure builds and everyone will have a sense of being misunderstood. If we have ever been judged and felt dishonoured or blamed and not forgiven, criticised or rejected then the pressure from each will be added to the problem of loving and we will have to make tough decisions through pain in our head and heart.

Feelings of confusion are natural and normal, and so are negotiations to establish a common standard, and when all is said and done there is no use in blaming others because in truth we are all at fault in some way. However, we can make the decision to care or not; we have the choice to abuse others and withhold nurture so others can hurt as much as we do; we can choose to use those around us for our own gain or serve them because we want to, regardless of how nice they are to us. It is our choice to get a free ride from someone else or contribute to help others.

If we refuse to offer help, guidance, support and love then we do so as a defensive mechanism. The question is, "What are we defending ourselves against?" Perhaps we do not want to continue the journey of change because others are unable to conform to our new standards, or maybe it is out of fear that we will be challenged too much or get hurt. This must be overcome, though, for if we ignore the pain we feel in our head and heart we are not truly living but only surviving. To live we must experience joy, love and mutual care.

Answer the following questions on courage in care:

1) Did you bastardise others in your need to be loved?
2) Did you use others in the process?
3) When true colours were presented did you judge, blame, criticise and condemn or did you state your view clearly and offer an updated deal that could be honoured and accepted by everybody?
4) Did you take responsibility for what you had created as best you could and limit the damage accordingly?
5) Did you maintain a quiet mind and have the heart to complete the job?
6) Do others feel safe enough around you to speak their truth?
7) Have you proved your trustworthiness to a satisfactory standard?

Freedom

The idea of being free can cause trepidation because it means we will be independent, and whether we stand on our feet or fall on our knees will depend entirely on us and our decision, rather than having our parents, culture or friends to blame. In our world of three dimensions (physical, intellectual and emotional) we are all but imprisoned under politics, commerce, religion, social and economic systems. As such, it is a delicate balance to stand alone while embracing all.

We may wonder how we are able to lead without knowing how to follow, but we have all followed and encountered people who dictate and control, murdering the free as they imprison others to enforce their own regimes and beliefs. A master of leadership will manage and while they may appear to be harsh occasionally they will always include themselves in their regime and as a result earn respect and loyalty.

Throughout life we may meet people who torture or enslave others through fear tactics, and in such cases self-responsibility and free choice are impossible.

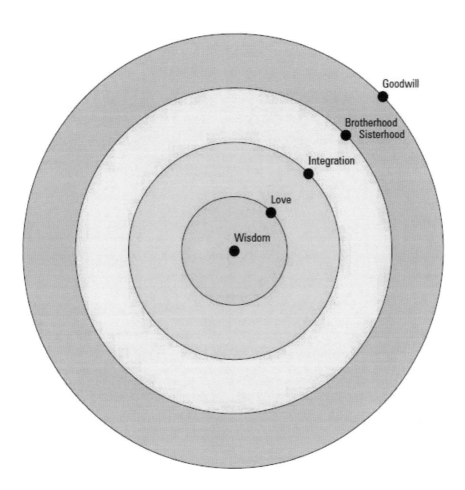

To become a master server we need to transcend the need for war, which ultimately comes to one side having to be right and the other being wrong by default – if everyone serves the same side there is no enemy and thus no need nor chance for war. This is not to suggest there will never be disagreement, but if we love and honour everyone and consider all views equally resolution can be found quickly and peacefully.

We may want to punish those who hurt us so we can return to everything being nice; the problem here is who decides what 'nice' actually is? Nice and not nice are intertwined and everyone needs the freedom to decide for themselves; when someone tries to fix something on behalf of another they are disregarding others by tacitly stating that their own opinions and standards are correct over those of others.

Under these circumstances every person will be disappointed that what seemed kind and friendly actually has no depth, and the dynamic will be changed by recognising that they have been manipulated by circumstances that suit someone else. These times require us to be aloof as a means of protection, so we are able to reappoint a more equal balance. If we offer a favour to someone it must be done graciously, because we want to do it out of our own goodness rather than to get something back.

Distrust is inevitable if freedom and cooperation are not gifted willingly without harbouring any malicious intent. It is important that we work in small groups where every member can give depending on their capacity and be honoured for their talent and input. When we are able to serve willingly we will be flexible enough to collaborate with everyone, and be able to care and share to the best of our abilities.

Answer the following questions on capacity:

1) Do you hold true to your belief regardless of others judging you?
2) Do you sell out because you could not stand the heat of collective challenge?
3) Are you able to put all to work within their own skill areas and wait to see if they will make use of the opportunities presented without interference?
4) Do you dispense justice or just wait in the space?
5) Do you feel impotent and frustrated and so become unjust or hostile? Or are you able to keep on remaining true to the original vision that all should be free?
6) Are you able to withstand being mocked, scorned, ignored, gossiped about, criticised and treated as if you were garbage?

Inspiration

Being in tune with Divine Guidance means that we need to cooperate and collaborate with "thy" will rather than "my" will, and doing so necessitates courage and determination no matter what the outcome. To represent a greater reality than we are used to requires a demonstration that inspires faith and belief, and inspiration is key: it is the antidote to sickness, disappointment and lack of faith. If we keep the company of uninspired people then it is a tough task just to keep sight of the calmness and serenity and shining countenance, all of which are omnipresent when we are under Divine direction.

The Management Upstairs would never work to divide a community and promote inequality, because that is the total opposite of the unity that we are striving for and the Management Upstairs is guiding us towards.

It is a gift when someone decides to care for us, and caring for ourselves is honouring the Spirit for the gift of life, which is something we must value and be grateful for without feeling envious of anyone else. The subtler realms will refrain from overriding our needs if doing so is avoidable, even when we feel we are being put out. If we do not want to be inspired then we may try to block off external input that we cannot control; instead, however, we must be dignified, courteous and caring, sharing the load to the best of our abilities. If we take care of the garden of life then our Spirit will become indomitable. We all provide all others points of reference as we move forward to becoming free, through choice rather than need, and these reference points will facilitate others on their own journey. As part of this, we meditate and communicate until everybody is free.

Answer the following questions on stamina:

1) Did you see the project entrusted to you through to a logical conclusion where you could take it no further?

2) Did you try to be popular or gain publicity by fighting, running away or running riot, thereby selling another out?

3) Do you give people the time they need to accept what comes, or do you barge in and assume you are correct in your assumptions?

4) Do you patronise, belittle, appear arrogant, superior or dismissive?

 Electric force from invisible to mobilise you.

 Magnetic attraction gathers together requisite people.

Union of both Provides current necessary for activation

 Circular magnet links to our work

 A linking of circular magnets form a grid – twelve grids link to an Earth vortex so as to magnify varying aspects which are reviewed periodically to access suitability, as adjustments that are required, are made.

Vertical connection – vortex to vortex

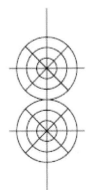

Spirit •————————• 4th dimensional vortex

Transformer •————————• 3rd dimensional vortex

Both must be in place to anchor a project to the Earth satisfactorily.

Selflessness

Selflessness is essentially resisting our survival instincts. By having no fear and being unattached to results we will have achieved total denial of the self-ego, self-life and self-mind, and this is the only way in which we can assume the spiritual mantle of the spiritual self. It is impossible to assume the spiritual mantle unless we are entirely selfless.

In order to correctly handle power we must release what we consider justice and injustice. If we are insecure to the point that we sacrifice ourselves or someone else then we will harm everyone in our vicinity. We have all been hurt and experienced fear but there is no need to hold onto that or burden others with the pain we have felt. Everyone has their turn with the good, bad and the ugly, and some have higher thresholds than others physically, emotionally and intellectually, but no one handles more than they are capable of even if they believe otherwise. The person constantly stating their feelings of woe and suffering is obsessive and compulsive in their demand for sympathy and attention, but they lack the realisation that these demands are self-fulfilling. When a person is selfish and demands all the attention they are not inclusive and they need to learn how to be fair to all. At some point we will get more attention and less at other times, so it balances out.

Self-pity gives way to the willingness to serve, and if we have been selfish then selflessness must be learnt before we can move forward.

Answer the following questions on caring:

1) Do you ask the correct questions and make the right comments so that people are gently led to make their own choices?
2) Do you demand and/or bully?
3) Do you lash out when your pride is hurt or your ambition thwarted?
4) If opportunities are slow in presenting do you feel lazy, greedy or try to get someone else to do your part of the job for you?
5) Do you consider yourself and others to be good enough?
6) Do you consider yourself and others have done well enough?

Non-attachment

Non-attachment means to live free of the demands and requirements of humans and instead to serve only one power: the Spirit. We can try to obtain non-attachment to physical life and its burdens initially through meditation, praying and/or fasting, and the benefit of obtaining it is that we can create sacred and holy space that will affect everybody who walks into it. In essence, it allows us to gift the world with radiance.

Certain places in the world, like Bahrain, Jerusalem, London and Lourdes, are energy vortexes, or places that produce a sound similar to an impulse bouncing off an earth mirror. These vortexes are thought-based and people will be attracted to them at different times, but regardless of when it happens it is the sound that attracts them. A good analogy for the vortex is the centre of a spider's web, where there are many threads coming off the centre that create a warp. In the vortexes these warps are known as Ley-lines, and they are always being updated and renewed.

There is no need to seek something out we already have; for example if our cupboards are full of food we do not need to purchase more, instead we must look for something else. A mouth can speak but not listen and an ear can listen but not speak, therefore to action something properly requires both. This is the same as how the Spirit guides us and how we care for others on Earth. We essentially become transformers for others and we can be 'plugged into' any vortex to enable us to be reached at any point and any time.

When we are connected to both the Heaven and Earth we might encounter a tingling sensation, which can occur internally as physically stored memories begin to be cleared away. This can cause us some confusion – and if necessary visit a doctor, but if you are informed you are in good health then you can be content in the knowledge that your body is simply doing some spring-cleaning.

Wisdom

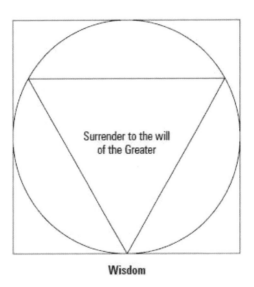

Letting go of control

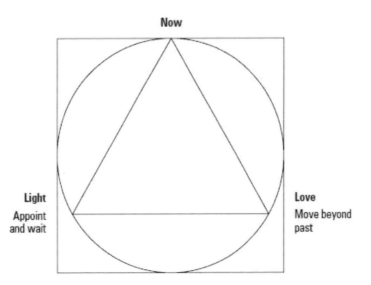

While wisdom can mean different things to different people, in actuality it means to embrace the states mentioned above in this chapter. It is to utilise silent influences and spiritual power, to apply it to life and be so tuned in that life is rich for ourselves and all those around us. It is being able to move without being affected by negativity, instead focusing on the joy. Wisdom is refraining from wondering what the point of something is, but instead progressing steadily and continually improving.

True happiness requires union with the head and heart, which requires us to be wise and not apathetic. Inertia must move over to make way for effort and we must release personal ambition, instead being inclusive of all. Jealousy and ego must be released and group equality must be strived for, regardless of our position in the group, and we must never resent inconvenience. People can and will cause us difficulties throughout life and we must learn to tolerate them and consider them there in order to make us stronger.

We should choose trust and be courageous enough to release the past instead of repeating it again and again. Our task now is to surrender everything to the Greater, and having done this we must wait patiently and lovingly for the past to be replaced with the next Chapter within our book of life.

As we have now dealt with the issue of the belief arena inside the head, we need to focus on the heart, where misconceptions negatively impact the work of the invisible, which still remains outside of our capacity to understand. We have stated that we are willing to help but still do not know what this means entirely, however it does reside inside our soul remit and we are reminded of this. The question now is what we have to remove from our heart so we can be of pure heart; possibly we have permitted others' pain to enter our space, and while this may have seemed appropriate at the time it is no longer so, and so we need to block re-entry to prevent disempowering them from being able to try to do it themselves. We might also have hated systems that we did not trust or embrace, but now our integrity is larger than it was we need to include those whose integrity has not increased yet.

We make an attempt to fuse the inner and outer and the heart and head in the same way as inhaling and exhaling are fused. As the heart and head fuse their rhythm will adjust, which may cause us some discomfort, at first in our head or emotionally and then our skin. This may require a visit to a doctor so we can minimise the discomfort and maximise support. We will be offering a shoulder to those in distress and we will quickly learn when to retain a smile in spite of being ridiculed or criticised by others, just as we will learn to be patient when we are informed we have not performed to the required standard. If our soul tells us to do so, we will wish everyone well and simply walk away.

Of course, it is helpful to take the path that has least resistance as we provide others with the time and space to learn what they want or need to learn without our interference. At the same time, though, we will be flexible to the point that we can adjust our plans at any given moment as we relay the updated requirements with honesty and without withholding any unpleasant aspects.

Complete the following self-reflection on update:

1) Redefine your personal expectations and complete a reality check.
2) Revise your ideal.
3) Review your potential in light of your skills and experience.
4) Renegotiate truthfully in cooperation with those interested.
5) Allow illusions to disperse as you collaborate with possibilities.

6) Honour disillusionment as it supports and encourages new probabilities.

7) Be grateful for the state of grace that allows the core centre to be cleansed and ready.

Before we are able to get into the movement our central core must purify as it balances with the pressures that are held inside the brain. The brain has its own misconceptions, though, and it might resist updating these; in order to expand beyond our previous limitations a contraction is required to push us into a new space, but this takes time and effort and we must be prepared for that.

Chapter 32: Spirituality

Back to Beginnings – Overcoming the Shock

Key to colour codes

	Purple	=	Discipline and willingness
	Violet	=	Cleansing and disinfecting
	Indigo	=	Capacity to hold vision; time management
	Blue	=	Expression; revision; review; update of truth
	Green	=	Rhythm; expanding some boundaries; working within others
	Yellow	=	Self-worth; self-respect; trust in adequacy to cope
	Orange	=	Balance of independence and interdependence
	Red	=	Creation and recreation from raw materials available
	Brown	=	Right use of entrusted power; stamina, persistence and endurance to steward and guard a project and to see it through to its logical conclusion

The innocence of childhood is not quite what it is cracked up to be, because we are never more vulnerable than we were as babies. We are unable to do anything for ourselves and rely on someone else for every single one of our needs, in addition to being in a state of recovery from the act of being born, which in itself causes confusion and disorientation. Far from childhood being the relaxing and comfortable state it is often lauded as, then, it is an extremely stressful time when we require round-the-clock care and attention.

When we develop and near adulthood most people make the decision to become more self-sufficient, and so we get jobs, learn to drive, cook our meals and find a home of our own. Too often, however, we forget or suspend the knowledge that without being dependent on others in the early stages of life we would not have made it to adulthood, and so no one can cast aside the goodwill we received from others, even if it was only in our infancy. This goes to show that as much as we may like to think otherwise, no one is an island, instead we are all inter-dependent, and this is true at all levels of life. We are dependent on others to provide our food, from the farmers to the factory workers and shopkeepers who sell it; we are dependent on employers or clients to pay us so we can keep our house, car and family; we rely on the community to serve our socialisation needs; and we depend on doctors and nurses to keep us well. The fact that we are dependent on so many reminds us that there is a greater force at work, and as soon as we acknowledge that fact we will begin to see things in a new light.

As our inner being matures as we age we encounter times when we realise that some of what we have from the past is no longer relevant and needs to be let go. This may be particularly true when we think back to our childhood, because in that time we not only receive the goodwill and nurturing of our parents but also their thoughts, opinions and negative vibrations, and these are often carried through to adulthood. As we develop independently, though, we can come to realise that some of their thoughts and ideas are not true, or at least not true to us, and so we try to shed them as our own ideas and thoughts take shape. This also allows us to turn resentment and frustration towards our parents into sympathy and understanding; the resentment and frustration coming from that which we received from them and us then blaming our problems or failures on that. However, as we move forward we can acknowledge that to blame is to remain in the past and we are responsible for ourselves, so as we release their teachings that we disagree with we also release those negative emotions.

There is no shortage of people who claim the best thing to do is put your childhood behind you – forget about it and move on. Instead, it is better to return to it: this does not mean act childishly, but be as open and trusting as possible, without being too vulnerable, and if we ever produce offspring then it is beneficial to meet them at the point that we once were and they are now.

Some people think communication really starts when we learn to talk, but in actual fact we respond to shapes and colours long before our speech develops. To prove this, simply observe a small child playing, or ask a visually-impaired person to identify the colour of clothing by touch and they will. Thus, it is beyond doubt that colour symbolises significant conversions that warrant investigation, as was done earlier in the book.

Expansion: Up the Spiral Staircase

It is an unfortunate fact that expansion and education are not always synonymous with the school authorities' thoughts. Many find that school serves as more of a test of endurance than training self-awareness or growing as people, and recollecting the experience can conjure images of dictatorship as we were subjugated to study subjects that did not interest us and learn theories that we could see having no use to our lives.

Release of misunderstanding

Stages of development in the acquisition of language

Average age	Language milestones	Motor milestones
6 months	Cooing, changes to distinct babbling by introduction of consonants	Sits using hands for support; unilateral reaching
1 year	Beginning of language understanding; one word utterances	Stands; walks when held by one hand
12 - 18 months	Words used singularly; repertory of 30-50 words (simple nouns, adjectives, and action words), which cannot as yet be joined in phrases but are used one at a time; does not use functors (the, and, can, be) necessary for syntax, but makes good progress in understanding	Grasping and realising fully developed; walking; creeps downstairs backwards
18 - 24 months	Two-word (telegraphic) phrases are ordered according to syntactic rules; vocabulary of 50 to several hundred words; understands propositional rules	Runs (and falls); walks stairs with one foot forward
2 - 5 years	New words every day; three or more words in many combinations; functors begin to appear; many grammatical errors and idiosyncratic expressions; good understanding of language	Jumps with both feet; builds tower of six cubes
3 years	Full sentences; few errors; vocabulary of around 1,000 words	Tiptoes; walks stairs with alternating feet
4 years	Close to adult speech competence	Jumps over rope; hops on one foot; walks on a line

Such forcefulness goes against the natural laws. Of course, all children need stimulation and encouragement and they may not always want to follow the guidelines that will be beneficial to them, but at the same time they need to be allowed to follow their own natural desires and gut feelings. In adulthood we have more freedom with our choices, partly because we do not have the same mandatory rigours as school or parental choices thrust upon us and partly because we simply realise that we can make our own choices. This can lead to new hobbies, talents, interests and activities. As a result of this we no longer feel the need to fight authorities and the limitations imposed upon us from them; instead we can participate and work with the efforts others have made. Thoughts, ideas and events change because life itself changes with each passing moment; this is not cause for concern or sorrow, though; instead we can look forward to what may come next even if we do not know what it will be.

We gain control, rather than lose it, when we persevere with self-awareness. While many people call this 'fatalistic', this approach to life permits us to act calmly and have freedom, letting us manage life without feeling weighed down with compromises, frustrations and disappointments. We acknowledge that everyone is simply one small part of a bigger pattern, something which is demonstrated at every single level of nature and evolution. We continue our ascent up the spiral staircase as time progresses, and even if we pass familiar space we must remember we are still moving and not mistakenly think we are stagnant or going backwards.

It is useful at this point to find others with whom you can share experiences, because once we experience something so unique and deep many people avidly try to further their explorations. As a result of this we may find ourselves now drawn to people and places that we previously had no interest in. Furthermore, now that we are more open-minded than we were before we find ourselves receiving more encouragement and direction, quite often from sources we would least expect it – as though we are being invisibly guided. Nonetheless, we must surge forward and avoid the temptation to be complacent, and finding others in the same boat as ourselves means we can both help and be helped.

Most people will consider this the greatest transition period yet to be had, and as can be expected it is neither smooth nor easy. In fact we may wonder if we are even in control of ourselves, because it can feel as though someone, or something, is guiding us.

Intuition

By training ourselves in self-awareness we will automatically become more sensitive to vibrations. To experience this is to hear with our mind and see with our heart, overriding the default ears and eyes respectively. We will have heightened awareness of what our senses tell our brain and we will be unable to ignore the warnings our body sends. It is possible that we will pick up on the vibrations in the atmosphere also, for instance we may enter a room and feel sad for no reason, or similarly we may feel elated upon entering.

However, as we become more sensitive we also become more vulnerable, because we realise we are not individual but part of the bigger picture and this puts us at risk from other people, places and stresses that surround us. So it is key that we learn when it is healthy to not plough on regardless but withdraw temporarily to filter our experiences. This is not being cowardly or being overprotective, instead it is just applying common sense to our survival. As we recognise this we may withdraw from familiar habits and patterns, which may alarm those close to us as they witness us shying away from things that we previously thoroughly enjoyed or even pursued. This is nothing but a perfect opportunity for us to practice compassion, because while these people may not understand us we can still extend love and understanding to them.

It is important that we become comfortable with our expansion and its process. We will notice that we constantly investigate and compare our thoughts of today with those of yesterday, all as part of the refining process. This should be considered an evolution rather than a change, and what we will observe is that life can be a continuous meditation where we notice what we used to just overlook. This extends our experience of life to one filled with richness.

During this time of transformation, and for the rest of our life, it is recommended to sit quietly to review past experiences and experiments and also to determine how we can offer our services to others. This may require us withdrawing from those we want to help for a while as we sort ourselves out and regain some comfort and certainty.

Throughout this period the invisible will start to become visible and we will begin to hear the updated vibration. We will need to make a space that is safe to explore in and we need time to discuss, in as simple terms as possible, until we stop wondering and just *know*. Our senses and mind will receive the same messages, meaning union has been achieved. This will mean we may feel fatigued and we will need to rest in order to regenerate to support the new.

Spiritual Responsibility

If we are so developed that we can see with clarity then we must also be responsible for what we see. This may, however, require a compromise between our ideal and our reaction to the reality of what is taking place, but there is no reason why the compromise cannot serve both sides.

Many at this stage will actively want to help others in whatever way is possible, and the good thing is this does not mean we have to choose a hospitable profession to do so. Each day of our lives presents an opportunity that allows us to demonstrate love and compassion to others, and when we are aware of our own motives and downfalls we find ourselves being more compassionate to those who do not have that same awareness. The lesson we must never lose sight of is our journey of growth is not strictly an individual one, but for the benefit of everyone.

Life should be considered an investment – certainly the more you put in the more you get out, but also the more interest is earned when more is put in, meaning there is more to work with and build from. At this point we are ready to take responsibility for the destiny of ourselves and, in turn, that of our friends, family and acquaintances. Naturally, this is no small feat and in actual fact it is a commitment that will last forever, but it is a noble task and one that is extremely rewarding, so there is no better way to spend our lives.

The diagram says "nature abhors a vacuum", and this vacuum can cause discomfort in the front of our bodies, as well as itching in the reproductive and excretory parts. If this does happen it is advised to consult a doctor, and if the all-clear is received then it is simply the body informing of the past being released and the future being anticipated.

The Soul Journey

The word 'soul' is extremely misunderstood, and yet when we stop to think about its meaning we are greeted with a cocktail of emotions including sadness, joy and wonder, because by merely acknowledging its existence we are recognising the indivisible eternal consciousness.

It appears as though we have struggled for a long time, weaving from crisis to crisis through confusion and doubt; when we are feeling more inspired we think our lives do hold some purpose but most of the time that purpose eludes us, especially because we must experience so much pain. The vibrant colours we experienced in childhood seem to have become dull before we even finished the picture, and a moment of reflection reveals the harmony and innocence of youth buried under our mistakes. Regardless of what we regret, each experience we underwent has served a purpose in its own way.

A dark night of the Soul

Affected area – Head and back

Issues: Depression; release of suppressed expression; negative expectation

Tasks: Raise standard; pray for wholeness; meditate and listen to new vibration;
contemplate balance of old and new; rest in natural simplicity

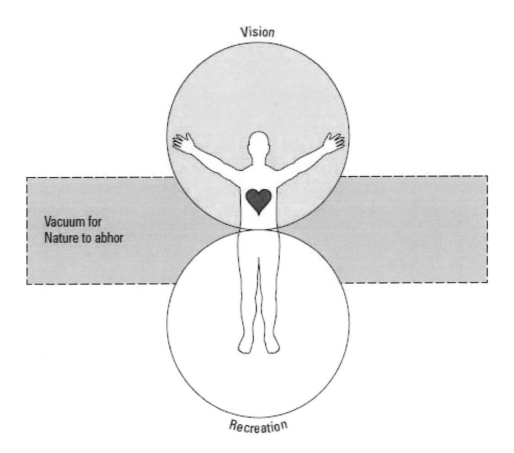

Affected area – Excretion centre and front

Issues: Insecurity; abandonment; rejection

Tasks: Reclaim past and administer it as correctly as you can – honouring all;
connect to future and organise it as best you can;
do the day and let go of anxiety as you surrender the need to help;
trusting total care systems

If we change our outlook just a tiny bit we will see that our soul has always been present. The problem is just that we get so caught up in performing for others that we often forget we are also supposed to take some joy and satisfaction from our hard work; when we do eventually remember this we can then tolerate our own shortcomings and the confusion of people in our company. What we feel at this point is similar to feeling the sun's warming rays after what seems like eternal rain, and despite our not being able to see it the sun never stopped shining above the clouds that blocked our vision to the sky, and this is true of our soul, too. This does not mean we have achieved all that there is to achieve on Earth, rather we have just learned how to create and subsequently how to use it and take responsibility. We must never become complacent or patronising just because we have acquired new abilities and knowledge.

Now that we have reached a certain point we can look back at all that has occurred previously and see just how necessary the experiences were that frightened, disappointed and imprisoned us; each helped shape and develop us in some way and if we are now self-confident, self-accepting and self-understanding then there is no need to censor the past or the truth, because we have the strength to unburden ourselves and carry on. No matter what life throws our way we are able to cope, and now that our sense of reality is deeper and all encompassing we move to a richer, more nurturing environment within our heads.

Answer the following questions on the way forward:

1) Do you feel that the past is a done deal or do you anticipate a compounding of unprocessed resentment and pain?
2) Do you feel able to look towards the future without a feeling of dread?
3) Are you able to carry hope on behalf of others when they are feeling a little under the weather?
4) Are you able to maintain a committed degree of faith as you gift love to all who surround you, yourself included?
5) Will you be led by your Higher Self/Mind or do you get in your own way with wanting what you want when you want it?
6) Lastly, ask to be shown the path towards Greater Light.

Our confidence of self-worth grows because we know our understanding of love and compassion has expanded and so we can help others on their own journey. Last but not least, our newfound ability to acknowledge the changes that occur from evolution, to recognise new opportunities for growth and new areas of work, meet new companions and explore new ideas, allows us to experience each moment as eternal. To then share the wonder and joy of our increasing awareness is the greatest reward imaginable.

ALSO BY JUDY FRASER

THE SOUL SEARCHER - SCENES FROM MY LIFE

Companion book to Second Aid.

www.judyfraser.com

Made in the USA
Lexington, KY
31 January 2012